CAPTURED *by the* CRUCIFIED

CAPTURED *by the* CRUCIFIED

THE PRACTICAL THEOLOGY OF AUSTIN FARRER

Edited by

DAVID HEIN *and*
EDWARD HUGH HENDERSON

T & T CLARK INTERNATIONAL
A Continuum imprint
NEW YORK • LONDON

T & T Clark International, Madison Square Park, 15 East 26th Street, New York, NY 10010

T & T Clark International, The Tower Building, 11 York Road, London SE1 7NX

T & T Clark International is a Continuum imprint.

The portrait of Austin Farrer on the cover is from George Speake's 1970 painting, which belongs to Keble College, University of Oxford. The publisher and the editors of this volume are grateful to Keble College for permission to use this portrait.

Cover design: Thomas Castanzo

Library of Congress Cataloging-in-Publication Data

Captured by the Crucified : the practical theology of Austin Farrer / edited by David Hein and Edward Hugh Henderson.

p. cm.

Includes bibliographical references and index.

ISBN 0-567-02510-1 (pbk.)

1. Farrer, Austin Marsden. I. Hein, David. II. Henderson, Edward, 1939–

BX5199.F29C37 2004

230′.3'092–dc22

2003027280

Printed in the United States of America

04 05 06 07 09 10 9 8 7 6 5 4 3 2 1

To the memory of
Austin Marsden Farrer
(1904–1968)
and in celebration of
the one-hundredth anniversary
of his birth

CONTENTS

FOREWORD

In his *Life of Mr. George Herbert*, Izaak Walton tells the story of Herbert's induction into Bemerton Church and of what he is supposed to have said to a friend that very night. Herbert sees a contrast between the "painted pleasures" of the court and the "fullness of all joy and pleasure" in God's service. He is resolved above all "to live well, because the virtuous life of a clergyman is the most powerful eloquence to persuade all that see it to reverence and love, and at least to desire to live like him. And this I will do, because I know we live in an age that hath more need of good examples than precepts." Of course, these words may say as much about Walton's purpose in writing Herbert's life as about Herbert himself. But we can take them seriously as a reflection of Herbert's true understanding of his vocation and, I suggest, as a way of understanding Austin Farrer's life and work. Forty years ago, at least in Anglican circles, one encountered Austin Farrer as much by the impact he had on people's lives as by his writings.

Farrer lived his life almost entirely in Oxford, where he was associated with the lively group of people that included C. S. Lewis, whose confessor he was. But his impact went far beyond Oxford through the succession of undergraduates whom he influenced. He was a scholar, but one impatient with the divisions created by academic "fields." Philosophy, theology, and New Testament studies were all grist for his mill. He was a priest — a chaplain, the warden of Keble College for eight years until his death in 1968, a preacher, and someone fully engaged in the cure of souls. But still more he was a Christian, concerned to exemplify what that might mean and to draw others into the church as the Body of Christ. Though he was a committed Anglo-Catholic, his true Catholicism may be understood as his ability to ignore divisions and boundaries, to be a scribe trained for the kingdom of heaven, bringing out of his treasure things new and old and uniting them in the interest of "plain practical religion."

Farrer's life shines through his writings. They are diverse in character — philosophical theology, New Testament studies, sermons, devotional tracts. But their diversity represents various paths that lead toward and intersect in a powerful exposition of the Christian life with the church as its context and union with the Trinity as its goal. While his thought is rigorously philosophical, Farrer's exposition is rhetorical and poetic. It drives toward a unified vision not only of Christian destiny but also of the paths that lead toward it. One might even argue that in understanding the Christian life as a journey that we undertake with one another, Farrer follows Augustine's insight that God calls us to move from the multiplicity of our rememberings, knowings, and lovings toward that unified cleaving to God's eternity where our restless hearts will find rest and peace.

As the essays that follow will show, two themes stand out. First, there is the paradox that God who holds for us our true happiness is both unknown and yet well known. Though God is incomprehensible, God has given us apprehensions we can trust, provided we have the curiosity and courage to seek their discernment. Second, the journey of the Christian life involves "double agency." God's grace is the persuasive activity of love that pervades our experience without in any way abolishing the freedom of our activity. Here we are closer to the Greek church fathers than to Augustine. Solving the theoretical problem appears less important to Farrer than showing how we can locate double agency in our own experience. In loving we remain free to act, even though there is a larger mystery in which we must locate our own agency.

Farrer's unified view also has the possibility of becoming a unifying one. In a sense, he has supplied us with a way to follow rather than with a fully achieved unity of perspective. Two examples occur to me. His New Testament studies are neglected partly because scholars tend to be unhappy with a literary and theological approach, but partly because Farrer did not go far enough to explain how his poetic reading of the texts could take account of the usual historical conclusions drawn from them. A second omission that can be discerned in Farrer's thought has to do with his failure to say much about what could be called the Social Gospel. It is possible to register some disappointment in locating lacks such as these. On the other hand, it is equally possible to argue that Farrer's work can challenge us to ask how his visionary perspective can be used to include these and other themes that attach to our concerns, questions, and difficulties.

The essays that make up this volume are primarily concerned with Farrer's thought, and they approach it from a number of differing perspectives. Nevertheless, they cohere with one another because they all lead toward the unifying glass of vision that can stand for the dynamic of the Christian life, the seeing darkly as in a mirror which is at the same time a movement into the vision of God. The essays point in two directions. They guide us toward Farrer's life as it is embedded in his writings. Reading what Farrer has written enables us to encounter his mind and his life. We find in his precepts his example. At the same time the essays point toward the readers' appropriation of "plain practical religion." The essays do far more than supply us with information.

We must be grateful to the essayists not only for calling to our attention the often-neglected life and work of Austin Farrer but also for giving us words that can inform our lives and be bread for our journeys. Indeed, what they have done supplies us with a kind of tract for our times. What we see in several quarters, I think, are divisions. The Academy in this country appears to be increasingly secular, sometimes not only indifferent but openly hostile to theology and to religious concerns save from a sociological or historical point of view.

On the other hand, the churches tend to be suspicious of the life of the mind. The issues that engage their attention are more often than not narrowly moral rather than theological ones, and are addressed with emotional heat rather than with the light of hard thinking. Even within the academic study of religion, including preparation for the Christian ministry, division often rules. Biblical studies drift apart from theology, and much that is written about "spirituality" remains uninformed by careful theological and moral examination. To the degree that this negative assessment is true, the example and thought of Austin Farrer supply a significant corrective stance. The contribution of this volume of essays, then, is a challenge to overcome the divisions that so often beset us.

ROWAN A. GREER
Walter H. Gray Professor Emeritus of Anglican Studies
Yale University Divinity School

ACKNOWLEDGMENTS

Happily working together in all other areas, the editors of this volume deemed it best to offer their words of acknowledgment and gratitude in separate sections.

D. H.:

I wish to thank, first of all, my colleague Ed Henderson, the person who, within this editorial duo, is the true Farrer scholar. Easily and fully, I came to trust in and to rely upon his fine ideas and excellent judgment. He is indeed the one who supplied so much of the spirit, the shape, and the focus of this work. His own high example as a person and a scholar, a professor and a churchman, elevated this entire effort.

For introducing Ed to me, I will always be grateful to David Baily Harned, former dean and professor at Louisiana State University, who first taught me when I was a beginning undergraduate at the University of Virginia and who's been a patient mentor and loyal friend ever since.

I am also glad to extend thanks to several institutions. All of them offered timely assistance during the period that I was working on this project. In July 1999, a travel grant from the Hood College Board of Associates enabled me to undertake research in England on Farrer's friend Hugh Lister. Through its award of a Hodson Faculty Fellowship, my home institution also provided an immensely helpful research leave during 2001–2002. In November of that academic year, as a Canon Lawton Memorial Scholar, I was able to make use of the splendid opportunities for research, writing, and companionship offered by St. Deiniol's Residential Library in Hawarden, Wales. The following April I enjoyed a two-week period of study, writing, and collegial conversation while a visiting fellow at the Episcopal Theological Seminary of the Southwest in Austin, Texas.

I am grateful, too, for opportunities to try out some of my Farrer-related work on various audiences over the past five years. For all of us who participated in the course on Farrer at Nashotah House in the summer of 1999, Ed Henderson, the seminar leader, deepened our awareness of this remarkable theologian and ably guided us as we pursued our own inquiries and presented our findings. At this historic Wisconsin seminary, where Farrer's former classmate Michael Ramsey spent many months after his retirement as archbishop of Canterbury, both colleagues and setting provided ample support and encouragement.

The subject of my Nashotah House paper, Hugh Lister, also became the focus of papers I presented at the April 2000 meeting of the American Society of Church History in Santa Fe, New Mexico, and at the World War II Conference, held at Siena College, Loudonville, New York, in June 2000. At both of these scholarly gatherings, respondents and audience members offered useful comments. I am also grateful to the Reverend Thomas L. Culbertson for his invitation to deliver the annual Theodore Parker Ferris Lecture at Emmanuel Episcopal Church, Baltimore, in October 2002. My leading themes for that lecture included Hugh Lister, Austin Farrer, and a practical theology of Christian friendship.

Major portions of the Hugh Lister section of my chapter here on friendship, sainthood, and the will of God first appeared in published form in the pages of *Theology* (2000) and *Anglican and Episcopal History* (2001). I wish to thank the editors and readers of these two journals for their helpful comments.

To the Reverend William Pryor of Oxford, England, I am tremendously thankful for his visit to the United States in the fall of 2002, on which occasion he brought with him the entire "Lister Archive," a large leather suitcase containing hundreds of letters and other documents by his uncle, the Reverend Hugh E. J. Lister. For the opportunity both to have access to these materials and to meet and spend time with Mr. Pryor and his charming wife, I am thoroughly grateful.

For their generous hospitality on my visits to Charlottesville in recent years, I wish to thank Julian and Elinor Hartt. Not once, of course, could I reenter the precincts of the University without succumbing willy-nilly to the lure of memory; it's that kind of place. One of those quarter-century-old memories always occasioned renewed appreciation: Like many others who were graduate students in religious studies at Yale and Virginia, I had my first in-depth encounter with the thought of Austin Farrer in a seminar taught by Julian Hartt.

Here at Hood College, I am particularly appreciative of the assistance given by Ms. Melinda Metz, who provides expert help to my colleagues and me, sorting out all sorts of problems, technical and administrative.

Most of all, I am thankful for the efforts of the contributors to this volume, who have worked hard and well to provide fresh treatments of significant themes in the work of an important and always challenging Christian thinker.

This book is intended to be of service and value not only to the present generation of readers but also to those who will eventually follow them; that is, to readers like my nephew, Charlie, born in 1987. He and his peers provide an immense amount of tacit, indeed unwitting, encouragement to us in our efforts. I hope that he and others of his generation will read Austin Farrer, and I trust that if they do apply themselves to the task, they will find riches, even many years from now. Then Farrer's writings will speak not only to those of us who are one or two generations beyond him but to those who are three and four generations on as well.

E. H. H.:

The idea for a book on Austin Farrer in the one-hundredth year after his birth came from my coeditor, David Hein. But David not only had the idea; in order to get it done he was willing to drive halfway across the country to spend the summer of 1999 at Nashotah House and to read and talk Farrer with someone he'd never met. In doing so, he turned my focus from Farrer's philosophy to his larger body of work and its practical meaning. The turn has been like heading home. Now David and I are friends — of the sort, I believe, that he discusses in "Friendship, Sainthood, and the Will of God." Without his experience, critical judgment, skill at keeping track of details, and tenacity in pressing the task, this book would never have come to pass. That it has proves the human analogy of double agency, two agents but one action.

Thanks also go to Nashotah House for inviting me to teach a seminar on Farrer in its Petertide term of 1999 and for providing so beautiful, hospitable, and congenial a setting for doing so. Special thanks go to Stephen Holmgren and Charles Miller, who were mainly responsible for the Nashotah House invitation. It was a summer of transformation for me. The students, all but two of them seasoned scholars and teachers representing a variety of disciplines and of colleges and universities, not only taught me much about Farrer but helped me with the turn from the theoretical to the practical. David Hein was one of those "students," though he became from the very first day the co-leader of the seminar, skillfully helping me deal with the challenges of that learned group: a human analogy of double agency again.

The St. James Center for Spiritual Formation, a program of St. James Episcopal Church in Baton Rouge, which was begun with the help of the Trinity Grants Foundation of Trinity Episcopal Church, Wall Street, New York, bears much responsibility for causing the focus of the book to fall on the meaning of Farrer's thought for the practical life of faith. The St. James Center, shaped by the contemplative instruction and practice of its director and my friend, George Kontos, incubated me in a dimension of Christian life I once knew only from reading.

Over the years there have been several conferences on Farrer — in Queens' College, Cambridge; Princeton Theological Seminary; Keble College, Oxford; Louisiana State University; the Center for Theology and the Natural Sciences, Berkeley, California; and the University of Durham. These conferences have been enormously important in bringing together those who have seen the extraordinary power and wisdom in Farrer's works, enabling them to learn from each other, and encouraging each other in the effort to awaken wider appreciation and use of his work. At the risk of forgetting an important name, I thank the following organizers and participants: Diogenes Allen, Charles Conti, Jeffrey Eaton, Brian Hebblethwaite, Ann Loades, Michael McLain, Basil Mitchell, Mark Richardson, Eric O. Springsted, and Margaret Yee. This book is not only indebted to their years of efforts; it carries forward their common intention.

David's and my hope in getting this book together was to honor Farrer in the centennial anniversary of his birth. We knew that it would honor him most if we could produce something that would generate readers for Farrer's works. Only time will tell whether we have succeeded. But we are confident that our authors have succeeded. They have given us complementary chapters of a whole, not a hodgepodge of essays. For that and for what we have learned from them, we are grateful.

Louisiana State University and its Department of Philosophy and Religious Studies have for many years given me the place and the means to teach, read, and write. One can only be thankful for being paid to do what one loves. In my years at LSU I have taught Farrer's philosophical books in several classes and, of course, learned more from the teaching than I could have learned in any other way. Thanks, therefore, to all the students in those classes. And special thanks to the students in last year's Christian Philosophy class for trying drafts of some of the material now in the book.

My wife and spiritual friend, Patricia Weems Henderson, keeps me in the real world, prevents me from getting lost in abstraction, and gives me the experience of marriage and parenthood as instances of double agency: God acting in our action. Support and encouragement flow intrinsically in such a sacrament, and I am deeply grateful both for her and to her.

Thanks also go to Clarke Cadzow and the students who work at his establishment, Highland Coffees. They have provided me with what my colleagues and students call my "other office." Most of my part of the writing has been done here (I say "here" because these words are being written "there"), and I am sure that it is one of the most civilized places in the world in which to work.

Finally, I join David in hoping that this book may encourage future generations to read Austin Farrer. Farrer taught us that words are meaningful only when we can use them to do something more than talk or think. May the words of this book take their readers to Farrer's own words in Farrer's own books. And may Farrer's words take them — and us — beyond words and thought into life in God, even the God who undertakes us, the God who undertakes to change us into persons who so live in God that we love God with all our being and our neighbors as ourselves.

INTRODUCTION

The Editors

> What, then, did God do for his people's redemption? He came among them, bringing his kingdom, and he let events take their human course. He set the divine life in human neighborhood. Men discovered it in struggling with it and were captured by it in crucifying it. What could be simpler? And what more divine?
>
> —Austin Farrer, *Saving Belief: A Discussion of Essentials*

This book aims to make the practical meaning of Austin Farrer's thought available to those who desire to integrate serious thinking with faithful living. Why should people committed to faithful spiritual life want to bother with theology? The answer is that "religion without theology," as the former dean of York Alan Richardson commented, "is like a body without a skeleton: it lacks that which stiffens and steadies it; it becomes flabby and weak and sentimental."[1] This is all the more true of spirituality when it tries to go it alone. When it is not tutored and strengthened by the discipline of theology, then spirituality, as the Roman Catholic monk Thomas Merton remarked, has "no substance, no meaning and no sure orientation." As Merton also observed, however, without the dimension of lived spirituality, theology has "no fervor" and "no life."[2]

The most important and oft repeated of Farrer's theological themes is the activity of God: in creating and sustaining, in forgiving and sanctifying. Christian spirituality must concern itself with this divine activity and with the proper human response to it. These matters are, in Merton's words, the "substance" and "sure orientation" of spirituality. Necessarily, authentic spirituality incorporates practical theology at its center. Practical theology, writes a theologian at the University of Edinburgh, "must first ask questions about God's activity and consider the practice of other agents within the horizon of the divine practice and as actual or potential participation in God's activity."[3]

The following chapters seek to make the rich spiritual content of the writings of Austin Farrer accessible to new generations of Christian pilgrims and thus to offer spiritual direction and sustenance for their journeys of faith. At the same time, this book, published in commemoration of the one-hundredth anniversary of Farrer's birth on October 1, 1904, presents an introduction to the leading ideas and approaches of his work.

Although he is not as well known today as some of his Christian contemporaries and friends — such as C. S. Lewis, Dorothy L. Sayers, Charles Williams, and J. R. R. Tolkien — Farrer is still widely recognized as a brilliant figure in the recent history of British Christianity. Indeed, he has been called "the one genius that the Church of England . . . produced" in the last century.[4] The English biographer and novelist A. N. Wilson has referred to Farrer as the "author of incomparably the most interesting theological books ever to come out of the Oxford Theology Faculty."[5]

After graduating from St. Paul's School in London, where he received excellent preparation in literature and the classics, Farrer attended Balliol College, Oxford, on a scholarship. At the University of Oxford he obtained a first in Mods and Greats (Classical Moderations and *Literae Humaniores*) and a first in theology. After studying at Cuddesdon Theological College, where the future archbishop of Canterbury Michael Ramsey was a fellow student, Farrer was ordained to the diaconate in 1928 and to the priesthood the following year. In 1931, following a curacy in a parish in Dewsbury, near Leeds in Yorkshire, he returned to Oxford as chaplain and tutor at St. Edmund Hall.

In 1935 Farrer became fellow and chaplain of Trinity College, where he taught both philosophy and theology. After his friend Katharine Newton graduated from Oxford in 1937, she and Austin were married; they had one daughter, Caroline, born in 1939. In 1945 Oxford University awarded Farrer the doctor of divinity degree. After failing to be appointed Regius Professor of Divinity, he became warden of Keble College in 1960. "He acknowledged a debt," his erstwhile colleague Basil Mitchell recalled, "to each of the colleges of which he was a member. Balliol taught him; St. Edmund Hall made him a teacher; Trinity mellowed him, and Keble gave him scope."[6] He died suddenly on December 29, 1968, at the age of sixty-four and after months of overwork and fatigue.

Farrer's most significant achievement was to make his philosophical, theological, and biblical writings — careful, critical, and rigorous as they are — into expressions and vehicles of faithful life. "We know, on our knees," he said.[7] The principle that the meaning of religious beliefs lies in the way that they can be lived was a basic tenet of both his academic and his devotional theology. Christians, he knew, do not deserve their doctrines unless they can pray them and live them, and no doctrine has meaning except insofar as it can be prayed and lived.[8] His own intentional practice of theology as an exercise of faith sets him apart from most academic theologians of the past fifty years.[9]

Farrer's thought speaks to a broad spectrum of Christians. His family upbringing was Baptist (his father taught scripture in a Baptist theological school), and in his college days he became an Anglican who felt most at home in the Catholic wing of the Church of England. His creatively Thomistic and Catholic sides were nourished by his Protestant attention to the Bible — and vice versa. His thought is rooted in scripture, in the sacraments, and in his Oxford philosophical and theological training, which in his time was centered on the historical greats.

Farrer spent his academic career attempting to demonstrate how the essential core of biblical and historical faith could be defended against the positivism and scientism that dominated intellectual life in the Oxford of his day. In carrying out this project, he developed a theology that incorporated a critical recovery of the riches of the Christian tradition: His theology revivified ancient wisdom and made it freshly relevant. Speaking at a conference on Farrer, the American philosopher of religion Eleanore Stump noted that we owe him an enormous debt for taking on the positivistic philosophers who ruled at Oxford.[10] He did so in a philosophically more credible way than did his better-known friend C. S. Lewis and succeeded in making historical Christianity intelligible in terms that were both traditional and contemporary, both orthodox and original.

Farrer's work is an instance, then, of the union of academic theology and lived faith. His scholarly life was in no way divorced from what he called "the practice of day-to-day religion."[11] Although his theology is often highly abstract and difficult, it is neither neutral nor detached. The concrete daily living of faith included his biblical, doctrinal, philosophical, and devotional writing, along with preaching, celebrating the Eucharist, giving spiritual counsel to students and friends, and tending to his administrative responsibilities as head of a college. His most technical philosophical theology is continuous with his devotional writing and sermons. The best way to understand him, two authorities on his life and work have pointed out, is to "think of him as one whose primary vocation was that of a priest dedicated to the care of souls, whether through the preaching of the Christian faith, the administration of the sacraments, or the writing of books for learned specialists and interested laity."[12]

We find Farrer saying in *Faith and Speculation,* for example, that "[God's] otherness for us lies in this, that his life is personal to him, it is not ours; that he has a will after which we enquire, a judgment to which we submit, a forgiveness we implore, a succour we seek."[13] But *Faith and Speculation* is no devotional work. It is a profound and subtle piece of philosophical argumentation. The words we have quoted occur in an argument about the real reference of language about God and against its reduction to language about morality. Such integration of faith with philosophy is found throughout Farrer's works.

This interpenetration of lived faith and rigorous thought came to fruition in the practical counsel of Farrer's sermons and in his devotional works (he called them his "pious" books). These writings incorporate ideas developed in and distilled from his academic theology, as in these words from a sermon on forgiveness in which Farrer makes use of the understanding of God as sovereign will, an understanding worked out and defended in his most important philosophical writings: "But God is not like the atmosphere either, for though air sometimes becomes wind and wind hurricane, yet for the most part air just lies about and lets itself be breathed. Not so God; he is never inert, he is master, he is the sovereign will, he is always at work on me; if he ceased from creating me I should cease to exist; he does not let me be, he continues to sustain me."[14]

The application of *sapientia* was a feature of Farrer's life as both theologian and priest. It shines through in his extensive practice as spiritual friend and guide to fellow academicians, to numerous students, and to many outside the academic world. His wife, Katharine, said that he was always generous of his time not only with students but also in response to the many other people who sought his spiritual counsel, despite the burden it placed on his own overworked self.[15] Both Austin and Katharine Farrer were lay witnesses to the civil marriage of C. S. Lewis and Joy Davidman. Farrer was Lewis's friend and confessor, and he administered Holy Communion to the popular Christian apologist and also to Joy when they were on their deathbeds.

Several decades after Farrer's death and in the midst of a widespread revival of interest in spirituality, many theologians are developing a new appreciation for the coinherence of thought and faith, of knowledge and contemplation, which Farrer's work exhibits.[16] Signs exist of a growing recognition of Austin Farrer as an exemplar of this old — and new — way of doing theology. The Chicago theologian David Tracy sees Farrer's theology as paradigmatic: a "wonderful" example, a "perfect model," of this union of theology and spirituality. Farrer is "the kind of person we need more of."[17]

In the modern West, the tendency in European and North American mainstream Christianity has been to preserve a sharp distinction between the rational discourse of theology — academic, intellectual, objective, elite — and the devotional language of spirituality — personal, affective, experiential, and often nonelite.[18] The process theologian John Cobb has observed, "[T]hrough the centuries the God of the philosophers and the God of Abraham, Isaac, and Jacob have remained estranged." But, in his view, "no one has done more to bring them together than Austin Farrer."[19]

The widespread attention given to spirituality over the past quarter century may suggest that this estrangement is now being overcome; and no doubt within much of modern Christianity, including feminist and liberation theologies, this rapprochement between theory and practice is taking place. For many denizens of our pluralistic culture, however, these two ways of addressing the divine reality — theology and spirituality — remain in opposite corners, situated even further apart than they were in Farrer's day. A large measure of what passes for spirituality in the present age is more shapeless and scattered, less tradition-based and other-regarding, more subjective and irrational than the older spiritualities ever were. Hence the need for regular reminders of what Christian theology and spirituality can and ought to be.

Farrer called the faith he sought to live and in whose defense he wrote "the catholic religion"; that is, traditional, orthodox, creedal Christianity. This usage and practice do not mean, however, that his thought was rigidly held within stultifying limits. "Tradition" is a dangerous word. To some it means an unambiguously clear and literal knowledge of those true beliefs that have come down to us from the past. On that view, traditionalists are those who affirm and fight for what they take to be unambiguous knowledge of the truth. They are prone to fundamentalism, to an absolutism about how to think and act, which leaves little room for the growth of wisdom. Such a traditionalism makes an idol of whatever the party of traditionalists has identified as simply "*the* tradition."

Against such traditionalists stand those who recoil from an idolatrous abuse of the past. Some, rightly seeing the abuse, think that everything from the past is a dead weight. Feeling no loyalty to tradition, no responsibility to press for its deeper truth, they are prepared to empty it of whatever content makes it hard for them to believe. Some such anti-traditionalists go so far as to call for the abandonment of belief in God.[20]

Austin Farrer was good at finding the right balance between these two extremes. He believed that tradition must be respected because Christianity is rooted in particular historical events believed to be particular actions of God in the world. It is not a philosophical system of abstract truths that we can either discover by pure reason or fabricate out of imagination. We Christians, therefore, should take the past seriously; but we should also do our best to view tradition critically. We must select from it what, from the standpoint of our best-educated but still limited perspectives, can be seen to embody truth and to be a fruitful resource for spiritual life. As part of this critical respect, we must follow "with devoted obedience the truth we [and the Christian tradition] have seen as true, pressing its meaning and bringing it into collision with the hard rocks of fact." In Farrer's day and in ours, that means bringing it into collision with the understandings generated by the natural and social sciences. If we will do so, then we can trust God to "correct, clear and redirect our vision, [and bring about] the perception of a freer and a deeper truth."[21]

Making good use of Farrer's thought may be inhibited, however, by his distinctive writing style. It is original, even brilliant, and he has always had a following of devoted readers. Yet in some places it seems parochial, addressed too much to the Oxford dons and students of his time, while in other places it seems too compressed and elliptical to follow.

But this perception is ironic. One of Farrer's gifts is that very writing style. It is no accident that his sermons have been continuously in print since 1960. While he does not write in the standard academic style of today, his words can strike deeply into those who are prepared to hear them. And in spite of instances when it seems quaint, his writing is punctuated with passages that can only be called poetic. One is tempted to call them "theological poems." They certainly are not poems in any formal sense, although they include many features of poetry. They compress much meaning into few words. They give statement after statement that cannot be explained or translated without blurring their clarity of insight and diminishing their power. They enable the attentive reader to see suddenly and directly the meaning and intelligibility of ideas that volumes of argumentative discussion could never make as clear. Even the philosophical essays are so sprinkled with poetic passages that whole arguments can be missed if the reader fails to enter into and to think in Farrer's own words. Indeed, Farrer's prose often exhibits what C. S. Lewis called the "phrase by phrase deliciousness" of poetry.[22]

While this poetic character sometimes makes Farrer harder to understand and, consequently, less popular than Lewis, this quality of his writing lifts him out of his place and time, makes his work a permanent gift to the church, and places him among her sage spiritual directors. Thus he is able to be a continuing help to those who desire to yield more intentionally to the transforming action of God.

The various chapters of this book offer Farrer to readers as a spiritual director. As spiritual nourishment for both lay people and clergy, for both academic theologians and nonspecialists, its chapters present some of the fruit of his integration of faithful life and hard thinking. This book is not a random collection of contributions. The following chapters move progressively through general theological and philosophical presentations to more concretely and practically focused discussions. But all of them, even those that focus on Farrer's philosophical theology, center upon his emphasis on the practical life of faith. The foundation of the Christian life is supported not only by his sermons and devotional writings but also by his most closely argued and abstract philosophical works. William Wilson and Julian Hartt call him "the philosopher of the believer's reasons." That is exactly right. Austin Farrer, at least as much as any other philosopher or theologian of recent years, thinks from within the lived life of faith. In doing so, he teaches us both the reasonableness and the vitality of traditional Christian spirituality.

We begin with Ann Loades's chapter, "The Vitality of Tradition: Austin Farrer and Friends," in which she describes the literary, philosophical, and theological matrix that was the Oxford in which Farrer was educated and in which he lived out his career as priest, scholar, teacher, and preacher. She reveals his familial, religious, and intellectual roots and describes the thought by which he was influenced and to which he addressed his own original contributions. Many of the day's luminaries were his friends, including Dorothy L. Sayers, C. S. Lewis, Charles Williams, Michael Ramsey, Basil Mitchell, Iris Murdoch, and Eric Mascall. But Loades also reminds us that Farrer's world was larger than the intellectual world of Oxford and England; there was the world of political turmoil, rife with the evil of Nazism and the suffering that World War II brought upon England. Farrer's books reveal the effects of these events, although he never let current events dictate the shape of his thought. In that respect he was more a citizen of the Church through the ages than a man of his times, and his best friends were those who shared this commitment to traditional Christianity as a living faith. Farrer's influence on the theological world has been considerable, and there are signs that this influence is by no means past but is indeed growing.

Moving beyond Oxford, England, and the twentieth century, Diogenes Allen places Farrer's spirituality in the larger history of Christian thought and practice. Allen defines the field of spiritual theology by means of seven questions and explains Farrer's answers to them in comparison with others given by notable spiritual theologians through the centuries. The most important of these questions, the most definitive for the shape of lived faith, are the first two: What is the goal of the Christian life? What is the path to the goal? Allen shows us that Farrer's emphasis on God's action in us by double agency is foundational for Farrer's response to these questions and, consequently, for his approach to the actual life of faith. For Farrer, the spiritual life is the action of God in us, on the one side, and our action in cooperative response, on the other side. God acts in our actions of faith; our actions of faith join with God's action: double agency. The goal of life is life-in-God, participation in God, being taken into the life of the blessed Trinity and perfected as participants in that community of reciprocal love. The path to the goal may take different forms but all will be activities in which the goal is anticipated; that is, activities that join the faithful now to the divine life that will transform and finally perfect them.

Allen completes his overview of Farrer's spiritual theology as he explains Farrer's answers to the other five questions: What motivates us to begin and to continue the journey of faith? What helps us make progress? What hinders our progress? How do we measure our progress along the path or assess our spiritual condition? What are the fruits of the Spirit in the life of faith? The chapters that follow will touch on many of the themes that Allen introduces, but they will concentrate on Farrer's understanding of the goal and of the path to the goal.

The next two chapters treat Farrer's philosophical thought, yet each one keeps its focus on the meaning-in-life of the theory discussed. "The God Who Undertakes Us," by Edward Henderson, explains how Farrer reconciles the traditional belief in God as a personal agent who acts effectively in the world with the scientific explanations of events in terms of natural causes. This reconciliation requires more attention to the idea of double agency, which was discussed by Allen in the previous chapter. Henderson also explains how Farrer develops a sound philosophical appraisal of our knowledge of God by taking the believer's reasons and experience as his starting point, an approach whose value Wilson and Hartt will also demonstrate in their discussion of suffering and evil.

Throughout, Henderson shows how Farrer's philosophical emphasis on action, God's and ours, encourages a spirituality best described as a participatory engagement with God. Showing how Farrer's philosophical ideas find frequent application in sermons and devotional works, Henderson encourages the reader in his or her journey along the path of life-in-God.

William Wilson and Julian Hartt, in the second of the philosophical chapters, examine Farrer's practical theological approach to the problem of suffering and evil. Farrer's "solution" to the problem of "Why does a good God allow so much evil?" is not to offer a theory according to which we can believe that all suffering and evil contribute to the realization of greater good. Such a theoretical solution could only be a form of willed credulity: believing what one wants to believe because it comforts one to do so. Instead, Farrer writes of the gift of God's Son as God's practical "solution" to the problem. Death, suffering, and pain are built into the very fabric of the kind of world God has seen it best to create. Faith is not a way to get around them. Nevertheless, for those who take up the life of faith there will be — even in the midst of suffering — an anticipation, a foretaste, of the fulfillment and perfection of life in which suffering and evil are overcome. And what is this participation in God's life that gives the faithful a taste now of the fulfillment to come? It is actively identifying with the sacrificial life of Christ by caring for, loving, and suffering with those who suffer and are in need of consolation.

Lived faith, the life of faith, life-in-God: In their different ways, the previous chapters show how this idea is the heart and soul of Farrer's spiritual theology. But the descriptions are abstract. David Hein gives us a more concrete account of the path of faithful life — and a more concrete anticipation of the goal — in "Farrer on Friendship, Sainthood, and the Will of God," in which he looks at the remarkable life of Hugh Lister. A priest of the Church of England, Lister led labor strikes in the East End of London in the 1930s and served as a combatant officer in the Second World War. He was, in Farrer's experience, both a friend and "the one saint" of his generation. His life makes clear the ideal shape of the spiritual life, and it shows us the goal of that life as well. The goal is perfected life-in-God, which is a life in which one's own will is completely identified with God's will and in which, paradoxically, one is made most fully oneself. The path to the goal is to take up the life of faith by doing God's will. We discover God in God's will, and we find God's will in doing it. Both the path and the goal are seen preeminently in those who do God's will most perfectly; that is, in Christ and the saints.

Saints provide concrete examples of what it is both to do God's will and to participate in the life of God; they thereby also provide what the theologian Brian Hebblethwaite has called the "experiential verification of religious belief."[23]

The last two chapters help us to use Farrer's work as aids to the spiritual life. Charles Hefling writes on Farrer's "scriptural divinity." He explains the peculiarities of Farrer's often-controversial efforts in the field of biblical scholarship and why it is unlikely that this work will ever become the focus of academic biblical studies. There should be little wonder about it, because Farrer's interpretations of the biblical texts, despite their scholarly detail, are finally preparation for and even instances of the spiritual practice of *lectio divina*. Farrer treats the biblical authors as creative writers whose work can be interpreted in terms of double agency. That means that we can reasonably believe, without falling prey to the naïveté and idolatry of biblical literalism on the one side or of academic skepticism on the other side, that God has acted in the biblical writings and that God can act in our efforts to meet God's will in them. The conclusion of the chapter brings out the spirituality of Farrer's scriptural studies as a model for a church that often has some difficulty — as the dean of the General Theological Seminary once observed — knowing quite what to make of the Bible.

Finally, in their chapter on Farrer's preaching, O. C. Edwards and David Hein discuss Farrer's sermons as a rich source of inspiration and direction for living the life of faith. They offer a historical and critical perspective on Farrer's homiletical art while bringing the spiritual power of his sermons to the fore. Five volumes of Farrer's sermons have been published, as well as a volume of brief paragraphs for the Eucharist and another of short homilies for various occasions. Since *Said or Sung* was first published in 1960, at least one volume of Farrer's sermons has been in print. They remain the most popular expression of his genius, the genre in which he brings to bear the practical value of his reflective faith. The authors of this chapter illuminate the techniques Farrer used to gain his listeners' attention, compare him with some of his illustrious predecessors and contemporaries, introduce the reader to some of the leading themes of Farrer's sermons, and bring these texts right into the spiritual life of the reader. The goal and the path as they appear in the sermons are put before us, and we are encouraged by the reminder that some, especially saints like Hugh Lister but perhaps from time to time all who are engaged with God on the path, "taste of the things [the sermons] describe."

We believe that, taken together, these chapters form an organic whole, or at least a complementary set. They should call to mind the unity of Farrer's thought, a mode of theological thinking that we have labeled both a spiritual and a practical theology. By these terms we intend to suggest several overlapping circles of meaning.

First, in speaking of practical theology we have no reason to disown its traditional reference to that branch of theology which, since Friedrich Schleiermacher's *Brief Outline of the Study of Theology* (1811), has been understood to have as its focus the work of training clergy in administering parishes, providing pastoral care, and so forth. The pages that follow have much to say about preaching, sacraments, priesthood, and the spiritual nurture of congregations, all of which we hope will be of benefit to both lay and ordained ministers.

Second, we wish to go beyond this older definition to point to a more comprehensive understanding of practical theology as theology for living the life of Christian faith. The task of theology is not confined to the pursuits of the scholar and the practice of the pastor. "Practical theology" can also mean the lively exploration of — including critical reflection on — theology and spirituality within Christian congregations. And, instead of restricting practical theology to its place in a sequence of theological subdisciplines (typically beginning with philosophical or fundamental theology), this broader understanding incorporates all the components of theology, including apologetics. Each branch of theology has a role to play in the transformation of Christians and their communities. Thus, as demonstrated in these chapters, even the results of Farrer's abstruse philosophizing have practical and discernible implications for communities of faith.[24]

Third, in employing this phrase we want to indicate a spiritual theology that is praxis-oriented, centered on the interaction between faith and conduct, between thought and practice, between contemplative prayer and love of others. Practical theology means doing theology as an intellectual and spiritual discipline that is concerned with living into Christian images and stories and living out the meaning of Christian truth-claims. This theology has entailments for the public realm, not just the private sphere, and so it supports the critical examination of Christians' relation to the larger society beyond the church. It directs our attention not only to Mary and Martha but also to Dives and Lazarus.[25]

Finally, calling Farrer's theology "practical" attempts to keep faith with his insistence that a necessary relationship exists between understanding and action: The meaning of religious beliefs lies in the way that they can be lived. The applicability of the terms "spiritual" and "practical" to Farrer's work should become clearer with each essay that follows. At this point the terms can at least serve as banners over the whole enterprise to alert readers to Farrer's constant stress on God as everlasting will and to his belief that practical obedience to that will—human beings' response to the activity of God—lies at the heart of any authentic spirituality.

NOTES

1. Alan Richardson, *Creeds in the Making: A Short Introduction to the History of Christian Doctrine* (1935; repr. Philadelphia: Fortress, 1981), 8.

2. Thomas Merton, *Seeds of Contemplation* (1972), 197–98, quoted in Alister E. McGrath, *Christian Theology: An Introduction* (3rd ed.; Oxford: Blackwell, 2001), 147.

3. Duncan B. Forrester, *Truthful Action: Explorations in Practical Theology* (Edinburgh: T & T Clark, 2000), 9.

4. Richard Harries, introduction to *The One Genius: Readings through the Year with Austin Farrer* (ed. Richard Harries; London: SPCK, 1987), ix. Basil Mitchell cautions against applying the term "genius" to Farrer, however, because "the word has romantic associations with the self-expression of a striking personality which are wholly inappropriate in his case." Farrer's "intention and . . . effect was to direct one's gaze away from the man to whatever was the object of *his* attention. There was a kind of transparency about him." Basil Mitchell, "Austin Marsden Farrer," in Austin Farrer, *A Celebration of Faith* (ed. Leslie Houlden; London: Hodder & Stoughton, 1970), 13.

5. A. N. Wilson, *C. S. Lewis: A Biography* (New York: Norton, 1990), 245n.

6. Basil Mitchell, "Austin Marsden Farrer," in Houlden, *A Celebration of Faith,* 14.

7. Austin Farrer, "History and the Gospel," Hulsean sermon preached in Great St. Mary's Church, Cambridge, November 14, 1948, in Houlden, *A Celebration of Faith,* 45.

8. Austin Farrer, *Lord I Believe: Suggestions for Turning the Creed into Prayer* (1958; repr., Cambridge, MA: Cowley, 1989), 9.

9. Among the notable exceptions to this general rule is one of Farrer's contemporaries, the Roman Catholic theologian Hans Urs von Balthasar (1905–88).

10. Dr. Stump, a professor of philosophy at St. Louis University, spoke at the Farrer conference sponsored by the Center for Theology and the Natural Sciences, Berkeley, California, in January 1992.

11. Austin Farrer, *Faith and Speculation* (Edinburgh: T & T Clark, 1967), 61.

12. Jeffrey C. Eaton and Ann Loades, "Austin Marsden Farrer," in *For God and Clarity: New Essays in Honor of Austin Farrer* (ed. Jeffrey C. Eaton and Ann Loades; Allison Park, PA: Pickwick, 1983), xiii.

13. Farrer, *Faith and Speculation,* 47.

14. *Austin Farrer: The Essential Sermons* (ed. Leslie Houlden; Cambridge, MA: Cowley, 1991), 28.

15. Katharine Farrer, journal, Farrer Papers, Bodleian Library, Oxford University.

16. See, for example, Mark A. McIntosh, *Mystical Theology: The Integrity of Spirituality and Theology* (Oxford: Blackwell, 1998); and *Spirituality and Theology: Essays in Honor of Diogenes Allen* (ed. Eric O. Springsted; Louisville, KY: Westminster, 1998). For a useful overview of the relationship between theology and spirituality, see Alister E. McGrath, *Christian Spirituality: An Introduction* (Oxford: Blackwell, 1999), chaps. 3–4; for a more advanced treatment, see Philip Sheldrake, *Spirituality and Theology: Christian Living and the Doctrine of God* (London: Darton, 1998).

17. David Tracy, quoted in Todd Breyfogle and Thomas Levergood, "Conversation with David Tracy," *Cross Currents* 44 (Fall 1994): 300.

18. Nathan Ng, "Spirituality and Theology," *Theology* 104 (March–April 2001): 115–22.

19. John Cobb, e-mail message to David Hein, March 19, 2002.

20. See Don Cupitt, *Taking Leave of God* (London: SCM Press, 2001).

21. Austin Farrer, "The Transforming Will," in *The End of Man* (ed. Charles C. Conti; London: SCM, 1973), 104.

22. C. S. Lewis, "Edmund Spenser," in *Major British Writers* (ed. G. B. Harrison; 2 vols.; New York: Harcourt, 1959), 1:102.

23. Brian Hebblethwaite, "The Experiential Verification of Religious Belief in the Theology of Austin Farrer," in Eaton and Loades, *For God and Clarity,* 163.

24. This second understanding of "practical theology" is akin to what two recent writers on spirituality refer to as "first-order theology," which they define as "the act of reflecting upon the meaning of God . . . by the ordinary believer. In this sense, first-order theology implies that every Christian must be a theologian." More precisely, this second understanding dovetails with their assertion that spiritual theology must *combine* first- and second-order theology — the latter being "a more conceptual or scientific way" of reflecting upon Christian faith. Robin Maas and Gabriel O'Donnell, "An Introduction to Spiritual Theology: The Theory That Undergirds Our Practice," in *Spiritual Traditions for the Contemporary Church* (ed. Robin Maas and Gabriel O'Donnell; Nashville: Abingdon, 1990), 12 (quotations), 13.

25. See ibid., 13–14, where the authors emphasize that spiritual theology (a phrase that we use almost interchangeably with "practical theology") must overcome the traditional separation between systematic theology and ethical inquiry; spiritual theology also must bring together reflection on the interior life with concern for the external expression of faith in worship and moral practice.

Chapter One

THE VITALITY OF TRADITION

AUSTIN FARRER AND FRIENDS

Ann Loades

Austin Marsden Farrer (1904–68) grew to maturity in a Europe in upheaval. He was an adolescent during the First World War and shared the experience of privation in Britain. He was a young adult throughout the period of the General Strike in the United Kingdom and the economic slump that followed it, observing at a distance the rise of National Socialism and Fascism in a Europe that had also witnessed the Russian revolution and the advent of Communist governments. The Second World War was associated not just with the aerial and saturation bombing of cities of civilians, but also with the unimaginable horrors of systematic mass murder, and not only in Europe. Although we associate Farrer with the Oxford in which he spent most of his working life, we need to keep this larger framework in mind if we are to appreciate him, the context that nourished him, and his world of friends of various degrees of intimacy that we are going to bring into focus in this chapter. We begin with Farrer himself, broaden out to look at his circle of friends and acquaintances, and return to him in the last part of this introduction. I want to pay particular attention to three key women thinkers of this period, because their influence is often underestimated.

EDUCATION

Austin was born the middle of three children into a lively, learned Nonconformist family, to whom he paid a profound tribute: "From first infancy our elders loved us, played us, served us, talked us into knowing them; and so the believer claims that he has been brought by mediated divine initiatives into the knowledge of God."[1] At St. Paul's School in London he received a predominantly literary and classical education, which included the invaluable practice of learning by heart both poetry and prose. He had no pretensions himself to be a poet of much significance, though write it he certainly could, and he was able to translate texts from the Western Church's inheritance of Latin liturgy and devotion.

Farrer's literary gifts were to be displayed in an inimitable prose style, especially that intended for oral delivery, as in his sermons; and his sensitivity to metaphor and imagery was to flower especially when he dealt with biblical texts. It takes someone thoroughly familiar with poetry in many styles and several languages to engage with the wealth of genres to be found in scripture. In this respect, he owed much to his schooling. It is worth recalling, too, that a person of Farrer's generation was nourished from childhood on a particular translation of the Bible, that of the Authorized Version, the King James Bible, a translation meant to be spoken out loud, its words falling into communities who might relish them and ponder them, so that they engaged heart and imagination, and seeped into speech and writing.[2]

No enthusiast for organized sport at either school or university, Farrer became a good runner, a mode of movement apparently characteristic of him in adult life, and a bodily expression of his own quicksilver intelligence. Both as schoolboy and as undergraduate at Balliol, he was an exemplary student, and certainly ambitious to do well. His gifts might have made him one of the great Nonconformist preachers of the twentieth century, but his life took a new turn when he became not merely a member of the Church of England, but found his vocation for ordination affirmed by his new communion.

Born in the same year as Arthur Michael Ramsey, another young man from a Nonconformist tradition who was accepted for ordination training, both coincided at Cuddesdon Theological College, just outside Oxford. Ramsey's own career was to take him out of the Oxford orbit—most notably to Durham as Van Mildert Canon Professor of Divinity (1940–50), then to Cambridge as Regius Professor, back to Durham as bishop, and then to Canterbury as archbishop—while Farrer's life centered on a series of Oxford colleges. But their friendship formed when they were young men was lifelong.[3]

Farrer's words on John Keble serve for Ramsey as well as for himself, and indeed identify just why Farrer became such a beacon of light for others of his day, some of them the most intelligent and perceptive Christian thinkers of their century. With reference to Keble, Farrer wrote that one must detect shams, clarify argument and sift evidence, and then make up one's mind what is most worthy of love, most binding on conduct: "It is this decision, or this discovery, that is the supreme exercise of a truth-seeking intelligence."[4] Both Farrer and Ramsey, it is worth noting, remained men of large sympathies in ecclesiastical terms, much liked and admired by lifelong members of the Nonconformist traditions they had left.

One particular example of such commitment to them is a Congregationalist, W. A. Whitehouse, who was to play a key role in chairing the commission that produced *A Declaration of Faith* to help toward the unification of Congregationalist and Presbyterian churches in the UK in the 1970s. Whitehouse had become well aware of the German Church Struggle just before the outbreak of the Second World War from a base in Mansfield College, Oxford, where he undertook his training for the ministry. It is from this period that he dated his lifelong admiration for Farrer's work, not least as a preacher, Whitehouse himself being notable for the same talent.

Farrer by this time had served a curacy in Dewsbury, near Leeds (1928–31), during a period of dire economic slump, and had been ordained priest by the bishop of Wakefield in 1929. He too had learned German and began visits to Germany, though he never developed the enthusiasm for German theology that precipitated Whitehouse into transmitting the work of Karl Barth into English-speaking theology from 1946, well before the volumes of the *Church Dogmatics* had been translated into English.

Farrer remained critical of Bultmann (whose work he knew well), attended seminars with Emil Brunner in 1932, and came to know of the immense significance of Dietrich Bonhoeffer. He was invited to work at St. Edmund Hall, Oxford, as chaplain and tutor (1931–35) and then moved to be chaplain and fellow of Trinity College, Oxford (1935–60). It was in this period that Farrer met and married Katharine Newton, who was reading for a degree at St. Anne's, whence she developed into a novelist. Once Whitehouse himself became chaplain and tutor at Mansfield College (1943–47), he and Farrer could become better acquainted, and Farrer's publications remained on his shelves through moves to Durham (with Michael Ramsey), to the new University of Kent, and into retirement. T. F. Torrance was also in Oxford immediately after the war, meeting up with Whitehouse at the SCM Theological Club. This friendship would lead to the founding of the Society for the Study of Theology in 1952.

If we ask ourselves what it was that held established and nonestablished churchmen together in such lifelong commitments to one another, the answer is the vigor of their engagement with theology, brought to birth in years of deep social and political distress, and the fact that their responsibilities as theologians included preaching, of such central and abiding importance in the Reformed tradition. That's why these men could readily appreciate such a book as Farrer's *The Glass of Vision* (1948), because what they saw there was not only the importance of clarity in communication but also the invocation of biblical imagery in both preaching and liturgy.[5] And Farrer's contacts with such men, as well as with admirable Dominicans such as Victor White, helped to keep his own sympathies large, so that he was stifled neither by his colleges nor by his ecclesiastical preoccupations.

DONALD MACKINNON, OLIVER QUICK, AND GEORGE BELL

In addition, for a time there was the critical presence on the Oxford scene of the Scottish Episcopal layman Donald MacKinnon, an Oxford graduate and a tutor in philosophy at Keble College (1937–47) before he returned to Aberdeen as professor of moral philosophy. From a disestablished and minority church of the Anglican Communion, MacKinnon was a persistent and acute critic of prelacy, as well as of some of the Church of England's clergy. Most notable among those criticized was Kenneth E. Kirk, the author of the 1931 masterpiece *The Vision of God,* written during his tenure of the Regius Chair of Moral and Pastoral Theology. As bishop of Oxford, Kirk was one of the core members of the Anglo-Catholic group that campaigned so disgracefully against Anglican participation in the scheme of church union that brought the Church of South India into being in 1947. And those who might have argued differently from this group were largely silent, Oliver Quick among them.

In the course of a varied ministry, Quick had become perhaps the most significant doctrinal theologian of the Church of England in the first half of the twentieth century with his books on the doctrines of the creed and on sacramental theology. From being Van Mildert Canon Professor at Durham for five years, he had become Regius Professor of Divinity at Oxford in 1939. For all his admiration for Quick, MacKinnon saw that he had not provided a more generous vision of Catholicity than that which prevailed. Two things might be said in his favor. Like others, including Farrer and MacKinnon himself, who were of course much younger men, Quick was too deeply disturbed by the horrors of the war and what was becoming known as the "final solution" to find the energy for narrow-minded ecclesiastical politics. And Quick was ailing, collapsing in August 1943 while reading a lesson in Christ Church, and dying early in 1944. Quick had hoped that Farrer would succeed him in the Regius Chair, but that was not to be, and Farrer had to sit tight at Trinity until he went as warden to Keble for what turned out to be the last phase of his life, 1960–68.[6]

Where Church of England clergy were courageous, MacKinnon gave them outstanding support. A key example was George Bell, sometime dean of Canterbury, lifelong friend of Quick, bishop of Chichester from 1929, and a major player in the ecumenical movement. Any discussion with Bell in the period of the war would involve discussion of the fate of members of the Confessing Church in Germany and its opposition to the National Socialist government. Bell had known Bonhoeffer since 1933, and the latter's *The Cost of Discipleship* was dedicated to Bell, who wrote the foreword to its 1959 English translation. One of Bonhoeffer's most quoted sentences is "When Christ calls a man he bids him come and die," and his last message before his execution in Flossenburg in April 1945 was for Bell: "This is the end — for me the beginning of life."[7] As well as supporting the opponents of the then-German government, Bell became a fearless critic of British saturation bombing of German cities — Dresden, Hamburg, and Lubeck being obvious examples. It was Bell who was to lead a delegation of British churchmen to the British Zone of Germany in October 1946, a delegation that included Whitehouse as the English Free Churches' representative, as well as representatives of the Roman Catholic Church, the Church of Scotland, and the British Council of Churches — a most exceptional group for its time, which speaks much for Bell. Pastor Dr. J. Rieger, dean of the German Congregations in England, went as interpreter for the delegation, whose task was to study the situation in Germany and to work out the needs and tasks of the churches there.

THE SECOND WORLD WAR

The point here is that Oxford, with Farrer in Trinity, was no haven from knowledge of the horrors of what was happening and had happened in mainland Europe or across the world. Some of the young men who had survived, more or less in one piece and sufficiently sane, would inevitably arrive or return, bringing with them inescapable memories and the legacy of suffering to share with anyone who had a shred of imagination and sympathy for them, not least their college chaplains.

Some seventeen years after the conclusion of World War II, Farrer himself was to recollect the harrowing lessons of that time (in his 1962 *Love Almighty and Ills Unlimited*). In 1939, he had attempted a conversation with someone about the usefulness of discussing "the rules and conventions of civilised warfare." The friend had simply replied, "We shall stick at nothing. There's nothing too bad to be true in war. When we think we've reached the moral bottom, another depth will open, and down we'll go." And that recollection was coupled with a bitter reflection on the end of the war in the Far East: "Martyr-breaking techniques are certainly bad; but not uniquely so, when compared, let us say, with the bombing of Hiroshima."[8] The writing of Farrer's *Finite and Infinite* (1943) had been concluded as the German armies were occupying Paris, "after a campaign prodigal of blood and human distress."[9]

These men of the first half of the twentieth century remained haunted by human inhumanity, and one of the most powerful evangelists of his day, C. S. Lewis, had firsthand experience of the battlefield, as indeed did those clergy on all sides who served heroically as chaplains and stretcher-bearers and medical orderlies with their armed forces. Lewis himself had started at Oxford, but then had enlisted as a volunteer in the British Army and arrived in the Arras area in 1917 on his nineteenth birthday. He was wounded, but survived to return to Oxford in 1919 to complete his degree, and by 1924 was ensconced in Magdalen College. Lewis's own memories of the first war surfaced in print in his 1940 *The Problem of Pain,* articulating the vulnerability of many another of his generation and the horrors lurking in their imaginations. His *Surprised by Joy* (1955) is also illuminating here. In any event, Lewis managed to stay in Oxford, and although he was to move to a professorship in Cambridge in 1954, Oxford remained his home not just for vacations but also for many term-time weekends. The friendship he had with the Farrers was to be crucial to both of them, in different ways, as indeed we will see.

EVELYN UNDERHILL

At this juncture, we need to be alert to the fact that several significant theologians of the day were members of the laity — we have already identified MacKinnon and Lewis. It was not just clerical Oxford, nor even just Oxford, that was associated with exciting developments in theology of different kinds. Nor were all the laity male. We will come back to Lewis and Farrer, but we need at this point to backtrack a little to take in the importance of some of the other theologians of the day. And the first of these is Evelyn Underhill, one of three significant women in theology in the first two-thirds of the twentieth century in Britain. The other two are Helen Waddell and Dorothy L. Sayers. None of them, of course, could hold institutional positions in theology in their day, either in universities or in theological colleges, which were themselves very small and primarily concerned with the education of all-male clergy. These three pioneers made their marks nonetheless.

So far as the Oxford Faculty of Theology is concerned, Evelyn Underhill was the first woman lecturer to appear under its wing. This was because a Professor Upton had established an occasional series of lectures in commemoration of his sisters, just after Oxford had deigned to admit women to BA and MA degrees in 1920. The Unitarian Manchester College invited Evelyn Underhill to give the first series of lectures, published in 1922 as *The Life of the Spirit and the Life of Today.* As a bestselling author, Evelyn Underhill outstrips many another theologian, with much of her work reprinted since her day, and she provides us with ready access to the theological world of her time.

Evelyn Underhill wrote and lectured as the married, childless wife of a distinguished lawyer. She struggled through her own pilgrimage of faith with a series of Roman Catholic and Church of England advisers; and, like Lewis, she shared her experience with a wide public, though her evangelistic style was different indeed from his. A somewhat dry-as-dust introduction to the Church of England as a child left her without nourishment, and she did not find her way back to the church of her baptism until 1921, by which time she had made her mark as an independent writer of theology.

For education, Underhill took full advantage of the newly opened "Ladies" Department of King's College, University of London, and found help from specialists in the British Museum and other libraries and from trips to mainland Europe. King's, to its credit, made her its first woman fellow in 1927. King's at the time was housed in Kensington Square, and there she discovered the Chapel of Maria Assumpta, one of the Roman Catholic places of worship in which she found a form of worship different from that of her childhood. She had balked at becoming a Roman Catholic, however, when, in 1907, that church condemned the movement known as modernism, whose representatives wanted to bring the resources of their tradition into engagement with new developments in the human and other sciences, as she herself was to do. In any event, it was to the Church of England's gain, though to begin with Underhill wrote as a student of religion rather than of specifically Christian theology. This is clear from her first major publishing success, her 1911 book on mysticism, which had reached its twelfth edition by 1930, just as Farrer got to St. Edmund's Hall.

Mysticism was a cross-cultural study that contributed to the immense interest in the phenomenon of its title current in Evelyn Underhill's day. The book stimulated interest in the mystics, which in time resulted in scholarly editions and translations of their prose and poetry by many different contributors on a scale of which she herself could hardly have dreamed. The difference between her publication and those of others (Inge, James, and von Hügel, for instance) was that she found a way of exploring and commending the mystics as lovers of the divine, whose lives were transformed by what they loved, to a fascinated public. She insisted that human beings cannot finally be explained as merely "natural," but they have something about them that renders them capable of striving for and responding to the divine, which pervades our world while being other than our world.

As for Farrer, he believed that intelligence and love are the keys to approaching and being approached by the divine. That is to say, aspiring to the completion of our knowledge, choosing more carefully, and orientating our love appropriately helps to give rise to our sense of God. Although he wrote with more precision as a philosopher, he seems to have shared Underhill's perception of something distinctive about human beings, which was to be identified in the lives and writings of the mystics — exceptional only in the degree of their aspiration, rather than possessed of some capacities not normally found in human beings.

During the First World War, Underhill did her bit by working in naval intelligence and for those organizations that endeavored to support the families of servicemen. With members of her family, she endured the loss of two of her male cousins, and like many others learned compassion not just for the physical wreckage of some of the survivors, but also for the traumatized men who rightly could not endure either what they saw and experienced or what they were commanded to undertake.

At the beginning of the war, however, as we can see from her *Practical Mysticism* of 1914, she could commend those mystics who found their self-discipline and their prayers giving them renewed vitality, courage, singleness of heart, and self-control — all "military" virtues of great value in times of national stress. But the impact of the war and the sheer fatigue of what seemed to be an unending and unendurable struggle turned her into someone with a rather different stance by 1939; but that was still to come, and stemmed specifically from her growth back into the Church of England.

By 1918, she was ready to speak at conferences and religious retreats, lecturing on the spiritual life and education; and by the mid-1920s, she had begun to give retreat addresses even to the clergy. One invitation came to her from George Bell, when he was still dean of Canterbury, to give a retreat address to women in the cathedral. And she, too, learned from European theology, not least from Barth's emphasis on the transcendence of God, the sheer "otherness" of the source of grace making human response to the divine possible. In addition, before von Hügel died, he had persuaded her of the centrality of Christ for her own religious life and conviction, and thence she re-found stability in the Church of England. Her work resulted in a series of specifically Christian publications, culminating in another major book, her 1936 *Worship*. Underhill was offered an honorary doctor of divinity degree by the University of Aberdeen in 1938, but she was too frail to go and collect it, suffering as she was from the asthma and bronchitis from which she died in June 1941.

Readers of Farrer quickly discover that he so much made his reading his own that he does not give away many direct clues as to what he had or had not read and when, but given Evelyn Underhill's stature by the 1930s, it is more than credible that men such as A. M. Ramsey and Farrer himself had read her work, including her profound reflections on the Christian liturgy, as in *The Mystic Way* (1913), *The Mystery of Sacrifice* (1938), and her *Eucharistic Prayers from the Ancient Liturgies* (1939).

Underhill's readers would have been faced with the way in which she came to focus more and more on the centrality of the cross and on Christ's cry of abandonment. They would have confronted her conviction that it was a vocation for at least some Christians to follow Christ in his self-giving life, a life conceived by Jesus himself as one of sacrificial love, of trusting in God to bring new life from death. A theologian as focused on some of the most characteristic emphases of Christian faith as Farrer of course also attended in his own inimitable way to the centrality and significance of "sacrifice" — both to interpret Christ's own understanding of his life and to make it integral to our own.

Underhill herself came to have a specifically sacrificial understanding of pacifism by the outbreak of World War II, while acknowledging that for some, war was one of the ways in which National Socialism must be resisted. It is also clear that she would have been on Bell's side in challenging the Allied policy of bombing German cities packed with civilians and refugees. For her part, she had come to believe that the ills of the world could be mended only by the love that expresses itself in union with Christ's own sacrifice, in the practice of intercessory prayer, including, unquestionably, prayer for the enemy, and in embracing the miseries of war for civilians.[10]

The centrality of the sacrifice of love is an important focus of *Worship,* and for Farrer, Underhill's perspective was identical with his, with worship meaning primarily the priority of God, and with the divine invitation to worship and our response to that invitation being the means by which we move through this life, undertaken to achieve the "transfiguration of the whole created universe, that shining forth of the splendour of the Holy," to quote some of the last words of her great book.[11] Compare this with the moving last paragraph of *Finite and Infinite,* written as Paris fell. As Farrer observed, rational theology of the kind he had written would not tell us whether the campaign "prodigal of blood and human distress" was an "unqualified and irretrievable disaster," especially to the men who died, but, he added, "it is another matter if we believe that God Incarnate also died, and rose from the dead." The one thing a rational theologian did know was that whether Paris stood or fell and human beings lived or died, "God is God, and so long as any spiritual creature survives, God is to be adored."[12]

In addition, for the great ecumenical theologians of the day like Bell and A. M. Ramsey, *Worship* was a gift, because Evelyn Underhill had had years of profoundly empathetic and deliberate experience of the practice of worship of Christians of many varieties, learning to get beneath the surface and see what was really at stake there. She knew also that to understand Christ and the roots of Christian liturgy she needed to understand the worship of the synagogue and the importance of the reading of scripture. The centrality of the Psalter made mediation on behalf of others possible as well as making moral demands on the self, providing also for lament, grief, anger, and recovery from harm. She could not know as much of the Temple liturgy as is possible for us in our time, but she warmed to its integration of prayer, festival, and sacrifice, satisfying both sense and spirit. The one passport to worship, she came to see, was a humility that "realizes our common fragility and need of pardon."[13]

HELEN WADDELL

Another woman whose work Farrer could not have been unaware of was Helen Waddell. Whereas Evelyn Underhill had provoked widespread interest in the mystics and their passion for God, Helen Waddell made an equally extraordinary contribution to recovering delight in the medieval Latin world, lifelong Irish Presbyterian though she was.[14] A little younger than Underhill and nine years older than C. S. Lewis, who became an enthusiast for her work, she had been born into the family of a missionary in Japan. She was eventually to arrive in Oxford in 1919, the same year as Lewis, after a traumatic childhood somewhat comparable to his own.

Waddell's mother died when she was two, with eight brothers and a sister, Meg, six years older, left to their father's care. When she was ten, she and the others were brought to the very different environment of Ulster (Lewis's Ulster) by their father, who himself died, leaving them all to the care of a difficult stepmother. Helen had the benefit of an excellent education at the then new Queen's University, Belfast, between 1908 and 1911. From 1915 onward, she wrote with a view to publication, despite the discouraging circumstances of having to look after her stepmother in the straitened war years. On the death of her stepmother after the war ended, Helen, aged thirty, was free to head off to Oxford in 1919 as a "living out" student of Somerville College. By 1921, she was a member of their Senior Common Room, lecturing in St. Hilda's Hall, then in Bedford College, University of London, between 1922 and 1923, as Lewis was trying to find a niche for himself in Oxford.

Lady Margaret Hall offered Waddell a scholarship for travel; her time in Paris and then in the British Museum (as Evelyn Underhill had done in her time) inaugurated a period of astonishing productivity. *The Wandering Scholars* (1927) was an astonishing success, to be followed by *Medieval Latin Lyrics* (1929). In these books, she opened up the medieval world to delighted readers. Waddell was versatile and catholic in her tastes, translating *Manon Lescaut* too, and by 1931 had been honored with the first of a series of LittD degrees, with Durham University acknowledging her first, to be followed by Queen's, Belfast, in 1934, and then Columbia and St. Andrews.

These honors were not just for the works already mentioned but most notably for what was to her the most cherished production of a dozen years of study, *Peter Abelard* (1933), reprinted fifteen times that year alone and translated into nine languages.[15] To penetrate into and to reflect on the world of Abelard and Heloise, on the new "schools" of learning which were to turn into universities, on the controversies about the doctrines of the Trinity and the Eucharist, on the interpretation of scripture, and on the liturgy and hymnody of Peter's twelfth century required exhaustive learning; her gift for writing made this world accessible to a variety of readers. Since her day, of course, more work has been done which illuminates Heloise's influence on Abelard's ethics, more of their letters have been discovered, and scholars have developed a deeper appreciation of Abelard's poetry, hymnody, and theology in the shifting theological world in which he was one of its most brilliant teachers. It was Helen Waddell, however, who brought him and Heloise back to public attention, along with the changes in theology and religious sensibility he embodied. If nothing else, the crucial point for her readers was the renewed vitality that could be generated by appreciating the past—and, above all, by recognizing that theology does change. It needs reappraisal and reappropriation if it is not to be mindlessly overlooked, but the past contains priceless resources not to be ignored.

Apart from the delight of her readers in her work, the implications of what she was doing, whether as translator or commentator or in her re-tellings of the past, were vitally important, as she helped her readers to transcend the boundaries of their normal lives and to see the world differently. Reaching back into the world of late antiquity, in the 1930s she published *Beasts and Saints* and *The Desert Fathers,* and, after the war, *Stories from Holy Writ* (1949). Like Dorothy L. Sayers, with whom she managed to sustain some sort of friendship despite occasional disagreement, she worked at new translations and studies during the blitz under aerial bombardment. *More Latin Lyrics from Virgil to Milton* was to be published in 1967, two years after her death. The last ten years of her life were tragic: She was helplessly but patiently more or less bereft of her intelligence, though still focused in moments of lucidity on personal devotion to Christ.

There are many ways of finding spiritual resources, and the clever and well-educated men who had studied Latin and Greek in their schooldays found Helen Waddell's work especially worthy of their attention. In theological terms, she helped her readers, many of them without that classical education, to rediscover the world of many centuries before the

Reformation, and to find in its lyrics and its hymns resources for themselves, especially when confronted with the agonies of Peter Abelard and Heloise, who by divine grace remade their lives after the tragedy that led to their separation.

DOROTHY L. SAYERS

Helen Waddell was one example of this new type of feminine scholarship, and Dorothy L. Sayers was another. She picked up Waddell's baton in the immediate postwar years, so far as the medieval world was concerned, by her own rediscovery of Dante and the publishing success of her translation of and commentary on his *Divine Comedy.* To understand her achievement here, we need once more to backtrack a little before finally turning from her to the world of Oxford theology after the war to Farrer's immediate circle of friends and colleagues and their lasting legacies in theological terms.

Sayers is still well known as a writer of detective fiction, but she also made major contributions to the theological education and reeducation of a wide public in her day, well before she rediscovered Dante.[16] An only child, she was the daughter of a clergyman who had taught the choristers of Christ Church, Oxford, before he went off to a parish in East Anglia.[17] Educated partly at home and for a brief period away at school, in 1912 she entered Somerville College and was among the first batch of privileged women able to take their BA and MA degrees in 1920. (In Cambridge, the same concession was not to be given until 1948.) She was of course thoroughly familiar with the Book of Common Prayer and with the Authorized Version of the Bible, with her religious life framed by the demanding theology of the Church of England's Matins and Evensong.

A published poet, Sayers earned her living in the commercial world and in advertising journalism. With *Whose Body?* (1923), she launched herself into the relatively new field of detective fiction. She had to earn a good living, not only for herself but also for her son, born as the result of a love affair in 1924. Her marriage, to a man who had survived the war, took place in a registry office, since he had been married before (and had children from his first marriage). Her son was raised in the household of a trusted friend, where she visited him regularly. She eventually arranged to "adopt" him, as he was told, long before he realized that she was in fact his birth mother.

Enterprising as she was in exploring new media, we can understand how her radio play *He That Should Come,* first broadcast on Christmas Day 1938 and focused on Mary, a mother with a newborn child, would be important for women whose children were conceived and born in problematic circumstances. Equally extraordinary was her contribution to the revival of religious drama instigated by George Bell when he was dean of Canterbury Cathedral between 1924 and 1929.[18]

Bell's initiatives had resulted in T. S. Eliot's *Murder in the Cathedral* (1935), a revolutionary play in theatrical terms, quite apart from its importance for Canterbury itself in representing the conflict between Becket and his king. Eliot had been baptized and confirmed in the Church of England in 1927, and was to play a useful role in getting Charles Williams's novels published.

Important in their day were such plays as Williams's *Thomas Cranmer of Canterbury* (1936) and Sayers's *The Zeal of Thy House* and *The Devil to Pay* of 1937 and 1939. The former play (taking its title from Ps 69:9 and John 2:17) was of the greatest importance to her personally, another example of how an incident from the past could illuminate something of value in the present. A monk had chronicled the fire of 1174 and the fate of the man who had rebuilt the cathedral. Out of this, she concentrated on the theme of the integrity of work and the problem of the artist who neglects God for it, but whose work finally redeems his personal weaknesses when acknowledged as a tribute to the divine Creator. She conceived of these plays as works of instruction, filtering the Latin Western tradition of Christianity through her own unusual literary and dramatic talent. And she did it because she was convinced that the orthodox belief of the Church was itself exciting and dramatic in essence, which was Bell's conviction too.

Bell was concerned not just with the recovery of drama for instruction and evangelism, but with art and sculpture as well. Most notable was his cooperation with Walter Hussey (a product of Keble and Cuddesdon), who had seized his opportunity while priest of St. Matthew's Church, Northampton, to commission work from an astonishing roll call of twentieth-century artists and composers: Britten, Rubbra, Tippett, Moore, Berkeley, Arnold, Berkely, Finzi, Sutherland, and Auden, all brought to wide public attention by reviews in newspapers and journals. In 1946, Bell dedicated Graham Sutherland's great *Crucifixion.* Bell managed to move Hussey to his own diocese of Chichester, and in 1955, Hussey was made dean of the cathedral—resulting in more Sutherland,

Leonard Bernstein's *Chichester Psalms,* and work from William Walton, plus a tapestry from John Piper and a window from Marc Chagall.[19]

Dorothy L. Sayers participated in this rediscovery of the many ways in which Christian truth can be conveyed to the imagination as well as to the intellect. We recognize this perception quite readily in the work of Sayers, Williams, and Lewis; but we need to applaud the common ground shared here in attention given to the imagination by both Eric Mascall and Farrer, with the latter the one who makes most of it in his philosophy.[20]

As it turned out, her radio play of 1938 on the nativity was preparation for the much more ambitious venture of writing twelve radio plays (the first broadcast was on December 21, 1941) under the title *The Man Born to Be King;* following its publication, C. S. Lewis reread it every Easter (her detective fiction was never to his taste). If Eliot's *Murder in the Cathedral* was groundbreaking for the theater, Sayers's radio plays were groundbreaking for broadcasting, arousing controversy because of the unfamiliar experience for some of the devout of hearing the "voice" of Jesus of Nazareth for the first time, on air. Moreover, this play included a number of excellent parts for women.

Sayers was unaware of helping to open doors to all sorts of versions of the Gospel on stage and screen. To a group of theologians, including MacKinnon, which met at Malvern in 1941 for the purpose of reformulating theology for their troubled times, Sayers, the only woman contributor, presented her understanding of what she was doing. In *The Mind of the Maker* of that year, she made her case for believing that human creativity gives us clues to divine creativity, while also making it clear (as in *Zeal*) that the artist is subject to the judgment of God and must not either misuse her material or regard herself as their creator. Such claims about the analogy between human and divine creativity were novel from the pen of a woman writer, but were nonetheless appropriate. In both *A Science of God?* (1966) and in a lecture of the same year given in the United States, included in *Reflective Faith* (1972), Farrer too was to use the analogy of God as playwright or novelist, getting characters "on stage" and then developing the "plot" by letting them be themselves.

By the early 1940s, Sayers had given up writing detective fiction, and was so well known for her radio plays and *The Mind of the Maker* that she was offered a doctor of divinity degree by the archbishop of Canterbury, William Temple, who had consulted Oliver Quick. This honor she declined primarily because she wanted to be identified as a writer and not confined within the category of "theologian." She had always been something of a poet and a scholar, but theology from a woman had not been much wanted in her youth. On the back of her reputation as a writer of detective fiction, she could now make her way as a learned woman of theological competence, but she would do it on her terms, as a freelance, unconfined by ecclesiastical approval. Certainly she continued most vigorously to contribute to theological discussion about the future of Britain and of mainland Europe after the war.

There may have been another reason for her keeping a certain distance from some kinds of approval, since, unlike either Evelyn Underhill or Helen Waddell, she was enough of a feminist to get the bit between her teeth on the subject of the lamentable legacy of Christian thinking about women, exemplified in her own time by C. S. Lewis before his marriage transformed him. She thought Lewis's views on the hierarchic superiority of men to women as those of a "rather frightened bachelor,"[21] but at least he had the weight of tradition behind him, and she knew that tradition inside out. She was uneasy about "feminism" if it meant the dramatic forms of political protest associated with the campaign for the vote — that crucial symbol of women's claim to have minds of their own — but longstanding problems remained.

To give one simple example: That women were not regarded or treated as beings as fully human as men was signaled in World War II, when, in the case of those women who had died in bombardments, compensation for their deaths was initially rated at less than that for men. Fortunately, this policy so outraged public opinion that the difference was abolished, so that at least equality in death from aerial bombing was achieved.[22]

If we ask on what theological resources Sayers could rely beyond the text of the Gospels and what she discerned therein about Christ and his relationships with women, and beyond the truths she deduced from the central claim that in the Incarnation Christ had taken our human nature upon himself, the answer is to be found in her rediscovery of Dante, which simply revitalized her as a theologian when she was in her fifties. She admired Lewis as the greatest evangelist of her day, but she believed Charles Williams (another of Farrer's friends) to be "a major prophet," even though she never came to know him very well.[23] It was Williams who provoked her to reread Dante during the blitz, just as Helen Waddell was working at her Latin lyrics.

We have noted that Williams's *Thomas Cranmer of Canterbury* was one of his plays first produced for Canterbury Cathedral, but there were others, in addition to his poetry, novels, essays, and theology (for example, *The Descent of the Dove: The Holy Spirit in the Church* [1939]). Ever alert to new provocations to deeply engaged religious reflection, he had edited Kierkegaard's *Philosophical Fragments* as well as *The Letters of Evelyn Underhill* in 1943. Also in that year, he published the book that mattered most to Sayers, *The Figure of Beatrice*. On reading it she plunged back into reading Dante in the original, exchanging an ecstatic series of letters with Williams during what turned out to be the last nine months of his life.[24]

In *The Divine Comedy* she found that Dante's love for and recollection of a living human person was for him a symbol of the full humanity of women. Dante's Beatrice was a mistress of philosophy and science as well as of theology. He represented her as the perfect integration of the intellectual, the emotional, and the bodily in her own great beauty, supremely well fitted for teaching Dante whatever he needed to know. Also, and of the greatest importance, she represented to him the sacramental mediation of grace and salvation.

It took time for Sayers fully to work out all the dimensions of Dante's importance, but just as Helen Waddell brought Peter Abelard alive in the twentieth century, so Sayers brought Dante alive for readers who had never before encountered him. We might expect C. S. Lewis, for instance, to be an enthusiast for her scholarship, as indeed he was, and he also admired the fact that she brought theology to a huge audience, just as he did. Sayers's theological appraisal of Dante has not been surpassed. Her audience included the readers and hearers of her translation and commentary on Dante, of her indefatigable lectures, and of another cathedral play. Important here was her friendship with a young lecturer in Italian at Cambridge University, Barbara Reynolds, during the last fifteen years of her life. Dr. Reynolds arranged Sayers's lectures in Cambridge and eventually completed her translation of the third section of *The Divine Comedy*, "Paradise."

When she came to read Farrer's *A Study in St. Mark* (1951), Sayers found fascinating analogies between the relationship of king and priest in Israel and that of pope and emperor in Dante; and the Farrers certainly had the opportunity to hear her lecture. Her paper "The Poetry of the Image in Dante and Charles Williams" was given at St. Hugh's College, Oxford, in 1952. Katharine Farrer was interested enough to want to chase up another lecture, one given to the Oxford Socratic Society in 1954.[25]

By that date, Sayers had put her finger on the importance of what Farrer said about love and the "truth-seeking intelligence," exemplified for her in Dante. She wrote in a letter to a friend that "where the intellect is dominant it becomes the channel of all the other feelings." She went on:

> The "passionate intellect" is *really* passionate. It is the only point at which ecstasy can enter. I do not know whether we can be saved through the intellect, but I do know that I can be saved by nothing else. I know that, if there is judgement, I shall have to be able to say: "This alone, Lord, in Thee and in me, have I never betrayed, and may it suffice to know and love and choose Thee after this manner, for I have no other love, or knowledge, or choice in me."[26]

Here she is at one with both Underhill and Farrer in identifying knowing, choosing, and willing as those characteristics of human beings that render them aspirants for the divine, but she had her own distinctive way of communicating her convictions to a wide public.

In revealing and interpreting Dante's intelligence and passion to a wide audience, she began by writing what she always considered to be her best cathedral play, *The Just Vengeance,* written for Lichfield Cathedral's 750th anniversary in 1946 — the title picking up a phrase from Beatrice's teaching of the doctrine of redemption from the experience of the grace, joy, and delight of salvation. Dante's great text had been written in a world of politically intractable circumstances, surpassed indeed by 1940s Europe, but sufficiently illuminating nonetheless.

Reading Dante in air-raid shelters, and being sufficiently aware of the bombing of German cities, she set the action of her play in the precise moment of the death of a bomber pilot, as he is shot down. In that moment, he learns of God's redemptive activity through Christ's cross, chooses it, and is embraced by it. Of much significance here is the last piece for the choir in the play, concerned above all with the praise of God, in which the redeemed are promised that they will praise God "with the holy and glorious flesh," with sensitive heart, and with "searching and subtle brain."[27] Here she was echoing the words Dante attributed to King Solomon in *Paradise*, where he appears as the embodiment of royal and divinely given wisdom (1 Kgs 3:4–13) and as the poet of the Song of Songs. It was to Solomon that Dante gave the praise of the promise of resurrection: "when we put completeness on afresh, / All the more gracious shall our person be, / Reclothed in the holy and glorious flesh" (Canto xiv).

No one in Sayers's day with a shred of sensitivity could ignore the evidence of the capacity of human beings to inflict unimaginable horror on one another, but her Christian conviction refused to let such evil have the last word. *The Just Vengeance* and, more importantly, the actual translations of and commentary on *The Divine Comedy* were richly satisfying texts for many reasons, but not least because of their concern for divine justice and for the promise of grace and redemption beyond it. In Dante, her readers could recognize the characters of their own day as she pointed them out: Chamberlain, "Butcher" Heydrich, The Lady-with-the-Lampshade-Made-of-Human-Skin, Quisling, and so on.

As it happened, Sayers was working on *The Divine Comedy* when E. V. Rieu was launching his Penguin Classics series, which began with his own translation of Homer's *Odyssey* in 1944. She made a notable contribution to the new venture. Her translation with commentary of Dante's *Hell* in 1949 led to the only academic honor she accepted after her first degrees, a Durham doctor of letters in 1950. *Purgatory* followed in 1955. With the translation of all but the last thirteen cantos of *Paradise* completed — but minus introduction, commentary, and notes — she turned to another medieval classic, *The Song of Roland,* published in 1957, the year in which she most unexpectedly died. The last thirteen cantos of *Paradise* on the vision of God were to be completed by Barbara Reynolds, incorporating the parts of the section that Sayers had already completed. The three volumes have rarely been out of print since.[28] Whatever the challenges to Christian belief, and there were and are many, Dante and his interpreter made belief credible, notwithstanding the political difficulties of his day, of hers, and, arguably, of ours.

C. S. LEWIS

At this point, we return to the Oxford scene more directly, and we do so by way of brief reflection on C. S. Lewis, whose name has already appeared a number of times in this chapter. We recall his origins in Belfast, in a grief-stricken family, in which in 1908 his father had lost his own father, then his wife (who died on her husband's birthday), and then his own brother. After an initial period in Oxford, C. S. Lewis saw action in the trenches in France, was wounded, and was back in Oxford by 1919, ensconced in Magdalen College between 1924 and 1954, and then in a professorship in Cambridge until his death in 1963. His colleagues may have experienced a mixture of exasperation and jealousy at the success of his Christian evangelism, some of it conducted by correspondence with those who read his books. From his first robust and controversial book of apologetics, *The Pilgrim's Regress: An Allegorical Apology for Christianity, Reason and Romanticism* (1933), through *The Screwtape Letters* of 1942, to the Narnia books of the 1950s, Lewis fought his battles with his eye always on the main point of attack, passionately concerned about the realities on which he meditated, as Farrer himself readily acknowledged.[29]

For an appraisal of Lewis by one of the circle closely associated with Farrer in the 1950s, however, it is worth noting some of John Lucas's words from a lecture of 1992, the fiftieth anniversary of Lewis's Riddell Memorial Lectures given in King's College, Newcastle on Tyne, in 1942, when Lewis lectured on "The Abolition of Man." What Lucas found so moving in Lewis's work overall was his preoccupation with the nature of God, and what God's love is like; how values collapse unless we put first things first; how prayers should be prayed and what things we ought to ask for. And finally, "in the Gethsemane at the close of his own life," with the questions of how a loving God "could subject him to false hope and final unutterable grief," Lucas wrote that Lewis was "the twentieth century's 139th Psalm."[30]

Lucas was referring to the death of Joy Lewis in 1960. Lewis first became acquainted with her through correspondence. She was an established professional writer, North American, of Jewish origin, baptized with her two boys in a Presbyterian church in 1948. By that time, Lewis was firmly established as a don, the product of a largely single-sex world in which most of his important relationships were with men. Both Katharine and Austin Farrer were firm enough friends with Lewis to attend his and Joy's registry office wedding in 1956, and Lewis's *Reflections on the Psalms* (1958) is dedicated to them. It was in October 1956 that Katharine had a premonition that something was wrong with Joy. She telephoned, but just before the phone rang, Joy tripped over the wire, felt her leg snap, and found herself helpless on the floor with the telephone receiver beside her, hearing Katharine's anxious voice at the other end. Austin, priest as well as friend, gave Joy final absolution on her deathbed, and read her burial service in stark Cranmerian form, under the stress of his own deep sorrow for her.

As Farrer was to recall in his commemorative address on C. S. Lewis, the latter had been put almost beside himself by Joy's death, as indeed his *A Grief Observed* (1961) most profoundly reveals. This short text, arguably the best thing he ever wrote, at first was published pseudonymously. Joy he referred to as "H"—the initial of Helen, Joy's first name.

And he called himself, the author, "N. W. Clerk," a pseudonym he had used on other occasions. The "N. W." derived from an Anglo-Saxon phrase meaning "I know not whom," and "Clerk" meant simply one able to read and write.

Farrer's *Love Almighty and Ills Unlimited* was published in 1962, and it is credible that its last chapter, "Griefs and Consolations," has Lewis's experience and work in mind. Only after Lewis's death in 1963 was the identity of the author of *A Grief Observed* revealed to the general public. Then, in his essay on Lewis as an apologist, Farrer could link this later book to Lewis's *The Problem of Pain* of some twenty years earlier.

Farrer may well have written here what he had actually endeavored to say to Lewis in person, trying to emend the way in which Lewis considered human beings in relation to God. Lewis in his opinion had viewed them too narrowly as essentially moral wills and thus their relation to God as no more than a moral relation, with pain as a moral remedy. Farrer wanted more allowance for the fact that the nature of the physical world carries with it "the chance of random and disastrous accident" to sentient creatures. Lewis had not sufficiently allowed for the requirements of the vast physical system that God as Creator is committed to uphold. In such a world, pain is better understood as "the sting of death, the foretaste and ultimately the experience of sheer destruction," which cannot be related to the will of God as an evil wholly turned into a moral instrument. Rather, he argued, pain is "the bitter savour of that mortality out of which it is the unimaginable mercy of God to rescue us."[31]

Not least because the many productions of *Shadowlands* hardly do justice to C. S. Lewis, it is important for readers of *A Grief Observed* to read not only Farrer's reflections but also Lewis's *Letters to Malcolm,* published posthumously in 1964, to see where Lewis had moved. The very last words of *A Grief Observed* sadly echo Canto xxxi of Dante's *Paradise* at the point where Beatrice "did smile and look on me once more, / Then to the eternal fountain turned her head," with Lewis writing of Joy, "She smiled, but not at me," then quoting Dante's "fountain" line in Italian. Lewis may, one hopes, eventually have recovered the perspective that he wrote about in the final chapter of *The Four Loves* (1960).

This, like his last book, tells us much about the way in which Joy changed his understanding and evaluation of women and about how all this was to be expressed in the language of his religious convictions. In the last chapter he had anticipated her death by claiming that in heaven "there will be no anguish and no duty of turning away from our earthly Beloveds," and had given two reasons: first, because we ourselves shall have turned to the Fountain — that is, "from the creatures He made lovable to Love Himself"; and second, because "we shall find them all in Him."[32] These words may have become among the most significant Lewis wrote, both for himself and for his readers, once the initial agony of his bereavement was over and he found himself approaching his own death.

POSTWAR CHALLENGES

We turn, finally, to the new challenges opening for Farrer and his friends in the world past the Second World War, picking up some recollections of John Lucas, who matriculated in Oxford in 1947, just five years after Lewis had given his Newcastle lectures on "The Abolition of Man." Lucas has written that the philosophical climate in which he grew up in Oxford was one of "extreme aridity." Much prized was the ability not to be convinced. A competent tutor could disbelieve any proposition, no matter how true, and "the more sophisticated could not even understand the meaning of what was being asserted."[33]

Undergraduates — and not only those reading philosophy — were avidly reading A. J. Ayer's *Language, Truth and Logic,* finished in July 1935.[34] The book rejected authority in both knowledge and morals; it had politically radical implications. Completed before Ayer's twenty-fifth birthday, undergraduates took to it like ducks to water: it had the singular advantage of being short and clear. It was well discussed in the philosophical journals, and Ayer's Oxford career seemed to be launched, first at Christ Church. After the war, in which he served in the Welsh Guards and undertook an extraordinary series of jobs in various postings, he was invited to Wadham College as tutorial fellow and dean. Within a year, however, and before he was thirty-six, he became professor of philosophy at University College, London, and so was out of the Oxford scene.

As John Lucas's comments reveal, however, Ayer's influence was long lasting. Nonetheless, Christian philosophers were not defeated. Some of them were at work in a depleted Oxford during the war years, staking out a rather different perspective on the world and its inhabitants. Farrer's *Finite and Infinite* (1943) was to be complemented by Eric Mascall's work. Working at Christ Church from 1945 to 1962 before, like Ayer, moving to the University of London (but to the very different climate of King's College, at which Theology was located), Mascall was a tough polemicist on behalf of Christian "orthodoxy." He published *He Who Is* in 1943 and a sequel, *Existence and Analogy*, in 1949. Both of these books appropriated the theology and philosophy of St. Thomas Aquinas for the Church of England. Two further collections of essays were to strengthen the theological riposte to Ayer and to those who agreed with him in finding theological language meaningless nonsense. A book edited by Ian T. Ramsey called *Prospect for Metaphysics* (1961)[35] helped to make the theological landscape inhabitable once more, but for our purposes the more significant collection was *Faith and Logic* (1957).[36]

The latter collection included two essays by Farrer (still at Trinity College) as well as essays by John Lucas (Corpus Christi College, Cambridge) and by colleagues at other colleges, including R. M. Hare (Balliol College and subsequently an Oxford philosophy professor), I. M. Crombie (Wadham College, Oxford), and M. B. Foster (Christ Church, Oxford, and the "Keble" presence before Farrer himself went there as warden). Another contributor, Christopher Stead, a classicist and philosopher, was fellow and chaplain at Keble between 1949 and 1971, before returning to Cambridge as a professor of divinity. Basil Mitchell, a fellow of Keble, wrote on the grace of God as well as the introduction, and then edited the whole collection. Apart from his account in the introduction of the impact of Ayer's work and the parting of the ways between philosophers and theologians, what is important for our purposes is the grateful acknowledgment by Mitchell of the fact that Eric Mascall had convened the group immediately after the war, keeping it going for its first ten years and providing the group's name, "The Metaphysicals." We will attend to the significance of Basil Mitchell's career in due course. At this juncture, we notice that he also acknowledged the contribution to the group of Iris Murdoch, who was bound to leave it as the nature of her convictions changed. There were to be others whose gratitude for membership in it was lifelong, such as the distinguished writer of Christian ethics Helen Oppenheimer.

IRIS MURDOCH

We attend first to Iris Murdoch, born in Dublin of Anglo-Irish parents, at school in England, and reading classics and philosophy at Oxford. After employment during World War II as a civil servant, she worked for the United Nations Refugee Relief Association in Belgium and Austria before returning to Oxford, to St. Anne's College, to teach philosophy. She was eventually able to turn full time to life as an independent writer. For some time before her death, she was receiving considerable attention from theologians, for the reason articulated by David Tracy: "Christianity's classic narrative of creation, fall, and redemption is deeply embedded in Iris Murdoch's imagination of the human drama."[37]

If we turn to some of her novels, we can to a degree be taken under the skin, as it were, of the religious sensibility of the women and men we have so far been discussing, and appreciate the depth of her perception of the shifts and turns of the human heart and its entanglement with living religious tradition — though we cannot deal with this exhaustively here. For instance, in chapter 14 of *The Red and the Green* (1965), a novel that draws on her Anglo-Irish world, there is a deeply perceptive passage about one of her characters, Barney, at the ceremonies of Tenebrae on Thursday of Holy Week, thinking about the mess of his life. He knows, clearly, that he "could make everything simple and innocent once again," and that if he lifted a finger to attempt that simplicity and innocence, "he would receive from the other region which had seemed so far away outside him, the inrush of an entirely new strength." He had thought himself lost, but all the time "he had been held so close that he could not escape even if he would."[38] Barney's tragedy is that in the end, he declines to lift that finger and sort out his life and the damage he is doing to others, so he declines that redemption which is at hand for him.

To take another example, we can recall the abbess in *The Bell* (1958) advising Michael that God would in God's own way and time complete our poor efforts: "Remember that all our failures are ultimately failures in love. Imperfect love must not be condemned and rejected, but made perfect. The way is always forward, never back."[39] Michael grievously fails to offer Nick love; after Nick's suicide, as he gradually recovers from the overwhelming sense of his own failure in love, knowing that he "should impetuously and devotedly and beyond all reason have broken the alabaster cruse of very costly ointment,"[40] he continues to attend Mass, making no movement and not reaching out his hand.[41] "He would have to be found and fetched or else he was beyond help. Perhaps he was beyond help."[42]

That human beings are not beyond help is evident in two other novels, but what they help us to identify is that for Iris Murdoch, that help is not precisely the identifiable help of divine grace as, let us say, Basil Mitchell wrote about it in *Faith and Logic*. Thus in *Henry and Cato* (1976) we have Henry engaging in an orgy of revenge for having been a much less-loved younger son, realizing that even his best intentions are simply beyond his moral level, but learning to focus on what is other than himself. A text significant for Iris Murdoch was Phil 4:8 and its injunction to think on those things that are true, honest, just, pure, lovely, and of good report. This for her meant attention to painting, landscape, and the independent existence of what is utterly other than ourselves, including other persons. Murdoch stresses the importance of imagination and attention in our efforts to do justice to these other realities, and Henry's efforts result in his gradually being able to love a woman and find happiness with her.

The tragic figure in this novel is Cato, a convert to Roman Catholicism from a family with a Quaker grandfather, who had continued to go to Quaker meetings without believing in God. He had taught Cato's father never to lie and that the world was godless almost in one breath. Cato is presented to us in the novel as one who despite his background has been "invaded by Christ," experiencing God as Trinity, "with an invasion of spirit which seemed totally alien to his 'personality' as he had known it before, but which became the very selfness of his self."[43] Becoming a priest and a member of a religious order, in mission work in a poor part of London he falls for a "baby crook," whom eventually he kills. His own egoism feeds upon the redemptive image of Christ and this leads him to disaster, identified at the point marked by Cato's reflection, "Not I but Christ. Now only I. There is only I to *be* Christ, thought Cato."[44] When with the aid of another priest, Brendan, he is stripped of his self-esteem, Cato learns something especially horrifying from Brendan. Cato says, "I loved that boy and I led him astray and I killed him." Brendan replies, "We live by redemptive death. Anyone can stand in for Christ." But Brendan also insists that everything we concoct about God is an illusion, that we have to forsake everything to be Christ's disciple, to quote Christ's own words.[45]

And this, finally, is beautifully exemplified in *Nuns and Soldiers* (1982). Anne is a Benedictine, released into "that other Love whose reality, as she experienced it, she could not doubt. Not I but Christ." Like Cato, she had lived with the passion of Christ, somehow inside the doctrine of the Trinity, but she comes to the conviction that she must move away from this life, and start all over again. She has to discuss leaving the community with her abbess, but rejects the latter's view that the change was in some sense the will of God, since for Anne it was clear that it was under "a negative and agnostic sign" that she must proceed.[46] A moving description of her encounter with Jesus himself has at its center her question, "Sir, what shall I do to be saved?" and his reply,

"You must do it all yourself, you know."[47] She leaves to find salvation in having nothing and being with those who have nothing, no longer believing in God.[48]

To put it briefly, what Iris Murdoch is offering through the medium of her novels is the exploration of what we might call a spirituality of renunciation. Spiritual growth may proceed by giving up the exercise of power, though perhaps in the process someone may find much happiness. It may mean giving up personal fantasies, especially those that have an identifiably religious character. It may mean the risk of giving love, and of enduring the renunciation of love, even when that love just might give us some hoped-for "fulfillment." But it also in a sense means giving up the God of our own idolatries, and to that extent she is in line with a central strand of Christian and indeed of many other religious traditions.

That said, Iris Murdoch's novels provide ample illustration of the degree to which she in fact parted company with the "Metaphysicals," and they would in any case be familiar with the position she worked out in the essays she wrote between 1964 and 1969 that were published as *The Sovereignty of Good* (1970) when she was still at St. Anne's.[49] The distance between her position and the explicitly Christian commitments of the group can be briefly indicated by reference to just one example from her texts, which might have been written by someone like Evelyn Underhill in her book on mysticism before she had become recommitted to Christianity. Iris Murdoch wrote: "No (conventional) God, no Church, no social support or protective institutions. No simple or secure connection with morality." Mystics dispense with these things, inhabiting "a spiritual world unconsoled by familiar religious imagery."[50]

Farrer, as we know, wrote eloquently about learning to acknowledge the inadequacy of our images for God, and of learning "to adhere nakedly to the imageless truth of God," but it is still God to whom he adheres.[51] In Murdoch's case, while her detachment of belief did not take her in the direction of A. J. Ayer, let us say, it certainly did remove her from unambiguous commitment of the kind that characterized Farrer and his circle, and from those who came to be associated with it, such as Helen Oppenheimer. Iris Murdoch's work continues to be of importance for anyone who wants an alternative to the view of the "moral self" that issues in the behavior of "I came, I saw, and I made it a desert," and there is undoubtedly a long tradition of "seeing" associated with a specifically Christian morality.[52] I think we have to conclude, however, that Murdoch's position has less to do with the vitality of the Christian tradition than with its enervation.

HELEN OPPENHEIMER

A near contemporary of John Lucas, Helen Oppenheimer had originally thought of reading English at university, but her mother and her headmistress put their heads together and between them encouraged her to read P.P.E. (Politics, Philosophy, and Economics), which she studied at Lady Margaret Hall. It was in philosophy and ethics that she was to find profound satisfaction, not least because, as we have seen, philosophy was undergoing some major and stimulating changes during her time at university. She lectured at Cuddesdon Theological College, Oxford, putting theological ethics firmly on the map there.[53] She was eventually to become president of the young Society for the Study of Christian Ethics, after a lifetime's writing on how to integrate theology and ethics, not least when writing about marriage and divorce law reform. The very existence of the new society represents a major shift in the priority given to theological ethics within the theological enterprise as a whole, at least in Britain, as compared with Helen Oppenheimer's pioneering days at Cuddesdon. In addition, along with Basil Mitchell in particular, she has had a long association with some of the Church of England's commissions of one kind or another. She has preached many sermons, beginning in an era when it was uncommon to find women doing anything of the kind.[54] Her commitment to the presence of women as well as of men in the lay as well as the ordained ministry of the church is part and parcel of a deeply orthodox faith, recognized in 1993 when she was awarded a Lambeth doctor of divinity degree—her first qualification in theology.

Oppenheimer's first book was dedicated to the "Metaphysicals," who roped her into their discussions and encouraged her first papers.[55] References to the work of Ian Crombie, Austin Farrer, Michael Foster, C. S. Lewis, John Lucas, Eric Mascall, Basil Mitchell, and Ian Ramsey invite us into their conversation, as it were, though of course by that time she had many other "conversation partners." Among this group, some have always been especially important to her. For instance, in her very fine book *The Hope of Happiness,* she recalled some of the twentieth century's prophets, "inspired with a positive vision of what Christianity is about," and robustly affirmed, "Anglicans should not quickly let Austin Farrer be forgotten."[56] And she included Farrer, along with St. Augustine, Julian of Norwich, Dante, Thomas Traherne, and C. S. Lewis, among those members of the communion of saints "who have put their imaginations to work in the service of their fellow Christians," thinking it right and fitting "to hearten us with positive images of God's purposes, filling in and enriching our hopes."[57]

BASIL MITCHELL

Among Oppenheimer's list of members of the Metaphysicals associated with Farrer is the name of the person who has made perhaps the most significant contribution to changes in the climate in which religious belief may be discussed, and that person is Basil Mitchell. He himself recalls the novelty in Oxford of the Joint Honours School of Philosophy and Theology in Oxford in the 1970s, evidence of the reconstruction of a relationship, even if sometimes an uneasy one, as compared with the days that produced *Faith and Logic*. For twenty years fellow and tutor in philosophy at Keble, in the year of Farrer's death (1968) he transferred to Oriel College and succeeded Ian Ramsey as Nolloth Professor of the Philosophy of the Christian Religion, remaining there until his retirement.

Mitchell was to write what continues to be the best short assessment of Farrer as a philosopher that has so far appeared, having come to know him exceptionally well.[58] He reminded his readers of Farrer's exhaustive knowledge of the entire Western philosophical tradition, "not excluding Augustine and Aquinas or Leibniz and Kant," and how he had never been intimidated by the so-called "revolution in philosophy" of the 1950s and 1960s, while sharing with it its concern for "clarity and precision of statement." It was not that the theological climate of the day was hospitable to Farrer's understanding of the tasks of theology either, but he simply carried on with the exercise of his particular gifts of philosophizing within the Christian tradition, insisting the while that "the tradition itself required a continuous effort of interpretation and criticism" if it were not to stultify.

Mitchell's own range is formidable. His first major book was *Law, Morality and Religion in a Secular Society* (1967), and besides making a major contribution to the work of the doctrine commission of the Church of England (1978–84), he also contributed to its reports on the issues of the 1960s and 1970s, such as abortion, sterilization, and the medical care of the dying. He was primarily responsible for setting up, in Oxford in 1985, the Ian Ramsey Centre for the study of further ethical problems arising from the interface of medical-scientific research and practice.

In 1987, Mitchell was honored with a volume titled *The Rationality of Religious Belief*, which included essays by two of the Metaphysicals, John Lucas and Ian Crombie.[59] And the Christian Philosophers Group instigated by Ian Ramsey flowered into the British Society for the Philosophy of Religion (the BSPR), which at its 1997 meeting on "Rationality and Religion" honored Mitchell on his eightieth birthday. At that meeting he was clearly delighted by the number and variety of those present, including, significantly, many graduate candidates for doctorates in philosophy and theology. In the meantime, the Royal Institute of Philosophy sponsored conferences on "Reason and Religion," "The Philosophy in Christianity," and "Philosophy, Religion and the Spiritual Life."

In the year 2000, at the Oxford meeting of the BSPR, Basil Mitchell heard Dr. Douglas Hedley of the University of Cambridge Faculty of Divinity give a main paper, "Imagination and Revelation," in which he discussed the work of Austin Farrer. At last, one might say, Farrer's "truth-seeking intelligence" is being honored once more, and that not least by those who became his friends, who in their turn have brought about the changes in the ways in which we think and believe and live, and which I have outlined in this introductory essay.

NOTES

1. Austin Farrer, *Faith and Speculation* (London: A & C Black, 1967), 129.

2. See Farrer's superb selections from the Bible and the way he connected them together in his 1956 *A Short Bible;* and his 1957 introduction and notes to *The New Testament,* as well as his more controversial biblical commentaries.

3. For the most recent appreciation of Ramsey by the current Van Mildert Canon Professor at Durham, David Brown, see "God in the Landscape: Michael Ramsey's Vision," *Anglican Theological Review* 83:4 (2001): 775–92, on the significance of Ramsey's lifelong possession of a reproduction he bought as an undergraduate at Magdalen College, Cambridge, in 1923, and which now hangs in Nashotah House, Wisconsin. The original of Perugino's 1483/1485 *The Crucifixion with the Virgin, St. John, St. Jerome and St. Mary Magdalene* is part of the Mellon Collection in the National Gallery of Art, Washington, DC.

4. Austin Farrer, "Keble and His College," in *The End of Man* (ed. Charles C. Conti; London: SPCK, 1973), 157.

5. See Kenneth Grayston, "Farrer Fares Far," *The Presbyter: A Journal of Reformed Churchmanship* 7:3 (1949): 10–14.

6. Paul Lucas, "Oliver Quick," *Theology* 96 (1993): 4–19; Donald M. MacKinnon, "Oliver Chase Quick as a Theologian," *Theology* 96 (1993): 101–17. See also MacKinnon's own early works of the war years published in 1940: *The Church of God* and *God the Living and the True,* and his essay "The Controversial Bishop Bell," in *The Stripping of the Altars* (London: Fontana, 1969), 83–94.

7. See *Brethren in Adversity: George Bell, the Church of England, and the Crisis of German Protestantism, 1933–1939* (ed. Andrew Chandler; Woodbridge: Boydell & Brewer, 1997).

8. Austin Farrer, *Love Almighty and Ills Unlimited* (London: Collins, 1966), 178.

9. Austin Farrer, *Finite and Infinite* (London: Dacre Press, 1943), 300.

10. There was much disruption precipitated by the evacuation of children, with or without their parents, to the countryside and to new ways of life wholly unfamiliar to them — with the alternative in the cities of sleeping somewhere underground.

11. Evelyn Underhill, *Worship* (London: Nisbet, 1936), 343.

12. Farrer, *Finite and Infinite,* 300.

13. Underhill, *Worship,* 175.

14. One major biography of her exists, written by a Roman Catholic Benedictine, Dame Felicitas Corrigan: *Helen Waddell: A Biography* (London: Gollancz, 1986).

15. The most recent major biography of Abelard is by Michael Clanchy, *Abelard: A Medieval Life* (Oxford: Blackwell, 1977).

16. It is to her younger colleague, Dr. Barbara Reynolds, an expert in Italian language and literature, that we owe the major biography, *Dorothy L. Sayers: Her Life and Soul* (London: Hodder & Stoughton; New York: St. Martin's Press, 1993), and the volumes of her collected letters published by the Dorothy L. Sayers Society, 1995–2000.

17. Dorothy L. Sayers's *The Nine Tailors* (1934) reflects the religious and cultural world of her Fenland childhood and upbringing.

18. See Kenneth Pickering, *Drama in the Cathedral: The Canterbury Festival Plays, 1928–1948* (Worthing: Churchman, 1985).

19. See Tom Devonshire-Jones, "Art-Theology-Church: A Survey 1940–1990 in Britain," *Theology* 95 (1992): 360–70; and Gareth Turner, "Aesthete, Impresario, and Indomitable Persuader: Walter Hussey at St. Matthew's, Northampton, and Chichester Cathedral," in *The Church and the Arts* (Studies in Church History 28; ed. Diana Wood; Oxford: Blackwell, 1992), 523–35.

20. David Brown, *Tradition and Imagination* (Oxford: Oxford University Press, 1999); and *Discipleship and Imagination* (Oxford: Oxford University Press, 2000).

21. *The Letters of Dorothy L. Sayers III 1944–1950: A Noble Daring* (ed. Barbara Reynolds; Bury St. Edmunds: Dorothy L. Sayers Society, 1998), 375.

22. See her essays "Are Women Human?" (1938) and "The Human Not Quite Human" (1941) in her collection *Unpopular Opinions* (London: Gollancz, 1946).

23. See Stephen Platten, "Diaphanous Thought: Spirituality and Theology in the Work of Austin Farrer," *Anglican Theological Review* 69 (1987): 30–50.

24. See Barbara Reynolds, *The Passionate Intellect: Dorothy L. Sayers' Encounter with Dante* (Kent, Ohio: Kent State University Press, 1989). Sayers's essay about reading Dante as a result of Williams's book is "And Telling You a Story," first published in C. S. Lewis's edition of *Essays Presented to Charles Williams,* a memorial volume of 1947.

25. See Dorothy L. Sayers, *Introductory Papers on Dante* (London: Methuen, 1954); and for the two essays on Williams, see her *Further Papers on Dante* (London: Methuen, 1957).

26. *The Letters of Dorothy L. Sayers IV 1951–1957: In the Midst of Life* (ed. Barbara Reynolds; Bury St. Edmunds: Dorothy L. Sayers Society, 2000), 138.

27. For the extract from *The Just Vengeance,* see Ann Loades, *Dorothy L. Sayers: Spiritual Writings* (London: SPCK, 1993), 159.

28. *The Comedy of Dante Alighieri the Florentine I Hell* (London: Penguin, 1949); *II Purgatory* (London: Penguin, 1955)—both volumes dedicated to Charles Williams; *III Paradise* (London: Penguin, 1962).

29. See Farrer's address in honor of Lewis after the latter's death in 1963: "In His Image: In Commemoration of C. S. Lewis," in *The Brink of Mystery* (ed. Charles C. Conti; London: SPCK, 1976), 45–47; and his essay "The Christian Apologist," in *Light on C. S. Lewis* (ed. Jocelyn Gibb; London: Bles, 1965), 23–43.

30. John R. Lucas, "The Restoration of Man," *Theology* 98 (1995): 445–56, at p. 453.

31. Farrer, "The Christian Apologist," 41.

32. C. S. Lewis, *The Four Loves* (London: Fount, 1987), 116.

33. John R. Lucas, *Freedom and Grace* (London: SPCK, 1976), ix.

34. Ben Rogers, *A. J. Ayer: A Life* (London: Chatto & Windus, 1999), particularly chaps. 8 and 9.

35. Important, too, was the work of Dorothy M. Emmet (author of *The Nature of Metaphysical Thinking* [1949], *Function, Purpose and Powers* [1958], and *Rules, Roles and Relations* [1966]), who always kept her eye on what Farrer in particular was writing. See the "Review Discussion of Farrer's *A Science of God?* (1966)," including Farrer's own response, in the journal for which she was responsible, *Theoria to Theory* 1 (1966): 55–75.

36. Ian T. Ramsey's *Religious Language* was published in the same year.

37. *Iris Murdoch and the Search for Human Goodness* (ed. Maria Antonaccio and William Schweiker; Chicago: University of Chicago Press, 1996), 73.

38. Iris Murdoch, *The Red and the Green* (Harmondsworth: Penguin, 1967), 176.

39. Iris Murdoch, *The Bell* (London: Triad, 1978), 235.

40. Ibid., 304.

41. For her use of the story about the woman with her box of precious ointment or the parable of the prodigal son (and see *The Good Apprentice* of 1985), see her essay "Vision and Choice in Morality," in *Christian Ethics and Contemporary Philosophy* (ed. Ian T. Ramsey; London: SCM, 1966), 195–218.

42. Ibid., 311.

43. Iris Murdoch, *Henry and Cato* (London: Triad, 1986), 34–35.

44. Ibid., 199.

45. Ibid., 347–51.

46. Iris Murdoch, *Nuns and Soldiers* (London: Triad, 1982), 63–66.

47. Ibid., 293–300.

48. Ibid., 506.

49. See Dorothy M. Emmet, "Why Theoria?" in *Theory to Theoria* 1 (1966): 10–18, for a comparable essay; and chap. 12 of her *The Moral Prism* (1979). Basil Mitchell discussed *Sovereignty* in his *Morality, Religious and Secular* (Oxford: Oxford University Press, 1980), 64–78.

50. Iris Murdoch, "Existentialists and Mystics: A Note on the Novel in the New Utilitarian Age," in *Essays and Poems Presented to Lord David Cecil* (ed. William W. Robson; London: Constable, 1970), 169–83, at p. 174.

51. Austin Farrer, "An English Appreciation," in *Kerygma and Myth* (ed. Hans-Werner Bartsch; London: SPCK, 1962), 222.

52. See the use made of Iris Murdoch's insights in Helen Oppenheimer, *Making Good: Creation, Tragedy and Hope* (London: SCM, 2001).

53. Helen Oppenheimer, *The Character of Christian Morality* (London: Faith, 1965).

54. For some introductory selections from her writings, see *Spiritual Classics from the Late Twentieth Century* (ed. Ann Loades; London: National Society/Church House Publishing, 1995), 1–45.

55. Helen Oppenheimer, *Incarnation and Immanence* (London: Hodder & Stoughton, 1973).

56. Helen Oppenheimer, *The Hope of Happiness: A Sketch for a Christian Humanism* (London: SCM, 1983), 2.

57. Helen Oppenheimer, *Looking Before and After* (London: Fount, 1988), 130–31.

58. Basil Mitchell, "Austin Farrer: The Philosopher," *New Fire* 7 (Winter 1983): 452–56.

59. *The Rationality of Religious Belief: Essays in Honor of Basil Mitchell* (ed. William J. Abraham and Steven W. Holtzer; Oxford: Oxford University Press, 1987).

Chapter Two

FARRER'S SPIRITUALITY

Diogenes Allen

The widespread use of the term "spirituality" is a recent phenomenon. In writing on it we face two problems. First, we have to specify what it is, so that we can know what we are looking for. Second, in dealing with Farrer we have a person who did not specialize in any particular field, much less in Christian spirituality. Although he mastered several specialized areas, such as New Testament studies, philosophy, and doctrinal theology, and made important contributions at the highest level to each, as a college chaplain he lived a life that was focused on teaching, preaching, celebrating Holy Communion, and attending to people's pastoral needs. He was, however, an unusual priest. He had a much deeper intellect and more wide-ranging interests than most priests, which drove him to seek "to spread the area" of his recognition of God's activity, as he put it, as far as his own area of thought reached: "Faith perishes if it is walled in, or confined. If it is anywhere, it must be everywhere, like God himself: if God is in your life, he is in all things, for he is God. You must be able to spread the area of your recognition for him, and the basis of your conviction about him, as widely as your thought will range."[1]

Farrer believed that because there were great changes in modern times in our understanding of history and nature, a pressing need existed to rethink orthodox Christianity in light of these changes, and in turn to share with others, both academically and pastorally, the results of his investigations. So it is no accident that he not only worked out with considerable theological and philosophical care a view of "double agency," but also in any number of sermons employed such a philosophically and theologically demanding notion. He believed that in spite of its sophistication, "double agency" fundamentally affects one's understanding and practice of the Christian life. It had to be included in pastoral teaching. Because Farrer did not isolate the results of his various inquiries or activities from one another, his reflections on Christian spirituality are deeply affected by his work in biblical studies, philosophy, and doctrinal theology. Once we have specified what the term "spirituality" means and have briefly looked at Farrer's spirituality in light of that specification, we will examine Farrer's understanding of the relation of Christian spirituality to Christian doctrine.

WHAT IS CHRISTIAN SPIRITUALITY?

Properly speaking, Christian spirituality is concerned with the work of God the Holy Spirit in bringing to fullness the work of Christ in both the Church and individual lives. Everything, whether it be philosophy, doctrinal theology, biblical studies, church history, preaching, or our behavior, is to be viewed from this perspective. The field of Christian spirituality or spiritual theology can be further specified as a subject that treats at least seven questions.

First, what is the goal of the Christian life? Classics of spirituality have described it as the vision of God, the vision of the Trinity, union with God, participation in God's life and being. Because the idea of union with God is unfamiliar to many Christians today, it is important to note that the familiar description of the Church universal as the Body of Christ rests on the conviction that Christ has united himself with us. All these ways of expressing the goal focus on the object of attention. Other descriptions of the goal found in the classic accounts concentrate on what *we* may become: We realize the image of God so that we resemble God more closely, or, as it is often put, we become more like Jesus. Sometimes it is said that our goal is to become holy, or to have a pure or perfect love for God in Godself, and not for the benefits we receive from God.

It seems that more than one way is needed to express the different aspects of the goal. A writer may emphasize one aspect more than others, or even neglect some aspects altogether, as we see in Farrer, who usually emphasizes that our goal is to participate in the life of God, Father, Son, and Holy Spirit. Farrer strongly stresses this union with the divine life, which for him and for the ancient Greek Fathers includes a union with the Body of Christ, the Church, both in this world and in the next. In spite of Farrer's deep regard for Aristotle and his appreciation of Thomas Aquinas, his sense of participation is more Eastern Church and Neoplatonic Augustinian, as is generally true of High Church Anglicans.

In contrast to the ultimate goal, there are proximate and more immediate goals, such as learning to control our emotions and to love our neighbors. Love of neighbor is the usual upshot of Farrer's sermons, and, more generally, he presents his understanding of such a love as a necessary result of our attention to God, whether through scripture, doctrine, meditation, or prayer. Any divorce between thought and practice is lack of faithfulness or obedience. One of the tasks of spiritual theology is to discuss the relationship between and the compatibility of these different accounts of the goal, as well as the relationship between the ultimate goal and those goals that are nearer to hand, which Farrer does explicitly in *Lord I Believe,* as we will see shortly.

The second question to ask of any account of the spiritual life is: What is the path to the goal? The classic path is the threefold way, which consists of purgation (ascetic theology), contemplation (contemplative theology), and union (mystical theology). There is, however, considerable variety in the description of the path among those who write on the spiritual life. This variety should not disturb us. On the contrary, it is wonderful that there is variety, because people differ in intellectual interests, emotional temperament, gifts, and roles in life; we also live in different periods of history and in different kinds of society. All these factors affect which path or part of a path will be most relevant to us.

For example, in ascetic theology, all accounts of the path stress the need for preparation and the purgation of vice. Although the lists of vices that need to be purged may overlap significantly, they are not identical, because the writers are addressing different audiences. Because his account of the Christian pilgrimage was directed primarily to courtiers, George Herbert, a seventeenth-century poet and priest, stressed the need to purge the vices of lust, gluttony, gambling, and idleness — vices that were particularly prevalent at royal courts. For a similar reason, Herbert wrote in verse; in his day, people at court prized poetry and wit, and, as Herbert put it, "A verse may find him, who a sermon flies."[2]

In general, Farrer treats the matters of ascetic theology or discipline in terms of commitment, and usually in the context of his sermons. He is aware of our frailty and of our lack of self-sufficiency, but he also stresses that through our struggle to remain faithful, we learn to depend on and to trust in God. He writes:

> No, we cannot commit ourselves in a day, because we cannot, merely by saying we will, put our whole trust in God. To trust in God is a thing which has to be learnt. We may stand up and make our profession of faith. . . . But we shall still trust ourselves to do our part in the new covenant we have entered. For we do not

> learn what dependence on God is, except through having our self-dependence broken in the mill of life, slowly and painfully. Many tears, much shame, continual repentance, this is the lot of those who pledge themselves to God. A paradoxical pledge; we learn to keep it by breaking it. True confessions, bravely and sincerely made to our confessor and absolved with the word of Christ, these are the means by which we learn distrust of ourselves, and trust in God alone.[3]

The first part of the path — ascetic theology — has as its goal our improvement in the love of our neighbor. The other two parts of the classic path — contemplation and union — stress our growing in knowledge and love of God. Contemplation is subdivided into two major parts: an increase of love and knowledge of God through the book of scripture, and an increase in love and knowledge of God through the companion book to scripture, the book of nature. Farrer gives enormous attention to both of these books of God. He wrote extensively on divine inspiration in scripture, and he published books on Mark, Matthew, and Revelation, as well as many essays on biblical issues. His criticism of the then very popular form-critical method, associated especially with Rudolf Bultmann, and his careful delineation of the medium of revelation as divinely inspired images, which are understood and elaborated by poetic imagination, are only now beginning to be taken seriously in biblical studies. Likewise, his commitment to reconceiving our understanding of nature and of its members as units of activity in constant interaction was extremely daring. His approach has yet to be properly appreciated by theologians and by those interested in the relation of theology and science.

In both cases, his use of the two books of God was not traditional. Rather than the classical practice of passive contemplation of God's power, wisdom, and goodness as reflected in nature, Farrer's ascent to God is through intellectual inquiry, an inquiry that increases our love for God even as it increases our knowledge of God. Although Farrer himself was a firm believer in the typological nature of scripture, he does not engage in the excesses of allegorical interpretation associated with the ancient school of Alexandria. So it is largely by means of intellectual inquiry, Farrer believed, not simply by prayer and meditation, that we grow in knowledge and love of God through the two books of God.

In his remarks on the last part of the threefold way, union with God, Farrer uses nearly all the traditional notions, except the notion of "mystical" ecstasy, in which we are in a trance or trance-like state, unable to use our normal faculties. Rather, he stresses that our destiny is to participate in the life of the divine Trinity, and that we begin that participation in this life especially through our membership and participation in the life of the Church. This participation calls for the union of our will with God's will:

> What I have spoken of is no exalted mystical ecstasy; it is just praying, or even, without the form of prayer, any attending to the presence and will of our Creator.... "We will come, and make our abode with him," says the Christ of St. John's Gospel. "We" — that is, the Father and the Son, by the indwelling of the Holy Spirit. And with whom will they take up their abode? With the man who "will keep my words," says Christ... drawing us into that happy converse, which brings the Trinity to earth, and raises earthly life to heaven.[4]

In the next section, on the relation of doctrine to spirituality, we will have more to say about Farrer's understanding of union in relation to the classic stress on God as surpassing all our thoughts.

The third question that is frequently treated in spiritual theology is: What motivates us to begin the spiritual life and to continue it? Here again we find a long list: fear, remorse or guilt, confusion, loneliness, a desire for justice, for truth, for understanding, and a sense of awe and mystery. And once again, variety is valuable because each of us begins to seek God for different reasons.

Farrer himself seems highly motivated by a desire for understanding, especially concerning the reason for the existence of the universe and to an extent the reason for its order. In *Finite and Infinite* he carefully, even painstakingly, argues that a finite, human mind can conceive of God by an analogy from both our own exercise of will and our degrees of knowledge. Unlike our will, God's is a perfect will, with nothing to limit or hinder it; and God's knowledge is complete, knowing all that there is to be known, without limit or hindrance. Farrer also claimed that the so-called traditional proofs of God's existence from the natural world are not demonstrations, as they are usually treated in philosophy, but means by which, through an analogical leap, we can with our intellect apprehend the One who is perfect will and mind. We can therefore claim that God's existence and perfect being are knowable *indirectly* (this is called "the way of eminence") by rational reflection.

Although Farrer modified the claim that God could not only be rationally conceived but also rationally known to exist through such reflection on our human nature *apart* from an active faith, he insisted throughout his life and writings that nature's order and existence were not self-explanatory and that this fact is rationally knowable apart from faith. Whether nature's order and existence must have an explanation, however, requires us to show that the Principle of Sufficient Reason applies not only to the members of the universe but also to the universe taken as a whole. But that nature's order and existence are not self-explanatory has been widely conceded in philosophy and science since Farrer's death.[5]

An awareness that nature's order and existence are neither philosophically nor scientifically fully accounted for can greatly motivate belief, as Farrer never tired of repeating. So, too, he often pointed out, do the lives of transformed people (saints), who far more clearly manifest the effects of divine grace than do ordinary Christians. In addition, we ourselves, when we examine our own lives attentively in light of the New Testament's and the Church's witness to Christ, recognize the accuracy of their understanding of our aspirations and failures, and recognize ourselves as sinners and as blessed by the gospel of salvation. We recognize in our own lives the effects of divine grace as being in continuity with the far greater transformation experienced by the saints. So rigorous philosophical study of the natural world's existence and order, attention to the witness of the scriptures and the Church, and the experience of divine grace operative in others and in ourselves can move us to a rational faith and enable us to remain in faith in such a way as to satisfy both the needs of the heart and the most demanding requirements of the mind.[6]

The fourth and fifth questions form a pair: What helps us make progress in the spiritual life, and what hinders us? Various types of prayer and meditation, fasts, retreats, and alms (or, more generally, acts of love of neighbor) are frequently recommended as aids by various writers on ascetic theology. Lack of faith, flagrant sins, and, paradoxically, pride in our progress are commonly cited as hindrances.

Farrer was often writing and preaching in an apologetic situation in which the credibility of religion and of Christianity in particular were at a low level among his audience. So he almost always gave accounts of the meaning of and the grounds for Christian convictions (as mentioned in relation to question three above) to help people to enter into a life of faith, and from this understanding and from the effects of divine grace upon them — comforting, strengthening, and guiding them — to a mature faith. Service to others would result. All of this formed the context of his references to the various stumbling blocks typically encountered in the life of faith, especially the hindrances of self-reliance and social custom. His sermons are peppered with references to these and other hindrances to growth into a mature faith. One of the few places where detailed advice on aids to the Christian life can be found is an account in *Lord I Believe* of how to pray the rosary. He made several revisions of it for reformed Catholics, as he used to describe the people of the Anglican Communion. From what he says about praying the rosary, this form of prayer appears to have played a major role in his own spiritual life.

The sixth question is closely related to the pair of questions concerning aids and hindrances: How do we measure progress? That is, on what basis are we to assess our spiritual condition? Luther strongly objected to the notion of a spiritual progression because to him it smacked of works righteousness and suggested that growth in God was something we could control. Rather than speaking of progress, Luther preferred to speak of Christian maturity. Calvin, in contrast, frequently spoke of progress.[7]

Like Calvin, Farrer strongly believed in sanctification: We as individuals and as a Church do or should progress in the Christian life, becoming ever more obedient to God and increasingly enjoying the divine life at work in us and among us. Farrer did not fear that our efforts and improvement would inevitably become acts of self-righteousness. As we saw earlier, Farrer stressed, "we do not learn what dependence on God is, except by having our self-dependence broken." Only by our efforts do we learn what it is to rely on God wholly. Farrer was all too aware of, and constantly preached on, our utter dependence on God's grace for our very breath at every moment, and for our powers and talents, and indeed for our ability to seek to improve in virtue and obedience. Even in his sermons, Farrer constantly reminded his hearers of divine and human agency as a "double agency," as we find, for example, in his sermon "Thinking the Trinity":

> God gave the world room to be itself. He would not so inhabit it as to make it the passive reflection of his own ideas; or like the machine which does no more than embody the design of its constructor, and perform the wishes of its manipulator. God made the world, but he did not just make it; he made it make itself; for only so could it be itself. He released a half chaos of brimless forces as alien from his own being as anything could well be; and

> they blinded away, not in the paths of a godlike wisdom, but according to the very limited principles of action implanted in each. Nevertheless . . . by an invisible art, and by a secret attraction, he has brought out of a blind interplay of forces many organized intricacies and much sentient life. . . . God made the world in unlikeness to himself; we look there in vain for the lineaments of his face. He made man in his own similitude, and it is in the face of man that we must look for the countenance of God. . . . We can achieve nothing truly human which is not also in a manner divine.[8]

Farrer's nontechnical remarks that the divine agency uses "an invisible art" and "a secret attraction" to bring "out of a blind interplay of forces many organized intricacies and much sentient life" suggest that there is no analogy or model for "double agency" — two agents, God and creature, resulting in a single event — a possibility often overlooked by commentators who have tried to devise models. So it would be no accident that Farrer, a master of analogies, never offered one.

Part of Farrer's view of double agency is that everything that exists does so only insofar as it is active. As he puts it in *Finite and Infinite,* "*ESSE* is not *PERCIPI, ESSE* is *OPERARI*" — that is, to be or to exist is not to be perceived, as in Berkeley's philosophy, but to act — "and an *operatio* . . . has a plurality of elements entering into it. It is a real concentration in which they are drawn together in a certain pattern, so that they could not exist nor be conceived to exist without it, nor it without them."[9]

So God as Creator creates units of activity. Every agent or being that acts is simultaneously an action of God's creative and providential power. Although we cannot specify the divine agency apart from creatures (and then only because of the insufficiency of creatures to account for their own existence and order), we can nonetheless show that double agency is the correct way to think of the Christian doctrines of creation and providence, so that creatures are not reduced to utter passivity. To show that double agency is the correct way to think of these doctrines, we need only the simple, elementary mathematical notion of "sets." God, as Creator and providential agent, and creatures, as active effects of God, belong to different sets. God as a member of a unique set is a way of referring to God's transcendence, which is sometimes popularly put as saying that God is "wholly other" or not "a being among beings." God acts by creating the set of beings and events that make up the world, without God being a member of that set.

Now imagine that in the set of creatures we find that C is brought about by the agency of A and B, with A as 50 percent of the cause and B as 50 percent of the cause. Then let us say that further investigation indicates that A actually is 60 percent of the cause of C. We then would reduce the causal significance of B to 40 percent. More work reveals that A is 70 percent of the cause of C, and so we reduce the activity of B to only 30 percent. Now whichever of the three relations of A and B to C may obtain, God as Creator and providential agent is 100 percent active in bringing about A, B, and C. This could not be the case were God a member of the same set as A, B, and C. Were God a member of their set, then God's 100 percent agency would reduce the agency of A and B to 0 percent. Only when agents are members of the same set does the increase of one member activity (A) in bringing about an event (C) reduce the agency of another member of the set (B). It is by failing to take into account that the divine agency is in a different set than the active creatures that God creates and providentially affects that it can seem contradictory to speak of double agency, divine and creature, in the occurrence of all events.

Divine agency is also compatible with human freedom. Even for us to disobey God, we use the power that God gives us to disobey, just as we use the power that God gives us to obey. The divine activity, through "an invisible art" and a "secret attraction," is perfectly compatible with creaturely agency. As long as we have reason to believe in God as Creator and providential agent, we can affirm double agency even though we cannot "model" or find an analogy for it among creaturely acts.

The seventh question frequently treated by spiritual writers is: What are the fruits of the Spirit? Among the fruits usually mentioned are love, joy, peace, friendship, discernment, and victory over death. The letters of St. Paul and St. John are particularly rich on this topic, while the classic biblical texts are Isa 11:2 (the seven gifts of the Spirit of the Lord) and Gal 5:22 (the fruit of the Spirit). Although Farrer treats these matters only in passing, since so much of his attention is on apologetic matters, their reality and significance are important. Otherwise his stress on the witness of the saints, who exhibit the fruits of the Spirit, would have no weight.

These seven questions do not by any means exhaust the number of questions that we might ask of the classic texts on the spiritual life, but they do precisely specify the field of spirituality, and they can guide us as we try, as I have just done, to distill from Farrer's writings and sermons something of his understanding of Christian spirituality, or the Christian life.

FARRER ON DOCTRINE AND SPIRITUALITY

Although today we tend to look to specific texts that are identified as classics of spirituality, many theologians of the past treated various of the seven questions that specify the field in the same texts in which they were engaged in philosophical or doctrinal inquiry. Augustine's attempt better to understand God as Trinity in his work *On the Trinity* is at the same time a spiritual journey into the life of God, as the mind, through its inquiries, gains a better understanding of the nature of the Trinity through a series of analogies. Intellectual inquiry and spiritual growth or transformation may go hand in hand, each assisting the other.

This connection is even more explicit in Augustine's disciple, Anselm. His famous ontological argument — intellectual inquiry par excellence — is preceded by several pages of heartfelt prayer concerning God's "otherness," or transcendence, and hence the baffling difficulty of even knowing where and how to look for God. Besides God's transcendent being, Anselm laments at length that our sinful nature greatly impedes our search. For Anselm such spiritual meditations are essential *every time* one seeks by intellectual inquiry to know or to understand God. Prayer and meditation on God's "otherness" and our sinfulness enable the mind to begin to rise from its customary way of thinking that is shaped and limited by its focus on created being, in contrast to the uncreated being that is God, and to be freed from the distractions caused by the cares of life. Only through such prayers and meditations can we hope better to understand or know God through intellectual inquiry.

It is not accidental that the longest chapter of John Calvin's *Institutes of the Christian Religion,* a recognized classic in doctrinal theology, is on prayer. It is only relatively recently, perhaps as late as the early nineteenth century, with the stress on the "scientific" (that is, impartial) nature of theological inquiry, that doctrinal inquiry and spiritual practice again became separated. It had happened in medieval scholasticism and for a time was reversed by the Reformation. For most of the history of theology, doctrinal inquiry and spiritual practices interacted richly. To make progress in doctrinal theology it was considered essential to mature in the spiritual life. Doctrinal inquiry without spiritual fruits was inconceivable.

Farrer is very much in this classic tradition. It is significant that *Lord I Believe,* one of Farrer's major works on the spiritual life, has as its subtitle *Suggestions for Turning the Creed into Prayer.* Christian doctrines make up the subject matter of prayer. His book begins:

> Prayer and dogma are inseparable. They alone can explain each other. Either without the other is meaningless and dead. If he hears a dogma of faith discussed as a cool speculation, about which theories can be held and arguments propounded, the Christian cannot escape disquiet. "What are these people doing?" he will ask. "Do not they know what they are discussing? How can they make it an open question what the country is like, which they enter when they pray?"
>
> To put the matter the other way round, suppose that our believing friends express bewilderment over the use and function of prayer. Shall we not ask them what they imagine their belief to be about? They may say it gives them a true description of the world in which they are called upon to act. Certainly; but not, surely, an obvious description, nor a description which, once learnt, continues steadily to illuminate the realities of life. . . . I believe in Jesus Christ, born, suffering, risen; yet I may leave the desk for the table, and find in my fellow diners the objects of my rivalry or the sources of my amusement, but never see the Christ in their hearts, or acknowledge in mine the Christ who goes out to meet them.
>
> Our creed shows us the truth of things, but when shall we attend to the truth it shows? The life of the world is a strong conspiracy not of silence only but of blindness concerning the side of things which faith reveals. We were born into the conspiracy and reared in it, it is our second nature, and the Christianity into which we are baptized makes little headway against it during the most part of our waking hours. But if we go into our room and shut the door, by main force stop the wheel of worldly care from turning in our head, and simply recollect; without either vision or love barely recall the creed, and re-describe a corner of our world in the light of it; then we have done something towards using and possessing a truth which Jesus died to tell, and rose to be. . . . Prayer is the active use or exercise of faith; and the creed defines the contours of that world on which faith trains her eyes.[10]

Here Farrer exhibits his fundamental understanding of spirituality. It is to have one's life and thought formed according to Christian doctrine.

God the Holy Spirit uses our understanding of doctrine (in this particular book, the doctrines summarized by the Apostles' Creed) to bring us to fullness of life in Christ. Accordingly, Farrer gives an exposition of the creed that we are to pray. He begins with the creed's fundamental Trinitarian structure by giving basic instruction on the nature of the Trinity. In succeeding chapters, he gives instruction on God the Creator, God the Son Incarnate and also Reigning, and the like in order that our minds and wills may be rightly informed and directed in our prayer.

At the same time, this very demanding but accessible doctrinal inquiry and instruction are given so we may be increasingly enabled by prayer and meditation to achieve God's will for us. It issues in action. Farrer follows this same pattern in his sermons. There is always instruction on the meaning of doctrine as he seeks to have us form our lives in accordance with Christian teaching. For Farrer, an obedient heart studies and seeks instruction, and a mind illumined by knowledge of God guides the will. Farrer does not, therefore, discount a knowledge of God or of Christian doctrines in seeking to give us advice and instruction in the pursuit of the Christian or spiritual life, as do so many so-called writers on spirituality today. He explicitly gives an exposition of fundamental Christian doctrines, and he explains that the person of God is accessible to us through this knowledge when it is used in prayer and meditation and when it results in obedience.

Farrer also shares Augustine's and Anselm's view that spiritual development is necessary for us to discern the truth of Christian beliefs. In his brief but important essay "Prologue: On Credulity," Farrer points out that a Christian "does not live long in a university without discovering that what passes there for philosophy does not oblige its practitioners to believe in God, and that history indeed obliges us to reckon with the Christian movement, but not necessarily to accept the Christian's account of the facts in which it originated."[11]

Farrer asks, "Is a Christian simply being credulous in holding to Christian beliefs?" He then speculates that a believer decides to turn to the New Testament to see if it provides any evidence for belief in a Christian God. What does the believer find?

> Not a word. Defence, indeed! They are putting their opponents through it, asking how men can look truth itself in the eye, and turn away to believe and practise lies. . . . A part of our own minds has often shared their view. We have often just seen (so we have thought) the inexorable truth that we are rebellious creatures under

> the eye of our Creator, and that our Creator has come upon us in Christ. Credulity, here, is the crime of pretending to believe that there is any way out of this situation but one — to reconcile ourselves to the truth of our nature, which demands our submission to the God who made us.
>
> Unless our minds in fact function in these two ways: unless we sometimes see God as truth, and evasion of him as credulity, at other times the proved facts of the special sciences as truth, and the outrunning of them as credulity — unless this is so, we are not confronted with the specifically religious problem of truth.... It is a matter of finding the proper relation between them, not of allowing one to oust the other.[12]

Farrer manages to find a proper relation between the two ways of thinking he has specified by distinguishing four kinds of truth. First, the truth of science. Here precision is obtained by limiting the subject matter. Modern physics refuses to consider anything but measurable physical processes. Such self-limitation does not mean that physical processes consist of nothing but the measurements. The same pattern of deliberate limitation of questions is present in human affairs:

> The economist may concentrate on man in so far as he is an economic agent, but if the economist concludes that *because* it is possible to get sound results this way, man is nothing but an economic agent and all the rest of his apparent action is economic activity under a disguise, then the economist is a fool. So, again, with the psychologist's study of man's subrational impulses, or any other limited inquiry.[13]

The second sort of truth is to move back from limited questions to deal with the whole reality that confronts us. With physical realities, we do not know nor can we guess what the whole being of a physical substance is. As Bertrand Russell, no friend of religion, put it, physics is so mathematical, not because we know so much about physical reality, but because we know so little. With human beings, we get to know them through interacting with them. We gain in this way a personal understanding. The third sort of truth has to do with our evaluation of the first two:

> Science is true when it conforms to certain abstract patterns which real things or processes exhibit, and personal understanding is true when persons are (or, in history, were) as we understand them to

> be (or to have been). It does not matter whether the facts are such as to be approved or deplored, whether the persons are acting a lie or living sincerely. . . . We open up a completely new dimension of questions when we ask what is that true essence of man which the insincere betrays and the fool misses and the callous ignores and the perverse distorts. . . .
>
> Now there are two ways in which the mind may relate itself to this essence of the truly human which it is our life's work to express. We may think about it abstractly, and that is ethical philosophy: we may think about it whole and in the round, and that is religion. The ethical philosopher is like other scientists of human nature—like the economist or the psychologist. He limits the issue and picks out a tidy question. . . . [The ethical philosopher says,] "let us talk about the limited fact of moral thinking—the recognition of obligation, the attempt to make moral rules consistent, the problems of particular duty."[14]

The other way of dealing with the essence of the truly human opens us to the fourth sort of truth:

> Just as you cannot become aware of the personal reality of your friend by trying on him preconceived questions of psychological or economic science, but only by undergoing the impact of his existence, so it is with awareness of your own being and destiny, and of its demands on you. . . .
>
> Now when the New Testament writers said that in Christ they had met the truth, they meant that in him they recognized what was demanding admittance through this door. It is of no use, of course, for Christians to pretend that on this ground everybody is bound to agree with them straight away, but anyhow on this ground their position is immensely strong and need fear no antagonist.[15]

The reason, then, that a Christian may look credulous is the failure of others to allow admittance of various other truths into their thinking. In fact, a person can stop with the very first sort of truth, as did the logical positivists in Farrer's day, and claim that there is only that sort of truth and all the other claims to truth are literal nonsense, because they do not conform to the first sort of truth. One may go further than the first sort but stop short of the third or fourth sort. Each instance ignores the reality of questions beyond the scope of where one stops.

Farrer's distinctions are important not only for doctrinal theology, which today frequently stops with limited questions, but also for biblical studies. Some biblical scholars tend to stop with delimited, manageable questions:

> Such men are not going to see truths of the [fourth] type breaking out at them through the façade of history, for they have discounted them from the start. . . . But the historian whose mind is open to the fourth type of truth, and who has some awareness of the abyss of divine being which underlies his own existence, may meet a voice and a visitant out of that abyss, when he weighs the strange history of the year 30 as it is mirrored in the witness of those who most intimately responded to it.[16]

Like Augustine, Anselm, and Calvin, Farrer too believed that all theological inquiry involves a personal element, a spiritual development, in order to be open to the divine presence and truth.

This need for personal engagement is not apparent in Farrer's first major work, *Finite and Infinite*. There Farrer sets aside the issue of the need for special revelation for us to pursue what he calls "rational theology." It is only much later, with *Faith and Speculation*, that he explicitly drops all pretense that his reasoning and, by that token, all Christian reasoning about God is done without a commitment to and actual interaction with God.

In a slightly earlier work, *Saving Belief*, Farrer already is in the process of transition to making this view explicit in a brilliant opening chapter on the relation of faith and reason. There he introduces his concept of "initial faith." The notion of God is not a neutral but a loaded term, to which we react positively or negatively. Farrer compares it to the concept of a mother. Even an orphan feels moved by simply entertaining the notion of a possible mother, whom he imagines he might still have but whose whereabouts is unknown to him. So too with God. If we do not find ourselves at all moved by the notion of the possibility of God, we will not be able properly to recognize the data that relate to the existence and reality of God. God will remain an abstraction, unable to move us toward a full faith. But if we are at all inclined to the possible reality of God, then this "initial faith" can turn into an explicit commitment as we carefully consider the testimony of nature, the gospel stories, the life of the Church, and the lives of saintly people. To pursue such intellectual work properly requires some positive engagement, some spiritual development in order to overcome the blindness of those who stop with limited questions and do not allow admittance to what has the power to wholly convince the mind and heart.

The didactic stress on doctrine in Farrer's sermons and devotional writings appears, however, to be contrary to a major teaching found in most recognized spiritual masters. Farrer himself raises the issue:

> No dogma deserves its place unless it is prayable, and no Christian deserves his dogmas who does not pray them. But if so, what are we to say to that high doctrine of the saints, which tells us when we pray to aim at utter simplicity, stilling first our imagination, then our thought, and adhering by naked will to a God we forbear to conceive? How strange this sounds! The saints who teach the doctrine are Christian saints, and they tell us, as any Christian must, that our salvation hangs on the revelation Christ achieved, and of which the shape is given us in the creed. They wish us to treasure the dogmas which our teachers laboured so hard to bring home to us; they wish us to be no less patient ourselves in handing them on to others. Can it then really be the intention of the saints that we should hold our treasures as a miser holds his wealth, and make no use of them? The sublime doctrines of our faith cannot affect our lives except through prayer, and yet, if we are to take the maxims of the saints at their face value, must not we make it our whole endeavour to forget the doctrines when we pray?[17]

Farrer here is referring to the relation of the *via positiva* (or, in Greek, the "cataphatic") and the *via negativa* (in Greek, the "apophatic"). Frequently these two ways to God are put into opposition, with the *via negativa* supplanting the *via positiva* among the spiritually advanced. We are said to begin with thinking of God in positive or affirmative concepts, such as power, wisdom, and goodness. God is also thought of in likenesses, such as Good Shepherd, Fount of Living Waters, and Father. But as we grow in faith and knowledge of God, as we make spiritual progress, we are more and more aware that all these terms are inadequate. God is wholly other, and not directly conceivable by our limited minds, as we find symbolized by the emptiness of the Holy of Holies in the ancient Jewish Temple, in which God was said to dwell. The best representation of God is no representation at all. So any and every positive designation, however helpful, is finally recognized as inadequate and misleading, even to be dropped altogether and replaced by "nothing" and approached by "silence."

The classic English treatise *The Cloud of Unknowing*, to which Farrer alludes, teaches a form of prayer for those few among contemplatives who are called to know God as God is in Godself. This is to know God without any doctrines, images, or words. By the practice of "forgetfulness," all of these are progressively left behind, and one remains only with love, which, stripped of all terms and images, is called a "naked love." With naked love as a dart, one pierces the "Cloud of Unknowing," and that naked love is then met by the divine love in the "Cloud of Unknowing." One is now beyond all concepts, words, and images, and fully in the presence of God.

Farrer pays his respects to those who are much more advanced in prayer than he. And in his attempt to instruct us in the doctrines of the Apostles' Creed for our prayer, he does not seek to oppose or to rival such masters. It is simply that the way of the mystic is not the way for beginners, nor is it his way, nor, he believes, is it the way of most practicing Christians. Besides, the two ways — the use of doctrines and the abandonment of doctrines — are actually integrally connected. Farrer explains their connection by means of a remarkably simple analogy, brilliantly harmonizing an apparent opposition between the *via positiva* and *via negativa* that has confused many people, including the philosopher-novelist Iris Murdoch (see her novel *Henry and Cato*) and the deconstructionist Derrida, who has recently admitted that his work is parallel to that of the *via negativa* — but his understanding of the *via negativa* is that of a total repudiation of the *via positiva*. Farrer writes:

> Those who fall in love may seem to themselves, and especially after the event, to have been simply swept away by the beauty they have seen. And it may sometimes be so. . . . But if we have loved the person, or the soul, we have loved what cannot be seen. . . . Our vision of the person is a knowledge of their thoughts and ways, acquired piecemeal from their conduct and brought together into a single view. And this bringing together is something that we do, it does not happen of itself. If we remember carefully we may recall a time of intense mental activity, when we were comparing the actions and opinions, the habits and expressions of our friend, and trying to make them fit. We thought we knew the person more vividly than we had ever known any one, and then found ourselves suddenly baffled; a stranger stood before us, and we began all over again.
>
> There was such a time, but it came to an end at last. . . . To bring our friend before us we no longer needed to make explorations

> in the field of memory. We had only to say the name "John" or "Mary" . . . to find ourselves at a point of mental vision like the convergence of the avenues in an old-fashioned park. . . . We had no need to explore the avenues to their ends . . . for we had often been there to look. . . . There was a time when the lover of God, like the lover of Mary or of John, was putting together his knowledge of God, gathered piecemeal from reflection on the ways and works of God, as they are delineated in the creed and recognized in life. But again, there was a time, not so soon reached but reached at last, when the knowledge of God gathered round the Name of God. . . .
>
> The saint is happy to be able to do this, and can do it, because he formerly explored and meditated the compass of the creed. . . . We, perhaps, are still plotting the circle of our faith, or have not even properly begun. If so, let us not leave off at the call of a false mysticism which mistakes the end for the beginning. . . . [18]

Farrer then proceeds to add to the analogy by showing how it is modified by God's actions on us, his view of "double agency." Our friends are not what God is, namely,

> the ground of our being, and principle of our growth; so that the way in which [the idea of God] develops in us becomes his own concern, for our whole growth is his concern. It is possible, then, for him to live and act in our idea of him as no friend can do, and our faith trusts him to do precisely this — to become in us an active, living truth. . . .
>
> Though God be in me, yet without the creed to guide me I should know neither how to call upon God, nor on what God to call. God may be the very sap of my growth and substance of my action; but the tree has grown so crooked and is so deformed and cankered in its parts, that I should be at a loss to distinguish the divine power among the misuses of the power given.[19]

In these remarks we see how Farrer's spirituality and intellectual investigations are actually of a piece. Those who have explored the many avenues of his thought — philosophical, biblical, and spiritual — in time find that his very name brings before their minds, not this or that particular brilliant exploration or inspiring sermon, but one who had so yielded himself to God as to become to them a never-failing fount of blessings.

NOTES

1. Austin Farrer, *A Celebration of Faith* (London: Hodder & Stoughton, 1970), 60.

2. *George Herbert: The Country Parson and The Temple* (ed. John N. Wall Jr.; New York: Paulist, 1981), 121.

3. Austin Farrer, in *Austin Farrer: The Essential Sermons* (ed. Leslie Houlden; Cambridge, MA: Cowley, 1991), 183.

4. Ibid., 80.

5. William L. Rowe, *The Cosmological Argument* (Princeton, NJ: Princeton University Press, 1975). See also Diogenes Allen, *Christian Belief in a Postmodern World* (Louisville, KY: Westminster/John Knox Press, 1989); and *Cosmos, Bios, Theos: Scientists Reflect on Science, God, and the Origins of the Universe, Life, and* Homo sapiens (ed. Henry Margenau and Roy Abraham Varghese; La Salle, IL: Open Court, 1992).

6. See Brian Hebblethwaite, "The Experiential Verification of Religious Belief in the Theology of Austin Farrer," in *For God and Clarity: New Essays in Honor of Austin Farrer* (ed. Jeffrey C. Eaton and Ann Loades; Allison Park, PA: Pickwick, 1983), 163–76.

7. See Book III of Calvin's *Institutes of the Christian Religion.*

8. Farrer, in Houlden, *Austin Farrer: The Essential Sermons,* 77, 79.

9. Austin Farrer, *Finite and Infinite: A Philosophical Essay* (London: Dacre, 1943), 21.

10. Austin Farrer, *Lord I Believe: Suggestions for Turning the Creed into Prayer* (Cambridge, MA: Cowley, 1989), 9–10.

11. Austin Farrer, "Prologue: On Credulity," in *Interpretation and Belief* (ed. Charles C. Conti; London: SPCK, 1976), 1.

12. Ibid., 1, 2.

13. Ibid., 3–4.

14. Ibid., 4–5.

15. Ibid., 5.

16. Ibid., 6.

17. Farrer, *Lord I Believe,* 10–11.

18. Ibid., 11, 12.

19. Ibid., 13, 14.

Chapter Three

THE GOD WHO UNDERTAKES US

Edward Hugh Henderson

> We must put our confidence in truth. But that doesn't mean sitting back and waiting for the truth to shine from above. . . . It means following with devoted obedience the truth we have seen as true, with an entire confidence in God, that he will correct, clear, and redirect our vision, to the perception of a freer and deeper truth. Go with the truth you have, and let it carry you into collision with the hard rocks of fact, and then you'll learn something.[1]

> The experimental evidence of God lies in the possession of our will by his and in nothing else. If an action and a will proceeding from the divine centre, and not simply from our centre is not convincing, nothing experimental will be so; if we are not assured that the integration of our will into the divine puts us where we belong, that the God who undertakes us is nothing less than God, then no experimental evidence is going to convince us.[2]

Traditional Christian faith is loving and obedient dependence upon the God who creates the world and acts in the life, crucifixion, and resurrection of Jesus of Nazareth, the Christ, to draw us into the divine life. By this action God undertakes to bring us finally to perfection in the divine life, where we will love God with all our being and our neighbors as ourselves.

Austin Farrer was one of that remarkable group of mid-twentieth century "Oxford Christians"[3] who held this faith as true and who bent themselves to interpret and defend it. Ann Loades has reminded us, however, that the larger Oxford environment — and, indeed, the Western intellectual world generally — was not hospitable to Christian faith. The positivist philosophy, claiming to speak for the sure knowledge of the sciences, called faith in the living God "nonsense." Now positivism has long since been discredited as a philosophical position, but its gospel is still very much with us. That gospel is that we are to take seriously only the kind of understanding provided by the sciences, the kind that explains in terms of natural causes and natural laws. Nothing else on this view counts as knowledge. But the world so understood leaves no place for God, especially not for the living God who acts to create and redeem the world and who undertakes to incorporate us into divine life and bring us to completion, and if that belief be excised, traditional faith is gutted.[4]

Many have responded to the naturalistic challenge by emptying traditional faith of belief in the God who acts. Let "God," they said, stand for a moral principle, and let stories of God be read for the encouragement they give to moral life.[5] The Oxford Christians, on the other hand, affirmed the robust substance of traditional faith. Among them, Austin Farrer developed the most constructive philosophical case.

Farrer's philosophical response was not primarily a matter of raising criticisms of the predominant naturalistic thought. He saw that it is not enough to point to the conceptual problems of rival philosophies. The Christian philosopher must rehabilitate the Christian imagination. That is, the Christian philosopher must show Christians how they can think about God's active and effective presence in the world along with the natural explanations provided by the methods of the sciences. The positivist's challenge, *either* science *or* faith, poses a false dilemma. Science and faith go perfectly well together if we understand God and God's action in the world aright. We can even thank the sciences — and the extremes of positivism — for saving Christian understanding from the idolatry of thinking that God is one of the forces that make up the world and compete with each other in the hurly-burly of natural causal process. No. God is the reason why there is a world and why the world is the kind of world that it is. God, therefore, acts in the world not as one actor or causal power competing with other actors or causal powers, but as one who acts in the actions of the creatures that make up the world.

The purpose of this chapter is twofold. First, it is to explain this most important and pervasive of Farrer's philosophical ideas: the idea that God is a personal agent who acts in the world by double agency. This is the idea that lets us see how to unite faith in the living God with the natural understanding provided by the sciences; it is the idea that sets the Christian imagination free to do its work of directing the practical life of faith.

The second, related purpose is to exhibit this understanding of God and God's action at work in enabling and encouraging the practice of traditional faith. Perhaps the power of Farrer's contribution to the life of faith can only be appreciated when his philosophical thought is brought together with the sermons and devotional works. These latter practical interpretations of the faith take Farrer's philosophical thought — and especially his thought about God's agency — and deploy it in ways that give direction to faith and enable the Christian confidently to enjoin life in God.

AVOIDING IDOLATRY

The Dialectic of Images

Because God is the transcendent creator of the world and not a created part of it, all thought and language fail to comprehend God. Therefore, it is necessary to use "the dialectic of images" to save us from worshiping ideas we have created instead of the living God.

> When we pray, we must begin by conceiving God in full and vigorous images, but we must go on to acknowledge the inadequacy of them and to adhere nakedly to the imageless truth of God. The crucifixion of the images in which God is first shown to us is a necessity of prayer because it is a necessity of life. The promise of God's dealing with us through grace can be set before us in nothing but images, for we have not yet experienced the reality. When we proceed to live the promises out, the images are crucified by the reality, slowly and progressively, never completely and not always without pain — yet the reality is better than the images. Jesus Christ clothed himself in all the images of messianic promise and, in living them out, crucified them, but the crucified reality is better than the figures of prophecy.[6]

God is the unique and transcendent Creator. Everything other than God depends on God for its existence, while God is altogether self-existent and dependent upon nothing other than God. God, being the reason there is a world, is not one of the things that make up the world; neither is God's way of being related to the world an instance of the way things in the world are related to each other. In order to emphasize that God is necessarily and inescapably a mystery beyond human comprehension, Farrer gave special attention to this ancient wisdom in his first book, *Finite and Infinite*. To know this truth is to know that no words can give unambiguous and comprehensive knowledge about

God, because we are parts of the created world, and we live our lives immersed in it. Whatever we say about God can only be said with words that come from our experience with the world. Whatever thinking about God we do must proceed by using images of God. It is easy to hide the images in abstract language, saying, for example, things like "God is infinite," "God is omniscient," and "God is the necessary being," thereby forgetting that behind such words are images. Whenever we think we possess the final and complete truth about God, we mistake an image of God for God and are in danger of worshiping an idol.

The caution against idolatry is an ancient theme. However, we must not take it to mean "because we cannot know everything, we cannot know something."[7] Farrer practiced a method that keeps the uniqueness of God and the limits of human thought ever before us, so that we are reminded that we can indeed know true things about God but at the same time are deterred from identifying the images with God. He called this the method of "analogical dialectic" or the "dialectic of images."[8]

The dialectic of images applied to thought about God consists in taking a particular image or analogy, allowing that God is like that image in certain ways, and then noting ways in which God cannot simply be what the image is. Then one goes on to another image and repeats the process. For example, suppose the theory of the cosmological "big bang" provokes the questions science can, as science, neither ask nor answer, and suppose that to ask and answer them we move into theology, saying that God "caused" the big bang and "chose" the values of the physical constants involved in it. This is to image God as the designing engineer of the world. The most the image can finally mean is that God is ultimately responsible in some way for the fact that the universe is and that this is the kind of universe it is. It should not be thought to explain how God brings about the world in the same way, for example, that a review of the chemical engineering processes in a pharmaceutical factory can tell us how a medicine is produced. It cannot mean that God simply is a designing engineer. Engineers are human beings who work with an already existing world that has already defined physical properties; their work is to discover what those properties are and how they can be manipulated to produce certain effects, in this case medicine. God, on the other hand, cannot be supposed to have brought about the very existence of a world by a manipulation of preexisting properties; it is that world of things with definite preexisting properties which depends upon God for its existence in the first place.

Once we have made ourselves aware of the image and its limits, we may go on to another image and repeat the process; for example, God is a painter;[9] God is Father; God is Mother; God is the soul of the world;[10] God speaks to us in scripture, converses with us in prayer, unites us with God's will, attaches us to God's life, and so on. God cannot be identified with any one image, but seeing from a variety of images provides perspectives that can lead us into a more faithful life in which more intimate and direct experience of God may be realized. Farrer shared this combination of the affirmative and negative ways with Dorothy L. Sayers, Charles Williams, C. S. Lewis, and Eric Mascall, but it was Farrer who made it clear that they concern our way of being far more than our way of knowing.

Living the Dialectic of Images

It is not enough to avoid fixation upon particular images of God; it is necessary to engage God with them by living the dialectic of images. God will then reveal to us their deepest meaning. Jesus himself is our example of this.

> What shall we say, then? Are the words "converse" as applied to prayer or "happiness" as applied to sanctity emptied out by God's actual dealings with men? Emptied out? Are the words emptied out? What was it Christ said of the words of the ancient law? I came not to dissolve but to fulfill. Not to dissolve, to melt away, to empty of sense, but to fulfill, to make full, to pack with all the meaning they could bear. . . .
>
> The discarding of the literal sense of God's promises is a trivial jest to the unbelieving philosophers, but to us it is nothing less than the crucifixion of Christ. Perhaps that is why we could not answer the philosophers: for how could one say in such a company, "That's the issue you are talking about: you are talking about the crucifixion of Christ"? Christ did not take the promises of God to be a jest, because they could not be literally fulfilled. He did not say "In the face of Roman power we can found no messianic kingdom here." He said: "In the face of Roman power, which excludes our messianic kingdom in the literal sense, we will see what sort of messianic kingdom God will make." He kept the words, and God changed the thing, and so we still call him Christ, Messiah, King, but not in the pre-crucifixion sense. He kept the words; and when Caiaphas asked him, "Art thou the Christ?" he said, "I

> am"; and when Pilate asked him if he were the King of the Jews, he did not deny. But God changed the thing. The body of Jesus, first living, then dead, was trussed up and crucified as the guy of literal messiahship, but God placed his true Messiah on the throne of heaven and in the hearts of his believers.[11]

With Christ as our example, we see that avoiding idolatry is not only an intellectual exercise; it is the heart of the whole life of faithful and loving dependence upon God. It should not surprise us: The first commandment is to have no gods before God.

No method can guarantee that we will avoid idolatry. No matter what method we use, we will still be prone to fix our minds on a limited set of images and to confuse them with the whole truth about God and God's ways with the world. Consequently, the way truly to avoid making an idol of tradition is to live the dialectic of images. Farrer saw the faith of ancient Israel as a lived dialectic of images, which unfolded over the course of its history of engagement with God.[12] The ancient texts of Jewish Scripture were not produced in a modern Western research university. They contained "lived" images. The criticism of the images came through reflection on the consequences of the life with God that had been shaped by them. The authors made the images and the consequences explicit. Thus in the Hebrew Bible we find the development of such images as "covenant," "kingdom," and "Son of God." Reflection on those same images continues in the gospels and the epistles of the New Testament as their authors reinterpret them through their experience of Jesus of Nazareth and as they understand Jesus of Nazareth through their reinterpretation of the images.

Farrer read the gospels as presenting Jesus himself as the exemplar of perfectly faithful life. What was the faith that defined Christ's life? It was a steadfast commitment to loving God and to loving one's neighbor, along with dependence on God to perfect that love in himself, the trust that God would indeed do so regardless of circumstances that might make that seem impossible, and the hope that doing so would bring him to the fullness of life in God. In short, faith, as exemplified by Christ, is life lived as loving dependence upon and trusting obedience to God. In the realm of understanding, the life of faith has the form of criticizing the images, images such as those Jesus had inherited from his culture. Faith trusts that God will bring to understanding the truth to which the images point.

Jesus' mind and life were formed by the images that dominated Jewish Scripture. They were for him more than interesting subjects of discussion: They were the means by which he saw reality, including himself, in relation to God and to Israel. More than that, they were the images by which he lived. It is no exaggeration to say that his life became a lived dialectic by which he discovered and lived into the truth of the images: Messiah, Suffering Servant, son of David, Son of God, kingdom of heaven.[13] These images defined for him "what there is most worthy of love and most binding on conduct in the world of real existence."[14] He let the truth contained in them carry him "into collision with the hard rocks of fact."[15] It became clear to him that he could not be Messiah or establish on earth the kingdom of God in the literal and expected sense. But he held on to the truth he believed, and he trusted God to make whatever messianic kingdom God would. He did not empty out the sense of those faith words "Messiah," "Son of God," "kingdom":

> [Jesus] pressed the sense of the words . . . so that he ran them clean through his heart; and that was how he discovered what they meant. . . . He did not empty out the meaning of the words, he lived it out, and found it wonderful; he died for it and found it transfiguring. His fulfilling of the words was not a matter of scholastic exposition, but of death and resurrection.[16]

Simply put, Christ lived the dialectic of images. The crucifixion of the images was part of the life of faith in which he offered his very self for crucifixion. The images were raised to new life with him.

In his scholarly vocation, Farrer attempted to follow the same pattern of sacrifice that he found exemplified in Jesus' life of faith. In the sphere of understanding, this pattern of sacrifice was the dialectic of images. Farrer believed that the God of scripture and tradition was worthy of unconditional love and absolute obedience. Armed with this conviction and trusting God to bring truth to light, Farrer engaged the Oxford intellectual world, allowing the usual ideas of God's way of being and acting to break against the hard rocks of scientific, scholarly, historical, philosophical fact. In doing so, he found old interpretations, of which we had been prone to make idols, broken. In their places were new ways of thinking the ancient faith. It was not a new and different faith that he found. It was the same faith understood in a way that fits with the modes of thought characteristic of our time.

If we are to think well about God, if we are to avoid idolatry in the realm of understanding, then we, too, must live the dialectic of images.

We must press the sense of the biblical stories, of the creeds, and of theological tradition by breaking them against the cold realities we encounter in living them and by trusting the God of truth to bring us into deeper understanding and more direct acquaintance with the God whose ultimate reality necessarily transcends all images. It will not be for us anymore than it was for Christ a merely intellectual or theoretical matter. We will not be able first to comprehend God and then proceed to a perfectly understood and safe life. Rather, we will have to risk sacrificial obedience and the crucifixion of our habitual ways of understanding in order to be brought through the problems and paradoxes of thought into intimate friendship with God.

> The saints confute the logicians, but they do not confute them by logic but by sanctity. They do not prove the real connection between the religious symbols and the everyday realities by logical demonstration, but by life. *Solvitur immolando*, says the saint, about the paradox of the logicians. It is solved by sacrifice. I can offer my life to the God who has shown me his face in the glass of riddles. The God who is seen in the sphere of religion takes control in the sphere of conduct, and there he gives me unworthy, the help of his Holy Spirit.[17]

There it is, then. It is important to think well about God, but there are going to be no merely intellectual questions and no merely intellectual answers. The dialectic of images will take us into the life of faithful obedience where God will help us discern what is most worthy of love and most binding on conduct. Farrer saw the beliefs of traditional Christianity as able to shape lives of free and obedient love, and he pressed their sense in his own life as a university priest and chaplain amidst the realities of a hostile intellectual culture.

SERIOUS PERSONALISM

God Is at Least Personal

Truly to affirm the existence of God is to affirm God as one who is *at least* personal.

> It is a popular attitude nowadays even with professed believers to wallow in theological indecision and in particular to refuse to affirm anything about the personal nature of God. But if belief does not assert that everywhere and in all things we meet a sovereign, holy

and blessed Will, then what in the world does it assert? If we don't mean this, let us confess ourselves atheists and stop confusing the public mind.[18]

We challenge anyone to tell us what middle position is tenable between a serious personalism in religion and that pious atheism which has no other god than the backside of human nature.[19]

Traditional faith proceeds through the full-blooded understanding of God as a personal being who has acted and who continues to act to create and redeem the world. The life of faith has the form of an engagement with this same living, judging, loving, and saving God who still acts in particular ways to draw people into the divine life and thereby to transform them at last and everlastingly into creatures who truly love God with all their being and their neighbors as themselves.

Under the challenges of philosophy and science, such full-blooded faith, especially among the more intellectual among us, has grown problematical. How often have we been told that "we can no longer believe" in a God who acts and with whom we can engage because, after all, we now know that everything has a completely natural or scientific explanation? Thinking thus with learned scientists and philosophers squeezes the belief in God's ongoing and particular action in the world right out of the "reasonable" and "educated" person's mind. If we do not press the sense of the God who acts in the world and trust God to show us its truth, if we simply accept the view that the scientific way of understanding events in the world is exhaustively complete, we will think that talk of God's action is at most a metaphorical way of defining the point and purpose of human life.[20] Its truth will be seen to be a truth about what *we* do, not about what *God* does. Talk of God's action, then, will be talk only of human life. Farrer appropriately calls this outlook "pious atheism," whose god is only the "backside of human nature."[21]

In a sermon to undergraduates at Trinity College Chapel, Farrer describes this theological approach as "emptying out the sense" of traditional faith.[22] Vividly describing the process, he imagines a Christian surrounded by "a ring of savage and keen-scented logicians" brandishing the natural explanations of phenomena and pressing for the reduction of the content of the idea of God to nearly nothing. Says the Christian:

"My believing in providence means that whatever happens it will be all right; not that one thing will happen rather than another." "Then why," they retort, "call it a faith in providence, governance,

> or management? The words sounded quite full-blooded and real when you began, but in the course of discussion you have been emptying the sense out of them bit by bit, until there is no more meaning left; or if there are still a few drops in the cup, we could make you empty them out too, if we pressed you a little longer." [Here we have] what is meant by the accusation of "emptying out." It means that religious language sounds quite full-blooded and ordinary, but when you press the religious believers they empty more and more of the meaning away, until they seem to be saying nothing at all.[23]

If we empty out the sense of "God," we are likely also to indulge in "double thinking." That is, in our liturgy we may continue to use the stories of God's redeeming action, to address God in personal language, and to implore God to act,[24] yet leave the liturgy and get on with our lives believing that God is not truly a personal agent who engages with us. We will think one way in worship, another way in the rest of life. But that is not living the life of faith; it is living life as something we must do by ourselves.

> Take the accusation of "double thinking" which is brought against us Christians.... Religious beliefs and ceremonies are just superfluous decorations. In fact [say the cultured naysayers of religion] all religion in a scientific age is fundamentally of the same character as the religion practised by a couple of sentimental atheists getting married in church because it sounds more comforting. But, you and I object, we are not sentimental atheists: We really do believe. To which the answer is given: You think you believe; but you are deceived. You are a double thinker: You have two systems of thinking which in fact you keep apart—you think, as people say, in watertight compartments. And when you switch from one system of your thinking to another, that is, from your religious thinking to your practical thinking, you turn a blind eye to the transition, the passage from the world of reality to the world of fantasy.[25]

Some theologians have given up and have agreed that pressing the sense of traditional faith against the realities disclosed by the sciences crucifies the personal image of God. It crucifies the personal image because it makes us think of God as one who can only act in the world by acting on the world, forcing things against the grain of the natural order that the sciences study. This puts divine causation in competition with natural causation. But no effects can be identified as effects that have a divine cause instead of a natural cause. Consequently, the personal God is squeezed out of the natural world and the most important content of traditional faith is emptied out.

The most radical theologians propose that the only way forward is to take leave of God and become "Christian" Buddhists.[26] Others propose to affirm God but not a God who acts to make differences in the world. They hope to avoid sentimental atheism by affirming the reality of God as the transcendent and unknowable Mystery while denying that personal imagery tells us any truth about the Unknowable One.[27] In the twentieth and twenty-first centuries, there are no end of examples. In fact, if we admit with Farrer that all images are ultimately inadequate to the mystery of God, should we not affirm God as mystery and go no further? But doing so would change the whole shape of the life of faith. Instead of faith as responsive engagement with God, its only appropriate form would be still and silent awe before the divine mystery. Many who believe that all religions come to the same thing recommend this approach. All paths, the idea is, lead finally to the same God and to true worship: sheer adoration of the great mysterious One.

Farrer disagrees. He argues that we can only affirm the radical otherness, the reality of God, by means of personal imagery.[28] There is much to be said for worshipful awe before the holy, but Farrer insists that the strong affirmation of God in those terms alone would amount to the death in practice of anything resembling traditional Christian faith. It would be another form of sentimental atheism. It is better — and truer — to say that God is *at least* personal or is *more than* personal than to say that God does not include the personal powers of loving, knowing, and doing. While it must be true that God goes beyond what we know in ourselves as the essentially personal activities of loving, knowing, and doing, we cannot without qualification deny the perfection in God of these attributes.

Denying personal characteristics of God amounts, in fact, to the denial of God's reality, because it reduces God to a principle in the human mind. The reason for this reduction is that truly to affirm anything as existing — in the sense of enjoying some degree of independent reality[29] — is to recognize something that makes a difference to other realities because of its own way of operating in the world. Farrer maintained that "to be is to operate."[30] For anything to be, to be real, or to exist is for it to do something to make a difference to the way other things operate. But if to be is to operate, then we only truly affirm the reality of something when there is something we can do in addition to speaking or thinking about the supposed reality. That is to say, we truly affirm the reality of something when we see it as something that can make a difference in our action. So also with affirming God.

But what can we do in relation to God? What can we do that amounts to a genuine affirmation of God's real otherness from ourselves? Is it a sufficient answer to say that we can worship or adore God? No. Truly to affirm God's reality means seeing God as one whose active being engages and makes a difference to our active being. It means recognizing that God's active will makes an unconditional claim on us to respond appropriately to it.

What can we do that will be a response to God's active engagement with us? We can acknowledge the will of God and obey it. We can depend on God and trust God to provide the obedience God commands. We can hope for and cooperate with God's transforming work within us. All of these actions on our part suppose a prior action on God's part. If we do not regard God as able to do such things, we will not be affirming the reality of God. We may be affirming a life principle, and we may even call the principle "God." But we will not be affirming the reality of God. For principles do not act in us; we act according to them.

To affirm God's reality, then, is to acknowledge the divine will and divine action as bearing upon us. It is also to acknowledge that God loves and knows, because an unconditionally binding will of God implies that God knows what possible ways there are for us to live and what ways are best. If God wills that we live in one way rather than another, then God loves or desires what God knows to be best. Thus the real affirmation of God will lead us to the use of personal language. While it is true that personal language or imagery does not simply describe God as God is in Godself, it can still be rightly called true and necessary. Therefore, to affirm God is to affirm the *at least* personal or the *more than* personal being of God.

We appear, then, to be caught in a dilemma. On the one hand, some say that belief in a personal God who acts particularly in the world is ruled out by the sciences, which provide natural explanations for all the goings-on in the world. There is nothing left for God to do and no room for God to act. On the other hand, belief in a personal God who acts in the world is the very form by which the life of traditional Christian faith must be lived. If we cannot think about God as one who acts in the world, then we will not be able to understand ourselves as engaged by God and saved into divine life. We will not, without emptying the action terms of their sense, be able to see Jesus of Nazareth as the incarnate Son of God, the sacraments as ways of God's active presence, Holy Scripture as a medium of revelation, or the Church as Christ's living body. We will not be able to hope for our ultimate perfection in God or for our transformation by God into persons who love God with heart, soul, mind, and strength, and our neighbors as ourselves. Nor will we be able to make good sense of our own experience of God. We might be able to hold to a strong sense of that divine Other beyond all human comprehension, but we will remain skeptical about the propriety of living life as an ongoing engagement with the living God unless we can understand how to think of God's action in the world without running afoul of the natural sciences.

We could solve this problem by deciding that we must after all learn to live without the belief in God's personal agency. To do that would be to empty out the sense of traditional faith. We would then either have to give up faith completely or modify it so as to see ourselves as responsible for our own transformation. Such a modification would be an abandonment of traditional faith.

In Farrer's view such a dilution of the traditional sense of God as a personal agent who engages us would not be pressing the sense of traditional faith hard enough to discover its truth. If we press harder, we will discover that an understanding of God's personal being and relatedness to the world and us is embedded in the life of faith. Making it explicit will help Christians to enter more intentionally into the life of trusting, obedient, loving dependence upon the living God.

DOUBLE AGENCY

Meeting God in the Exercise of Faith

Truly to believe in God is to take up and enter into life lived in a personal relation of trusting, loving, and obedient dependence on God. If we take up this life of faithful relationship, then we can hope to know God intimately, as one with whom we are engaged from day to day. Here if anywhere we may hope to experience God's action in the world without having to think of God as one who smashes in to act by overthrowing the created order of things.

> We are perfectly clear that for us there is a positive and practical value in asserting the otherness [i.e., the real existence] of God.

> For it means that we exercise our relation with him as a personal relation. God is not, indeed, out there in space beside us, like one of our neighbours; he is at the causal root of our being, and of every being; and it is through our root . . . that we receive his grace. But his otherness for us lies in this, that his life is personal to him, it is not ours; that he has a will after which we enquire, a judgment to which we submit, a forgiveness we implore, a succour we seek; that the personal character of relation with him is the very form of it, not a metaphorical trapping which can be thought away while any substance remains.[31]

> But God does not stand alongside us or on a level with us, nor do we become aware of him through any external collision, mutual impingement or interaction between his activity and ours. How could we? He is related to us in quite another way: as the will which underlies our existence, gives rise to our action and directs our aim. To look for God by the methods we use for examining nature would not be scientific, it would be silly. A microscope is a scientific instrument, but it is not scientific to look for a note of music through a microscope. How can we have experimental knowledge of the will behind our will? Only by opening our will to it, or sinking our will in it; there is no other conceivable way. We cannot touch God except by willing the will of God. Then his will takes effect in ours and we know it; not that we manipulate him, but that he possesses us.[32]

Embedded in the faithfully lived relationship with God, we find a different image of God from that of a coercive agent who smashes into the world from outside, nullifying or overthrowing the created order of things in order to accomplish the divine purpose. The image of God in lived faith is personal, but it is an image of God as one who acts within the actions of creatures. Farrer develops this understanding of God by examining the experience of faithful persons who live the relationship.

It is important to say "*lived* faith" and "the *life* of faith" because faith is often taken to be some special kind of knowing that bypasses the evidence and reason that we ordinarily think are essential features of human knowing. Thus we are inclined to say that we "take on faith" those things for which we lack rational explanation and justification. In this view, faith is blind, groundless, and wholly outside the usual methods and processes by which people know their worlds. But Farrer avoids the usual confusions about faith by emphasizing action. For him the term "faith" almost always refers to the life of faith. He shows how faith as a way of living involves its own distinctive rationality.

The "life of faith" refers to a particular way of being in the world and of undergoing its active reality. Life in the world is always lived by means of ideas about what is real, how it works, and what is most important. The ideas we use will shape our way of living and at the same time our experience and understanding of reality. The peculiar ideas or ways of understanding by which traditionally faithful Christians live their faith in the world constitute faith's embedded rationality.

We can appreciate the appropriateness of faith's rationality if we consider it in relation to other aspects of our experience and understanding. Begin with sensory experience. How and what we see, hear, smell, taste, and feel are due both to the way our sensory organs operate and to the way the world they encounter operates in turn upon them. We may say that the embedded "rationality" of plain sensory experience is the way our neuro-sensory mechanism operates. Seeing and hearing, for example, are ways that our bodies interact with the world around us. If we wish to see, we must "act seeingly"; to hear, we must "act hearingly." That is, we must open our eyes and look and open our ears and listen. The substance of what we see and hear will not simply be the world as it is in itself (or as it is to God); it will be the world as it affects the bodily activities of looking and listening.

Moving to a higher level than sensory recognition, we may wish to know whether a person has, for example, a particular disease. In order to find out, we must act in relation to that person in the way appropriate to the reality we want to know about, in the way that will let us know the kind of truth we are looking for. In our modern culture that will mean subjecting the person to the appropriate set of diagnostic tests: x-rays, blood tests, CAT scans, and so on. These are designed and directed by the understanding provided by the biological sciences. They are also ways of acting toward the person based on that understanding. Only by acting in just those ways will one have the experience that confirms or disconfirms the presence of the disease.

When we turn to the activity in which we come to know persons as friends, we find that the way of acting toward the person in order to know him or her as a friend must be significantly different from the way we would act to diagnose the person's disease. As Farrer puts it, we must undergo the full impact of the person as a whole.[33] If one would know someone as a friend, the rationality of diagnostic medicine will not work. One must enter into friendly life with him or her: converse, sympathize, cooperate, and the like. It is possible for the same person to know someone both as a friend and as the subject of diagnostic tests, but he or she will have the two kinds of knowledge only because he or she engages in the kinds of activity using the kind of rationality necessary for the two kinds of knowledge. In knowing the person as diseased, he or she will not know all there is to know about that person but will know the person only as he or she affects diagnostic activities. In knowing the person as friend, he or she likewise will not know the person as the person ultimately is to God, but as the person responds to and interacts with him or her in activities of friendship.

So it is with God. If we are to know God and God's way of acting in the world, we must first act in a way that will allow us to know God; that is, we must act in a way appropriate to the reality we seek to know. And that means using the kind of rationality that makes faith the kind of activity it is. It means taking up the life of faith.

To know a person as a friend, we must be friends with the person. To know God, we must live faithfully with God. And if we do, we can reasonably believe that we encounter God acting within our own action. "We cannot touch God except by willing the will of God. Then his will takes effect in ours and we know it; not that we manipulate him but that he possesses us."[34] The knowledge that results will be anything but groundless and irrational. The degree of its concreteness and accuracy, however, will depend on how authentically and fully one lives the life of faith.

The life of traditional Christian faith is a complex way of acting in and interacting with reality. It is what it is because of particular ways of thinking, valuing, and feeling; that is, because of its embedded rationality. Jewish faith, Muslim faith, Sikh faith, and so on, are other ways of being in the world. Each is ordered by its distinctive understanding. So Christian faith is ordered by its use of the ideas and images of Christianity; one cannot experience reality as traditional Christians do unless one lives the life of faith in those terms. It follows further that living in terms of those ideas and images generates experience that is peculiar to the Christian life. The distinctive feature of that experience is that as one actively and intentionally submits to God's will, God's own action is present and enabling. Yet one's freedom and personal integrity are not thereby canceled or minimized, but are, rather, fulfilled.

Jesus Exhibits Double Agency

Taking Jesus as the paradigm of faithful life makes clearer just what the embedded rationality of faith is. Here, too, we find the necessity of personal imagery for God most strongly demonstrated. And here, too, we see that it is not the imagery of the god who smashes in to force things against their grain; it is the imagery of interpersonal communion and cooperation.

> The Christ of faith is not some figure remotely supernatural about whom ingenious doctrines have been propounded by theologians. ... For consider; what do we mean, when we call the man Jesus, Christ and Son of God? We mean that the action of Jesus was simply the action of God. But what was Jesus? Was he a divinely mesmerized sleepwalker, a jointed doll pulled by heavenly wires? Was he a painful pedant, carrying out with pharisaic exactitude a part which had been written for him by a divine hand? He was all the reverse of this. Never was there a man whose words and action were more utterly his own. The spontaneity of his compassion moves us to tears. The blaze of his indignation shocks us; his speech is an unforced poetry, the coinage of his heart; the sacrifice on which he spent his blood was a decision personally made in agonies of sweat. If any man made his own life, Jesus did; yet what was the impression he left on his friends? That his whole life was the pure and simple act of God. What Jesus did was simply what God did to save us all.[35]

Jesus of Nazareth, the Christ, is the ideal case of the life of faith, and it is the life in which God is most fully and directly known. Farrer aptly describes it in various sermons and books as a life of loving and obedient trust in God, whom Jesus called Father, and of hopeful dependence upon the Father to do what he had promised, even though the prevailing circumstances and conditions made it impossible for Jesus to see how it could be done. What we call the perfection of Jesus' life is unconditional, obedient, loving, trusting, and hoping dependence on God. This was Christ's way of being in the world. It defines the ideal of the traditional life of faith.

Embedded within such a life of faith is the image or understanding of God as a perfect personal agent who acts in and through the faithful actions of persons. We could well call it an *inter*personal or social image. It remains an image, but as we have pointed out, it is not one we can do away with and continue to practice Christian faith. For Christians it holds a privileged place among all images of God, not primarily because it helps us make theoretical sense of God's action in the world, although it does that, but because it is the image by which and through which Christian faith must be lived. This interpersonal image of God gives faith its defining form as life in cooperative dependence on God. Christians say that Jesus lived it perfectly. The rest of us struggle to live it — and meet with greater and lesser degrees of success. Spiritual growth is all about being transformed into people who live the life of faith more completely. It begins in the present life as a struggle to bring our wills into conformity with God's will. Its fulfillment is eternal life.

The obedience that is an essential part of the life of traditional faith is obedience to the will of God. But how do we know the will of God? There are several ways. We know it by interacting with the history of the effort to live in response to God. For Christians this means interaction with the Old and the New Testaments in the context of worship and service and in the tradition of theological interpretation that continues the same interaction into the present. It means especially attending to the life of faith as Jesus lived it. And it means attentiveness to the claims God makes on us through the world, especially the part of the world that meets us in the neighbors with whom we live.

The general will of God is clear. It is to love God with our whole being — with heart, soul, mind, and strength — and our neighbors as ourselves. Therefore, the life of faith is a life in which we recognize those great commandments as the very will of God for us and, consequently, as laying an unconditional claim on our whole selves, for there are no circumstances or conditions in which we may say that these commandments do not apply.

In the case of Christ, we see one who lived a life of unconditional obedience to these commandments. His life was an interpretation of and a commitment to doing what they required, even if he could not clearly see how the consequences would fulfill his messianic call. His obedience, therefore, was rooted in the love of God; that is, in the deep desire to do what God commanded. If God commanded that he love his neighbors, that meant desiring for them what God desires for them. And what God desires for them is, in broad terms, what God desires for us all: to be persons who do — in thought, feeling, and deed — love God with all our being and our neighbors as ourselves.

Jesus' life of faith included trust, trust that obedience would ultimately lead to the good of all neighbors and the fulfillment of God's call to him to be the Messiah. That loving his neighbors required unconditional trust is clear from the fact that he saw that such love was leading to the cross. In obedience, he trusted the God he loved and whose will he embraced to fulfill the promise to establish the kingdom as a life in which the will of God reigns. He trusted God to accomplish God's purpose in spite of the fact that his very obedience seemed to be leading to the crushing of that purpose.

Trusting and depending on God to provide what God commanded, Jesus hoped for the ultimate fulfillment of the kingdom of God: all people loving God with their whole being and their neighbors as themselves. That would be life eternal. It would be joy, blessedness, peace, freedom.

Such being the character of the promised kingdom, Jesus' faith also had to be an obedience that placed him in complete dependence on God. He depended on God to fulfill the promise of the kingdom because he knew that he himself by himself could not do so, either in himself or for others. The temptations described in Matthew and Luke were, in fact, ways in which he might have attempted to accomplish the kingdom by himself.[36] It is essential to Jesus' faith that he rejected those ways. Doing so was an act of unconditional dependence on God to accomplish what he trusted God to do.

Traditional Christian faith is for us that way of being in the world in which the faithful become part of Christ's own life of perfect faith. That means being part of Christ's loving, obedient, trusting, hoping, and dependent life. Thus the Christian's faith in God is mediated by faith in Christ. As Christ's life is a participation in the will, that is, in the life and being of God, so the lives of faithful Christians become participation in the life of Christ and thereby participation in the life and being of God. What the faithful see in the life of Christ is that here, even if nowhere else, we must say that God is active in the world, not in the general way of giving the world's processes universal laws to follow, but in saying and doing particular things. God acts in the world by acting in the actions of Christ.

What we see is paradoxical. We see that Christ was most fully and completely himself, most fully and completely rational and free, in his trusting obedience to God's will. He responded to God by sinking his will without reserve into God's will. He chose and enacted his life freely by giving himself up to God, and God enacted the divine purpose for redemption within Christ's life of committed and free obedience. Here, then, we have two agents, each free and enjoying integrity of being, yet each the agent of the same events in time and place.

Our Experience of God's Action as Double Agency

We experience the action of God in our own experience of active faith, and we experience it as an action that takes effect without forcing us against the grain of our nature as free agents. Cooperating with God's action, we are more ourselves and more free than when we act without regard to God.

> We can, in the only possible way, experience the active relation of a created energy to the Creator's action by embracing the divine will. Everyone who prays knows that the object of the exercise is a thought or an aspiration or a caring which is no more ours than it is that of God in us. . . .
>
> We know that the action of a man can be the action of God in him; our religious existence is an experimenting with this relation. Both the divine and the human actions remain real and therefore free in the union between them.[37]

"Our religious existence is an experimenting with this relation" between God and ourselves. That is a strong claim. The heart of the life of faith is the loving, trusting embrace of God's will. We can only embrace God's will in our free action, but embracing it is at the same time a dependence on God to do in us what we cannot do by ourselves. We are free, yet submissive to the will of another. We are obedient to the will of another, yet thereby most fully in charge of ourselves. Thus, what one experiences in double agency is not the effect of external hammer-on-nail force but of two agents cooperating in one action: God acting in and through us, such that God's action is effective in our own but in a way that lets us be ourselves and retain our identity and integrity. In fact, the believer's experience is that God's action not only respects one's integrity but even makes one more fully who one is than one otherwise could be. Generalizing, we can say that God achieves the divine purpose by letting creatures be themselves. The more the creature is consciously cooperative and intentionally obedient, the more it aims at what it takes the divine will to be, the more God's letting the creature be itself is also at the same time God's action in the creature to fulfill its nature. In the case, then, of free human obedience to God, we can say both that the act of obedience is the person's own free action and at the same time the action of God. The action is something the person freely does, and it is at the same time something God does.

Cooperative agency among creatures cannot be exactly the same as God's action in creatures. In the case of creaturely actions, we can distinguish the different agents clearly and in principle specify which part of the double action is done by one and which by another. Furthermore, we can describe or explain the way each creaturely agent works. But it is impossible to "locate the causal joint" between God's action and the creatures' actions and impossible to describe how God's action takes effect in the actions of creatures because we have no access to the interior life of God in God. What we experience is the *effect* of God's action in our action; we experience what God does in us rather than the mechanism or process by which God does it.

What God reveals to us can only be revealed by God's acting in the world, and what we experience will always be the effect of that action. That is true whether the effect be internal to us, God's acting in our experiencing and knowing, or external to us, God's acting in creatures other than ourselves. We could have an explanation or description of the process by which God acts only if God's action were an instance of the same kind of actions people perform in their cooperative interactions with each other; then perhaps we could know how God's agency takes effect by knowing how ours does.[38] But if we could give that kind of explanation, it would mean that God and God's agency would be parts of the world rather than the reason why there is a world and why that world is the kind of world it is. God, as we said, is unique, as is God's relatedness to the world. We should in principle always be able to explain the *natural* principles according to which the divine effects occur, for the effects will just be events in the world. As events in the world they will have natural descriptions and explanations. What we will never be able to do is describe or explain what goes on within God to bring about the effects. The uniqueness of the relation makes it essentially a mystery, irreducible in principle to any instance of the relatedness among the creatures that populate the world.

The mystery of how God's action takes effect does not mean that we do not experience double agency any more than the mystery of how our decisions take effect means that we do not experience our intentional control over our own bodily movement. Indeed, St. Paul said of the whole life of faith: "not I but Christ who lives in me" and "for me to live is Christ." Farrer points out that the experience of God acting in our action is the heart and soul of the Christian life, that "the whole mystery of practical religion comes down to that familiar phrase of our daily prayer, 'whose service is perfect freedom.' "[39] Therefore, believers say that they experience the action of God in the actions of their own lives and that the experience is not the experience of being coerced against the grain of their own natures, of being diminished as persons, of losing their freedom, or of ceasing to be finite human beings; rather, it is the experience of being enhanced and fulfilled as the very persons they are.

There is no proof that it is God's action in ours that we experience. We cannot use biochemical or psychological tests to catch out God's action and demonstrate that it is in fact God's action. If we could do that, God would be a creature among creatures rather than God. Nevertheless, the experience of being most free and most oneself just when one is most obedient and most given over to God's own will is undeniable to those who are on the path of faith.[40]

Experiencing God's action in a life of faithful response does not mean that only good things happen to those who live the life of faith. If that were what God's action means, then we would know that all good things are things that God does, while all bad things are not. But that would be locating the causal joint that connects God's action with its worldly effects; it would be reducing God to a testable and finite natural cause that we can manipulate. The experience of God's action is rather the experience that in faithful life one is more free, more oneself, and more the person one is commanded to be than one could be outside the life of faith. That experience is certainly not a simple and indisputable given fact; it involves an ongoing implicit judgment — as do all modes of experience. In this case the experience is that one's effort to love God and one's neighbor is strengthened, aided, abetted, and carried forward in spite of one's natural inability simply to accomplish such love, and it is also the experience that in the process one is thereby made more truly oneself. But the experience of God's action within one's life is compatible with any external or measurable characteristics — as much with pain, defeat, shame, and boredom as with pleasure, success, recognition, and interesting fulfillment.

> It is natural to expect that the integration of our will with the Creative Will should enhance, enrich and bless our personal being, and others through us. On the supposition that God is truly what we believe him, it would be odd if our giving ourselves to him made us on the whole more restless, more frustrated, less able to manage our relations with others or to discipline our own passions, less

> generous or outgoing, less alive all over. The signs of blessing can fairly be looked for; but at the best they are confirmatory evidence of a relationship which must be its own proof. No one can say that wherever such enrichments of life are present, there is bound to be an active dependence on the divine will. We may go farther; there may be a heroic service of God and no such blessed signs be visible at all. For sometimes the will of God which his servants must embrace is not aimed at their present or personal advantage; it pursues a more distant creative purpose. The individual's service may be a martyrdom, with no fruits in the world but agony and personal destruction. So Christ was crucified.[41]

Some may object that we are talking nonsense, that the nature of free action is that it cannot have two agents. If, say the objectors, it is God who acts in us, then we do not freely act; we are but the instruments by which God acts or the media through which God's actions proceed. To say that we experience our own free actions as things that God does is absurd. We cannot possibly experience the actuality of something that is logically impossible.

But the objection is mistaken. Double agency is not logically impossible. If God's action operates in the world in its own peculiar way, the inability to give a scientific account of it cannot rule it out as an impossibility. To insist that it does indicates that one is thinking in terms of external physical causation, of physical force on physical force. Or perhaps it means that one is a metaphysical naturalist, committed in advance to the decision that only explanations in terms of external physical force may be admitted to thought. But our free actions cannot be understood that way; neither can God's action in us be reduced to that model. There is no contradiction in saying that our own free actions are also actions of God, because God is unique, and God's relation to the world is unique. We know that double agency is possible precisely because we experience it. Therefore, there is no contradiction in saying that the relation of God's action to our action is a matter of double agency.

Nevertheless, even if we cannot explain the inner workings of God, we can render the experience of God's action intelligible by looking to creaturely relations that are analogous to the cooperative agency of God in people. The action of God in our free actions can be thought after the model of cooperative human undertakings. Consider two examples.

The first is that of a parent teaching a child to ride a bicycle. Both parent and child intend the same outcome, and the child's actually riding is continuous with and at first inseparable from the parent's holding up the bicycle and running beside the child. When the child learns, the accomplishment may truly be said to be something the parent did and also something the child did. Furthermore, the action of the parent did not overthrow the free action of the child but made it more fully what it intended to be. However, God's action in the free action of a person cannot simply be an instance of this parent-child relation. In the latter, the action and motion of each can be separately described. We can say where one leaves off and the other begins, and we can describe the mechanics of the parent's action and how it takes effect in the child's riding. Furthermore, once the child learns to ride, he or she can continue on his or her own and in the absence of the parent. By contrast, people of traditional faith do not think their obedient response to God can ever proceed on its own; faith is not a matter of learning how to operate independently and on one's own in a way that makes God's continued action unnecessary.

This analogy can be extended further by taking the more complex example of an ideal parent-child relationship as a whole, thinking of the loving care of the parent over a lifetime as one complex action of forming the child into a mature adult of good character, able to live well among the people of the world. The extended action may certainly include times of coercion, but it succeeds only insofar as the parent's action increasingly brings the child's action into freedom and independence. It may be difficult to say where the parent's action leaves off and where the child's begins. Most importantly, the parent's active relationship with the child achieves its greatest success and operates most effectively in the free and responsible life of the child. If the parent is truly wise, the child will become more truly himself or herself, more independent, more responsible, more free, as the effect of the parent's own free action. But, again, the parent-child relationship cannot be the same kind of relationship as that which holds between God's action and ours. If parents are successful and children become mature, they will leave continued dependence on their parents behind and learn to be themselves on their own.

We could multiply examples. In them we can, in principle if not in fact, locate the joint where the different agencies come together, and we can more or less clearly describe or explain the mechanism of their respective agencies. But we shall never have access to the inner working of God's life and so will never be able to describe God's side of the action whereby God acts in us. Nevertheless, the analogies show that events in the world cannot be completely explained as the coercive impact of one thing on another. Especially when it comes to the intentional and purposeful lives of people with one another, we have to acknowledge the mutual cooperation of agents in a way that preserves and enhances the freedom and self-fulfillment of the agents.

Double Agency in the Wider World

Although it is in the life of Jesus and in our own lives of faith that we most clearly see the action of God in the world as noncoercive double agency, those instances become the clue by which God's action at all levels of being can be understood.

> Wherever we come up against the living process of nature, we meet the thought and will of God. Not in the gross and outward show of things, with which they strike our senses; but in the intimate process of activity by which they are themselves. In so far as our science strips away the sensory show and lays bare the rhythm of active being, it approaches the divine creative thought.[42]

> When we contemplate the physical creation, we see an unimaginable complex, organized on many planes one above another; atomic, molecular, cellular, vegetable, animal, social. And the marvel of it is that at every level the constituent elements run themselves, and by their mutual interaction, run the world. God not only makes the world, he makes it make itself; or rather, he causes its innumerable constituents to make it. And this in spite of the fact that the constituents are not for the most part intelligent. They cannot enter into the creative purposes they serve. They cannot see beyond the tip of their noses, they have indeed, no noses not to see beyond, nor any eyes with which to fail in the attempt. All they can do is blind away at being themselves, and fulfil the repetitive pattern of their existence. When you contemplate this amazing structure, do you wonder that it should be full of flaws, breaks, accidents, collisions and disasters? Will you not be more inclined to wonder why chaos does not triumph; how higher forms of organization should ever arise, or, having arisen, maintain and perpetuate themselves?[43]

> What moves believers to worship moves atheists to ridicule. A thought living at once on every level of natural process and thinking all levels into a single story is to believers the wonder of omnipo-

> tence and to sceptics the height of absurdity. Perhaps we cannot make those who come to scoff at us remain to pray with us. It will be something if we can help those who come to pray, pray with a more understanding adoration.[44]

That the clearest case of God's action in the world is the case of God's action in one's own intentional cooperation with grace does not mean that God acts only in the lives of faithful people, or that God's action in the world is restricted to people. It does not even mean that we experience God's action only when God acts in our own selves. Farrer argues that God acts in all levels of the created order. Everything that is exists only insofar as God's creative action preserves it in being. Nothing is left out. All things depend on God for their existence, and not for their existence only but for being the kinds of things they are and for making the world to be the kind of world it is. Furthermore, these two dependencies of the world on God do not belong simply to some action of God in the past. They are effects of God's continuing action in the different levels of things. Therefore, God's action in the world is not limited to God's action in people. The question is how to understand God's action at levels below free human action.

Farrer takes the experience of double agency in the life of faith as the clue to understanding God's action at all levels of existence. God acts always and everywhere by acting in the creatures — and in a way that does not cancel, overthrow, or force them against the grain of their natures. "God not only makes the world, he makes it make itself."[45]

Farrer is clear that the action of God in making and sustaining the entities that operate below the level of conscious will — subatomic and atomic particles, molecules, chemical compounds, microscopic life, and so on up to human beings — is not the same as God's action in the freedom of people. It is "double agency" at all levels, but when we speak of operations below the level of consciousness, we are extending the term "double agency," which comes from our experience of life in God, beyond all but the most minimal analogical understanding.

To say that God acts by double agency at the subatomic level means that God acts at that level in a way that does not overthrow what the subatomic particles are or force them to operate contrary to what they are. It does not explain *how* God brings this about. It is only a way of saying *that* God does. And it is a way, therefore, to affirm God's action intelligibly without having recourse to the smashing-in image of God's action. Although it does not explain the process by which God both lets the creatures be themselves and gets the world out of them, double agency nevertheless helps our understanding. It extends the principle that God can act in our actions without canceling our natures to the action of God at other levels of the world's make-up. We know that God's relation to the world and to its creatures is unique. We know that God does not smash in and negate our integrity and freedom as persons. Therefore, we may reasonably say, "Yes, God can respect the reality at all levels of creature, let them be themselves, sustain them in being themselves, and yet get the world and its complex order out of them."

The best creaturely analogy for God's action at the nonhuman levels is that of thoughtful bodily action.[46] This is an example of creaturely double agency in which one of the creatures is the human body with its skeleton, musculature, organs, and nervous system; the other, the thoughtful person. When one thoughtfully decides to perform an action, one's decision in no way overthrows or forces bodily action against its nature. Rather, the free and conscious agent decides and acts, and the body responds. That is what bodies properly do. Effort may be required, but the body does what bodies are naturally able to do. What the body does can be described in purely natural terms. The body is itself, even in being directed by a decision. Suppose, for example, someone waves an arm. The waving can be understood in physiological and neurological terms. Yet, that understanding will not be complete if the waving is being done by a person acting consciously and purposefully. One will not understand the waving without understanding what purpose it is intended for. Does it mean "hello," "go away," "look at me," or "watch out"? Thus, there is the person and there is the person's body, two distinguishable constituents of the world. The decision of the person to wave takes effect in the body without canceling the body's nature as a body or going against the grain of its nature.

Analogously, Farrer says, God "acts as the soul of the world."[47] God achieves God's purposes in the world by acting in the world without smashing its natural order. This, again, is not an explanation of how God accomplishes what God does; it just says that it is reasonable to believe that God does it. Just as we can freely decide on bodily movements without understanding or being able to explain how our decisions take effect in our bodies, so God can surely act in the operations of the constituents of the world without our being able to explain the process by which God does it.

ALL THAT GOD SEES IT BEST TO BE

The traditional understanding of God as personal in nature is not the understanding of God simply as a person. Certainly God is not a person on the same level as human persons. Practicing the dialectic of images, Farrer proposes that we can best think of God as the one "who is all he wills to be, and wills to be all he is."[48] We should take the formulation as one that drives us beyond all images rather than as placing limits around God in the manner of a definition.

> God wills and knows all He is, and is all He wills and knows.[49]

> God is will, and as such is an agency to which our own voluntary and intellectual being offers the sole analogy or clue. How, then, does the divine act differ from ours? God must be such that he can will for every sort of creature once it is created, and also will what created forms there shall be. Such a will can only be defined by its unrestricted freedom. It is not the will of a determinate being, operating within a certain charter of function or scope of effect. It is all that it does, and chooses to be all that it is.[50]

> And thus, proceeding from the "Why is it so?" question, we may reach the God who is all he wills to be, and wills to be all he is: for his act is himself, and his act is free.[51]

> The very meaning of the name [God] is a free, untrammelled Spirit, who is all that he sees it best to be.[52]

When we say that we must think of God as personal, we will all know that God's personal being is both like ours, which is why we call it personal, and unlike ours, which is why we say things like "God transcends the world," "God is unique," and "God is perfect being." God's being must be like ours in involving knowledge, love, and the ability freely to decide, do, and bring to pass that which is decided. Farrer takes action to be the essential reality here, for knowing and loving—and even passive receiving and being affected—are themselves modes of activity, ways of operating. "To be is to operate."[53] To be a finite creature is to operate according to patterns over which the creature has limited, if any, control. Being conscious agents who aspire to act on the basis of the best possible knowledge and the most appropriate desire with the greatest power of realizing our ends, we think upward to God as the one who is the perfection of the existence we know in ourselves as imperfect.

We know the imperfection of our existence in many ways. As much as we might like to, we cannot bring about our own existence or assure that it will continue. Nor can we know everything as it truly is, not even ourselves. We also cannot know what is the best and right thing to do in every circumstance. We cannot do everything we see it best to do, be everything we see it best to be. We confess as much when we acknowledge that we do not love our neighbors as ourselves. But our aspiration toward a more perfect freedom rooted in a more perfect knowledge of how things are and ought to be leads us to the idea of God as Unconditioned Will. It is anthropomorphic imagery, yes; but it points beyond the human to the unique and transcendent God. Were we to dispense with the personal imagery of God as Supreme, Perfect, and Unconditioned Will, we would find ourselves thinking of a being who is less than God, not more.

Farrer, therefore, refines and qualifies the personal image of God, compressing it into two similar formulations. The first of these is that God is the being "who is all he wills to be and who wills to be all he is."[54] A slightly different formulation is that God is the one who is "all that he sees it best to be."[55]

There are reasons to prefer the second formulation. It makes clear that God's being is not imaged as a sheer power of capricious will but that it includes knowing ("all God *sees*...") and loving ("all God sees it *best* to be"). In our own experience, knowledge, love, and will are distinguishable from each other. We can know without loving or without acting on the knowledge. We can act without loving or knowing. We can love without knowing or acting. But in God, as the best of beings, these distinguishable features must be perfectly realized and perfectly united. Knowing, God loves the best and does it. Loving, God knows the best and does it. Acting, God knows the best and loves it.

God, therefore, cannot be conceived by us as anything greater than one whose being is a perfect knowing-loving-doing. Hence the statement that God is the one who is "all that he sees it best to be." This refers to God's own being. Who God is, Farrer proposes, is just who God sees it best to be. God knows what that is, loves it, and unfailingly and eternally goes about enacting it. Nothing other than God limits or determines who God is. God's being, therefore, is not relative to or dependent on the world. On the other hand — and we shall see that it is important in Farrer's coming to terms with suffering and evil — God can choose to wait for God's creatures, can make the divine action relative to the action of creatures.

Apart from the knowledge gained through lived relationship with God, we can say very little about the God who is all that God sees it best to be. Nevertheless, saying that little bit is an important part of avoiding idolatry. We can say that God's being is not distinct from God's acting. We can say that what God sees it best to be is Creator of a world that does not have to be. God is the reason why there is anything at all other than God. Furthermore, God is the reason why there is the kind of world there is. This does not mean that God sees it best for everything that occurs to occur. It does not mean, for example, that God sees it best for terrorist acts to occur, for homes and livelihoods to be destroyed by flood or fire, or for nation to respond to nation with war. It does mean that God sees it best for there to be the *kind* of world in which these kinds of things can occur. The philosophical assertion that God is the Creator of all things does not explain how God creates. It is only the assertion that God is the reason why there is something rather than nothing and why the something that is has the general character our world in fact has.

To say what we have said in this chapter about God and about God's action in the world is not to claim that we comprehend God. It does not reduce God to a clear idea we can get our minds and experience around. It does not tell us what the life of God is like to God or give us the definite content of God's being. On the other hand, it does tell us that the logic of thought about God combined with the human experience most suited to representing God require us to say that God is at least who God sees it best to be. Philosophy can tell us little more, but it does tell us that we cannot say less.

The God who is all that God sees it best to be has seen it best, Christians believe, not only to create a world and to set the divine life in Christ in the midst of it, but also to undertake our fulfillment by attaching us to Christ and thereby making us participants in the divine life of reciprocal self-giving love. To cooperate most intentionally with this grace, we must take up the personally ordered life of loving, trusting, obedient, hoping dependence upon the living God: Father, Son, and Holy Spirit. Acting in us, God will crucify us, but God will also resurrect us and ultimately bring us to completion as persons who love God with all our being and our neighbors as ourselves. This is the Christian hope, and it is what the God who is all that God sees it best to be sees it best for us to be.

NOTES

1. Austin Farrer, "The Transforming Will," in *The End of Man* (ed. Charles C. Conti; London: SPCK, 1973), 104.

2. Austin Farrer, *God Is Not Dead* (New York: Morehouse-Barlow, 1966), 110.

3. I borrow this term from Ralph C. Wood, who for some years has taught a course called "The Oxford Christians." As Wood uses the term, it refers to those who used imaginative literature to express, interpret, and defend Christian faith: Dorothy L. Sayers, J. R. R. Tolkien, C. S. Lewis, and Charles Williams. I extend the term to include also the Christian philosophers whose life and work overlapped with the literary figures. Ann Loades has noted their place in the Oxford of Farrer's day. They are mainly Farrer, Basil Mitchell, Eric Mascall, Donald MacKinnon, and J. R. Lucas.

4. Austin Farrer, "Emptying Out the Sense," in *Austin Farrer: The Essential Sermons* (ed. Leslie Houlden; London: SPCK, 1991), 117–20. Hereinafter cited as *The Essential Sermons.*

5. Iris Murdoch is a case in point. She went with the Metaphysicals in bucking the antimetaphysical tide, arguing for a version of Platonism by affirming the reality of "the Good." She could not, however, bring herself to believe that the Good could be a God who acts. It was this inability, says Basil Mitchell, which led her in the interest of honesty to withdraw from the Metaphysicals.

6. Austin Farrer, "An English Appreciation," in *Kerygma and Myth: Rudolf Bultmann and Five Critics* (New York: Harper, 1961), 122.

7. Alan Jones, *Living the Truth* (Cambridge, MA: Cowley, 2000), 18.

8. See especially Austin Farrer, *Finite and Infinite* (2nd ed.; Westminster: Dacre, 1959), parts 1 and 3; and *The Glass of Vision* (Westminster: Dacre, 1948).

9. For Farrer's use of this image, see "The Painter's Colours," in *The Essential Sermons,* 1–4.

10. Farrer discusses this image in *God Is Not Dead,* 85–86, and in *Faith and Speculation* (Edinburgh: T & T Clark, 1988), chap. 10.

11. Farrer, "Emptying Out the Sense," 119–20.

12. This does not mean that Farrer thought of the lived historical dialectic of images — after the manner of Hegel or Marx — as though it were the inevitable expression in the world of the inner logic of divine Spirit or the directional development of political and economic structures. The historical dialectic of the Hebrew Scriptures, rather, is the development of their understanding of God through the experience of interaction with God.

13. Many biblical scholars argue that Jesus did not think of himself in these images, that they were used later by followers to theologize his life. Farrer certainly agrees with those who think that Jesus did apply them to himself. However, the point is not critical to the present purpose. Say, if you like, that the authors of the gospel accounts portray Jesus *as if* he lived the dialectic of images. But in that case, the gospel writers themselves thought by means of a dialectic of images. The method remains a proper one for the spiritual life.

14. Farrer, "Keble and His College," in *The End of Man,* 156–57.

15. Farrer, "The Transforming Will," 104.

16. Farrer, "Emptying Out the Sense," 117–20. For another discussion of the practical spiritual thrust of Farrer's work, which also makes use of this same passage, see Richard Harries, " 'We Know on Our Knees': Intellectual, Imaginative, and Spiritual Unity in the Theology of Austin Farrer," in *Divine Action: Studies Inspired by the Philosophical Theology of Austin Farrer* (ed. Brian Hebblethwaite and Edward Henderson; Edinburgh: T & T Clark, 1990), 21–34.

17. Farrer, "Double Thinking," in *The Essential Sermons,* 88.

18. Farrer, *God Is Not Dead,* 92.

19. Farrer, *Faith and Speculation,* 48.

20. The active movement of philosophers and scientists who call themselves "religious naturalists" makes a credo of what Farrer calls sentimental atheism. Summing it up, Michael Cavanaugh says: "Religious naturalism is a belief in the natural order as understood by ongoing scientific investigation, underlaid and supported by a strong and positive emotional feeling about the wonder and efficacy of that natural order. Religious naturalism is philosophically materialistic, but with an affirmation of the sense of mystery that accompanies our contemplation of the emergence of matter. . . . " See Michael Cavanaugh, "What Is Religious Naturalism? A Preliminary Report of an Ongoing Conversation," *Zygon: Journal of Religion and Science* 35 (June 2000): 241–52.

21. Farrer, *Faith and Speculation,* 48.

22. Farrer, "Emptying Out the Sense," 117–20.

23. Ibid., 118.

24. According to Robert Towler's research, on almost any pew in any church on any Sunday there will sit five people with five radically different theological orientations. See Robert Towler, *The Need for Certainty: A Sociological Study of Conventional Religion* (London and Boston: Routledge, 1984). I owe this point to Michael Cavanaugh.

25. Farrer, "Double Thinking," 86.

26. Don Cupitt, *Taking Leave of God* (London: SCM, 2001).

27. In Farrer's background perhaps we will think of the Evelyn Underhill who had not yet returned to her Anglican roots. The unwillingness to affirm the at least personal being of God also calls Iris Murdoch again to mind.

28. See Farrer, *Faith and Speculation,* chaps. 2–4.

29. We refer here to what Aristotle called primary substance. A less hoary term is "entity" or "individual entity." Whatever is or exists, Aristotle said, and Farrer implicitly agreed, either is a real individual entity or a quality or relation or effect of a real individual or, for the real individuals that are persons, an experience, idea, emotion or action of an individual. When we affirm real existing entities, we mean that they are other than ourselves; they do not exist only in our minds but enjoy independence of the minds that recognize them and of the other real things with which they interact. This in no way denies the interconnectedness of things; it only says that to be interconnected, things must have some independence or otherness of their own. They must be their own centers of operation or activity. It also does not mean that affirming God's existence reduces God to being one entity among many other entities and another constituent of the world along with them. No. God is not an entity in that sense. God is the reason why there is a world at all, not simply one of the things in the world. But to say that God exists is to say that God enjoys more

independence of being than any entity that is simply part of the world and that God is in no way to be understood as the effect or relation or idea or experience, etc., of something other than God.

30. It is the heart of Farrer's thought about the nature of real entities. It was central in his first book, *Finite and Infinite,* and it was reasserted in every book afterwards right up to and including his last books, *Faith and Speculation* and *God Is Not Dead.*

31. Farrer, *Faith and Speculation,* 47.

32. Farrer, *God Is Not Dead,* 106–7.

33. Austin Farrer, "Prologue: On Credulity," in *Interpretation and Belief* (ed. Charles C. Conti; London: SPCK, 1976), 1–6.

34. Farrer, *God Is Not Dead,* 107.

35. Farrer, "Grace and Resurrection," in *The Essential Sermons,* 138.

36. One of Farrer's best works of devotional theology, *The Triple Victory* (London: Faith, 1965), is an extensive exploration of the temptation story as presented in *The Gospel according to St. Matthew.* A Lent book published at the request of the archbishop of Canterbury, Michael Ramsey, it is one of Farrer's most extended christological discussions.

37. Farrer, *Faith and Speculation,* 66.

38. In fact, we do not truly have an explanation in detail of how our intentional, conscious decision making takes effect in our bodily action. It is still a raging debate in philosophy of mind whether we shall in fact be able to explain it in terms of events in the brain. Farrer's Gifford Lectures, *The Freedom of the Will* (2nd ed.; New York: Scribner's, 1960), address this very issue and come down on the side of saying that the explanation cannot in principle be given wholly in terms of physical events in the brain. Nevertheless, we know that conscious intention does take effect in our bodies as well as we know anything, and we experience the process of conscious choice in bodily effect. Knowing how it works or knowing the "mechanism" by which it works, in our case as well as in God's case, is not necessary to our ability to recognize intentional agency or to perform it.

39. Farrer, "David Danced Mightily," in *A Faith of Our Own,* 216.

40. See "Experimental Proof," in *God Is Not Dead,* 92–111.

41. Ibid., 110–11.

42. Farrer, *God Is Not Dead,* 86.

43. Farrer, *Saving Belief,* 39–40.

44. Farrer, *God Is Not Dead,* 78.

45. Farrer, *Saving Belief,* 39. Farrer develops this theme at length in several of his books: *Saving Belief, God Is Not Dead,* and *Faith and Speculation.* It also plays a prominent role in *Love Almighty and Ills Unlimited* (Garden City, NY: Doubleday, 1961).

46. Speaking of "mind and body" does not entail metaphysical dualism. Farrer, in fact, is not a metaphysical dualist. Mind and body are different levels of operation or activity: "*ESSE* is *OPERARI*. . . . " See Farrer, *Finite and Infinite,* 21; and *Faith and Speculation,* 114.

47. Farrer, *God Is Not Dead,* 83. Farrer makes an issue of saying *acts as* the soul of the world because he does not wish to say that God is precisely related to the world as human minds are to human bodies. God as soul of the world is an image,

not a literal description. The human soul has as an essential function to animate its one body; we must not say that the essential function of God is to animate the world. For God is God, and we must believe that being God, God enjoys fullness of life all apart from God's relation to the world that God creates and redeems.

48. Farrer, *Faith and Speculation,* 118.

49. Farrer, *Finite and Infinite,* 58.

50. Farrer, *Faith and Speculation,* 111. Notice Farrer's use of the impersonal pronoun here. Although he and his generation commonly used the personal and masculine pronoun "he" to refer to God, this passage shows that he was well aware that the masculine pronoun is an image that is not to be taken as defining God as God is in Godself. This, of course, is exactly what one would expect from someone who placed the emphasis he did on the limits of human understanding and on its dependence upon images and analogies.

51. Ibid., 118.

52. Farrer, *God Is Not Dead,* 35.

53. Farrer, *Finite and Infinite,* 21; and *Faith and Speculation,* 114.

54. Farrer, *Faith and Speculation,* 118.

55. Farrer, *God Is Not Dead,* 35.

Chapter Four

FARRER'S THEODICY

William McF. Wilson and Julian N. Hartt

THE BELIEVER'S REASONS

For all of his erudition and the severe difficulty of much of his writing, throughout his career Austin Farrer remained the champion of the man or woman of simple Christian faith and the guardian of what he called "plain practical religion." In many ways the same can be said of all the great twentieth-century theologians. By the end of the First World War, whether it be Karl Barth, Karl Rahner, Emil Brunner, or Paul Tillich, virtually no theologian any longer believed that the human mind is capable of coming up with a purely rational religion, one that could say to humble piety (as Farrer worded it), "the One you ignorantly worship, Him I declare unto you."[1] The killing fields of Verdun and Ypres, not to mention the Nazi ovens or Stalin's Gulag, put an end to this dream.

Every major theologian also came to see that there is a conceptual difference between the "God of the Philosophers" and the "God of Abraham, Isaac, and Jacob." A purely philosophical construct simply is not, it was argued across the board, the deity of mystery and awe who finds us out at the River Jabbok. There was no denying that philosophical concepts and categories must be used to order and present this faith, but conviction and assent are in no way based on this human ingenuity. The certitude of belief — and its tenacity as well — is a gift of grace and of grace alone.

Farrer shared these opinions on the autonomous power of the mind to know God, and he shared as well the verdict on the nature of the human animal this past century renders. But his turn back to the faith of the simple believer was nonetheless very different. He declined the basic distinctions of his colleagues — distinctions between a God of reason and a God of biblical faith, between knowledge by way of proof and knowledge by way of grace, between the autonomy of philosophy and the dependence of faith — and he did so because he denied that the primary question for modern theology to face was one of pathways, or approaches, as these distinctions assume. For him the question "Should our approach be by reason or by faith?" was entirely wrongheaded.

Rather, Farrer held that we must return to the believer, because there we can find the pathway already trod and the connection already established (at least in principle). The role of the theologian is not to draw a line of connection but to retrace that line which the believer acknowledges in claiming to have faith, whether this retracing is accomplished by ordering and clarifying the tenets of revelation or by examining and criticizing faith's philosophical presuppositions. When all is said and done, the theologian "must know," Farrer argued, "that he is examining or articulating the assumptions of the believing mind."[2]

The examination of these assumptions required Farrer to delve into several areas of theology, including philosophical treatises, biblical studies, and devotional and doctrinal literature. Given his unique approach, none of these studies is like any other in his time. For instance, his philosophy is completely subordinated to the task the route of faith sets for it. His biblical studies were far more than simple exegesis or textual criticism. Instead, Farrer sought to demonstrate how the basic images of scripture grow into inspirational—in the dogmatic sense of the word—patterns of verse that seize the mind like a poem. In his writing on doctrine and creed he demonstrated that formulated articles of the faith, once carefully analyzed, turn out to be the rudimentary prayers of the faithful.

In this essay we will demonstrate how Farrer's theodicy—his inquiry into the problem of evil—is also a retracing of the believer's connection with God. His careful balancing of reason and revelation put him in a good position to carry out this vital exercise, because in theodicy one must take the articles of revelation, like the resurrection of the dead and the destruction of sin by Christ's cross, and defend them rationally to an audience that will include those who are either dismayed or outraged that this God of revelation can be said to rule a universe filled with gratuitous pain, suffering, and treason. The defense Farrer mounts, as we will see, is not so much a defense of God and of God's ways as it is an explanation of how the believer keeps the faith and finds the redemptive hand of God at work come what may.

Here is another major difference. The air of twentieth-century theology was filled with the heated and passionate questions that the evil of this past century raises. What sense can it make to speak of divine providence in an era of world wars? Is it moral to cancel the sin of the

Nazis? Farrer stayed out of this fray, and he did so for the sake of the plain practical religion that he struggled to maintain and defend. *That* faith, he proclaimed, can always find a way to see the direction of God's action and follow it, and the theologian can follow along with whatever conceptual tools are at hand — metaphysics, the poetic structure of scripture, or the channel of prayer in the bedrock of doctrine and creed.

"THEODICY"

The word "theodicy" is a composite of two Greek stems: *Theos,* meaning "God," and *dike,* meaning "justice" or "righteousness." For most of the Christian tradition, the word was used to draw a distinction between "theology," the human study of God and of all things divine, and what the tradition came to call the "justice of God," which culminates in the cross of Christ.

The cross was understood to reveal, above all else, justice, for several reasons. For one, justice signals the proper completion of an action, and at the cross what God set out to accomplish in restoring all of Israel's covenants was fulfilled. Another reason underscores justice as a moral category. In his suffering and dying, Christ pays a price that is owed. Sin destroys even the liberty to make recompense; thus the mission of Jesus, the incarnate Son, is to make recompense vicariously. This offering of a sinless self to God is of course not simply a raw act of "payback"; rather, Christ's recompense for sin gathers the other virtues along with it. For example, mercy is clearly at work in a vicarious suffering, and love is the motive for an execution of justice that aims to restore, through Christ's offering, the original dignity of one's people. This is a further example of the way in which the death and resurrection of Christ constitute an act of completion and fulfillment: God's justice gathers up, fulfills, and perfects the other virtues that make up the moral life.

Finally, justice confirms that the cross, as a self-contained and already fulfilled action, is also a verdict, a decree — a word spoken about us that is uttered through no contrivance or initiative on our part. Notice how the Synoptic Gospels not only destroy our expectations as Christ expires; they also, so to speak, cordon off the cross. They show us an outward event of a hidden transaction: The death gasps of Jesus, we tremble to read, are also the out-breathings of the Holy Spirit. Accordingly, "theology," the human word about God, at this point draws to a close; and "theodicy," the setting forth of an otherwise hidden justice, takes over.

But in modern theology, "theodicy" is a completely different sort of exercise. Rather than walk the circle of a closed mystery, the modern theologian must face down a problem: How can God in any way be understood to practice justice when the world is so plagued by gratuitous pain, suffering, and tragedy? One recalls Sigmund Freud's statement that if there are pearly gates and he is fortunate enough to reach them, then the first thing he would do is demand from God a reason for allowing children to suffer from bone cancer. In modern theodicy, God, not humanity, is on trial. The forum, too, is entirely different. Now the theologian must stand outside the tradition and defend the faith without the grist of the Christian scheme, such as a freedom destroying sin or a mercy that is perfected by justice. In modern theodicy such notions are taken to be the prejudices of but one religion and are thus ruled out of the discussion.

As this "problem of evil" is universal, modern doubt and unbelief now require a universal language. Witness the title of the recent bestseller by Harold S. Kushner: *When Bad Things Happen to Good People.*[3] No longer do we deal with the likes of sin-fraught Adam; we deal simply with "bad things." No longer can we plead the example of sin-conquering saints; we need only refer to "good people" in the round.

Indeed, modern language has strayed so far from the Christian idiom that many theologians are not only steering away from theodicy but also claiming that it was a bad idea in the first place. Faith, they argue, has nothing to do with explaining or avoiding the tragedies and suffering of life. God's justice inspires the believer to confess an all-consuming resolution to embrace suffering as Christ did, and in the face of evil to take up a cross. When others suffer, the Christian should enter into it with them and, when possible, take it on vicariously. In this view, it is the death knell of the faith to water down its vocabulary in order to enter a universal conversation, and the world cannot possibly be served at all if the particularities of belief are forsaken for it.

FARRER'S APPROACH

Austin Farrer's principal work in theodicy has a title that seems to fit the modern type perfectly: *Love Almighty and Ills Unlimited.*[4] This phrase suggests the general problem: Some people profess belief in an almighty love, but all people experience evil. Anyone who takes up the task of theodicy, we might plausibly infer, must answer for this universal problem of evil. And, indeed, after reading this book we might well conclude that Farrer belongs in this modern camp. He openly embraces the thorny questions posed by doubt and unbelief: Why are there cancer cells? Why a world of pain? How can anyone morally say that years of gratuitous suffering nurture character and strengthen faith? And he works his way through these tough questions with any tool at hand, be it from the tradition or not. But there are many parts of his theodicy that challenge such an interpretation, and if a person reads widely in Farrer's other writings, he or she can easily find not only passages that are severely critical of the way theodicy is currently carried out but also assertions that beyond doubt place Farrer in the older, justice-of-God tradition.

Consider this passage from his devotional literature:

> God does not give us explanations; we do not comprehend the world, and we are not going to. It is, and it remains for us, a confused mystery of bright and dark. God does not give us explanations; he gives up a Son. Such is the spirit of the angel's message to the shepherds: "Peace upon Earth, good will to men . . . and this shall be the sign unto you: ye shall find a babe wrapped in swaddling clothes, and lying in a manger." A Son is better than an explanation. The explanation of our death leaves us no less dead than we were; but a Son gives us life, in which to live.[5]

What could be more unlike modern theodicy than this statement that waves off the command to explain evil and leaves us in a world that is "part dark and part bright"? And what could be more like the traditional theodicy that finds in scripture the justice of God cordoned off from the world, complete in itself and fulfilled, and breathing new life as it crushes human pride?

Or consider this passage from a late sermon, delivered four years after the publication of *Love Almighty and Ills Unlimited:*

> There is no denying, for a Christian, that God knows what he wants with this baffling universe; only we do not. . . . [W]hat great purposes he is working out in this unimaginable form of things, we do not know. . . . Shall we put together the cosmic puzzle, and so justify the ways of God? No; God will justify himself, by His deeds. . . . [H]e is not obliged to patch up a solution out of the old pieces. . . .[6]

In the phrase "justify the ways of God," Farrer is citing the preface to John Milton's *Paradise Lost,* a phrase that has come to stand for the very project of modern theodicy; and his answer to its challenge is a clear "No."

Spot-citing passages in this way leaves the novice reader of Farrer simply confused, and many, perhaps most theologians who have taken on his writings in their entirety have put him aside because they find him to be unmethodical, contradictory, and completely without antennae for the conventions of modern theology. But the persevering reader will discover that the contradictions are superficial, and that once he or she makes this discovery, the method becomes quite clear and seriously challenges contemporary theological conventions.

If we take the current matter and look at it carefully, for instance, all that we see at the outset is Farrer responding to a grief-stricken person by offering the supreme consolation of resting in the Christian promise. What could be more natural? And it is not as if Farrer adopts a "blind faith" approach in doing this. Quite the contrary: He gives a solid *reason,* which is that God gives no explanations. God offers no secret wisdom; God gives God's Son instead, and with the Son comes a new community, a new and certain hope, and the consolations of grace.

But it remains to ask why Farrer should delve into the passionate discourse with outraged suffering at all if the gospel is the sole reason for adhering to the faith in the midst of the turmoil of life's unlimited ills. This question contains the probe that works at the heart of theodicy. We should note, however, that it also probes the heart of all theology. Why should there be *any* science of God if the most pointed and poignant of human questions are answered by an unimaginable gift from the Lord of all? The question is so basic that one is often embarrassed to raise it, but it is entirely proper if for no other reason than that it courses through the career of any serious theologian, professional or amateur.

The question, however, reflects confusion, and so much so that the wayward heart of the believer is exposed. For one, the question takes Farrer's claim to mean that the gift of the Son is *the* Explanation of explanations, so entirely wonderful that none other is required. But a little reflection will reveal that this is exactly what Farrer did not say. Rather, he said that the gift is no explanation at all. The gospel is an event, an action, a bloody battle fought out and forever won. Second, Farrer's claim did not say that we should not ask our questions and seek explanations. He simply said that the gift of the Son, not being an explanation, would not answer them. Thus, to refer back to the first confusion, it is of course proper to engage in theological explanations, and especially while engaged in a consideration of the heart of the faith:

God's gift of Christ to the world. We need only remember that these are *our* explanations, not God's.

RESURRECTION

With these considerations in mind, let us address two other passages similar to the others we have looked at, but which indicate a direction for us to follow toward a proper understanding of Farrer's position. In the first passage, Farrer makes his point firmly and then allows us to listen in on the typical rejoinder.

> It is absurd for any Christian to undertake a defence of God's good providence, or to justify his tolerance of the evil he permits, without speaking of the resurrection. "Come now," says a skeptical antagonist, "the resurrection of the dead is the supreme improbability. You can't expect me to consider that until you have shown me the prevalence of divine goodness in human affairs apart from such hopes. Bar out the life to come, and strike the balance of God's dealings with mankind without it."[7]

The "skeptical antagonist," Farrer is saying, assumes that the resurrection is a glorious explanation of what would otherwise be a sheer tragedy: Jesus took on the role of the Messiah of Israel and was lynched for it. And the antagonist's point is that we cannot accept this explanation and take it for an interpretative key to the "problem of evil" until we have established, by surveying and interpreting the unlimited ills of life, that divine, providential care and intervention accompany all our suffering. We must know, in other words, that God cares for us and uses our suffering for the betterment of all before we can tackle the large and looming question of whether we survive death. As Farrer goes on to say in this passage (speaking for the antagonist), we cannot take the most improbable of beliefs and use it to verify our general conviction that life, despite all the ills, is finally beneficent. We must establish this conviction first, then show that the survival of death is probable.

The central error of this position is the assumption that the cross and resurrection are on the same footing with ordinary suffering and tribulation, whereas we have seen that they constitute a unique revelation of God's justice. Typically, we cannot clearly discern, in particular cases of human suffering, what specific good God wills to bring out of God's creation. But let us give the antagonist his or her due. Chapter 8 of *Love Almighty and Ills Unlimited* ("Griefs and Consolations") is in large measure given over to the voice of this antagonist trying to find the good in gratuitous suffering and in numbing sorrow. What we find is fairly homespun theodicy, which often "sounds like a flock of ducks quacking in chorus."[8] A young woman dies, but it is a blessing because she is finally relieved of her pain. A man is struck with rheumatism, but it is all for the better because now he is free from the painful chore of tending his garden. A boy is bedridden for eighteen months ("at the age when boys grow strong and daring"), but he is now more thoughtful and mature than his peers.[9]

Farrer admits that these typical responses by faith to tragedy are well intentioned, and he also allows that they are proper, "because there is little other wisdom to be had."[10] We simply do not know what else to say by way of consolation, and consolation is a Christian duty toward those in grief. But these responses obviously are not a rendering of God's providence. Rather they are examples of wisdom after the fact, which point out nothing but the general balance of nature: Pain subsides at death; we reach a point in life when we can no longer labor; the crushed expectations of young people temper them for the harsh realities and inevitable disappointments of adult life. Unbelief, however, can offer the exact same solace.

But when the general balance is taken for divine providence, then unbelief must find injustice. Should the ends (unbelief will argue) — painlessness, cessation of labor, early maturity — be had by such cruel means? The young girl suffers no more, but the young girl *is* no more. The old man no longer labors, but he must sit out his days in an armchair. A case for justice must square ends and means, and in these readings of divine providence it seems that the ends can be justified by any means at all.

At this point the believer has no recourse but to introduce the resurrection as the sole justification for evil, and unbelief will find this move to be what the "skeptical antagonist" admitted at the outset (and which set him on this quest): the admission of the most improbable explanation of them all. Then the entire Christian case crumbles. This move will not simply render the core of the faith a last-ditch belief; it will also be an admission that God's ways are unaccountably cruel and that we can only look to an unproven event for hope. This attempt at defending God's justice is not a case for providence, therefore; it is but a further admission that this last-ditch belief is no belief at all and that Christian hope is simply blind.

THE GIFT OF HEAVEN

If this first passage leads us to the dead end of assuming that the gift of Christ is God's final explanation grounding our independent theodicizing, then this second quotation will offer the way out that Farrer's approach offers: "Heaven *alone* gives final meaning to any earthly hopes; and, to take it the other way round, we have no way to grasp at heavenly hopes than by pursuing hopeful tasks here below."[11]

We ought not try to confirm and establish the great hopes of the "heavenly things" like the cross or the resurrection by construing on our own how the tragedies of our lives might be shown to be events of hope nonetheless. We must do the opposite. The causes of suffering must be taken on and explored in the light of the gift of the heavenly things. The nonbeliever of course might construe this effort to be an invitation to give up on our own reasoning and intellectual autonomy and simply swallow the miracles whole and show a bright face to an unkind world.

As we have seen, however, such criticism assumes that heavenly gifts are explanations of God's ways because the critic considers them doctrines that the believer relies on for his or her general hopefulness. If such were the case, then the non-believing critic would be perfectly correct; and there is no doubt that this approach is one that many of the faithful attempt, and thereby sacrifice the intellect.

But the heavenly things are gifts and should be embraced as such. There is all the difference in the world between accepting a gift and swallowing a doctrine. These two activities look very much the same because neither is based on the believer's having entertained and assented to a rational case, and both activities may plead the assent to be a matter of grace and a gesture of God's kindness toward us which is quite beyond our fathoming. But taking on a gift does not necessarily involve a blind acceptance. The disbelief that accompanies receiving a gift is due to the fact that we do not warrant it. The disbelief that goes with blind faith is a result of willful credulity. The nature of the hope that ensues from the acceptance differs greatly as well. A willed credulity has no structure to its hope and thus no real motive for its actions, whereas the receiver of the gift, if his or her thanksgiving is sincere, will go out into the world and, like the Good Samaritan, treat others without asking for warrants, conditions, or rewards.

What is more, by performing such deeds of grace toward others, "we grasp at Heavenly hope"; we take it on, and, as Farrer implies in this passage, we slowly come to understand the ways of God toward us; and although we can never know God's final purposes for God's creation, we can come to understand how to bridge the conceptual gap between a world of divine love and a cosmos of unlimited ills.

IDENTIFYING WITH THE SUFFERER

How do we learn to discover the hopefulness of the world by taking on suffering and identifying with the sufferer? Farrer offers two answers. First, the example of Christ's death shows that God is not out for wholesale pain and malice. The event of the cross clearly indicates that God takes suffering to be the pathway to redemption. Through whatever way we enter into another's calamity, be it by relieving the agony, by grieving alongside the victim as if his or her woes were our own, or simply by honoring the state of poverty and misery (no place of shame for the Christian), the walls between people break down. New eyes are given to the sufferer because somebody has demonstrated that the evil is not to be feared. Also, as Farrer says, although present pain is far more forceful than future hopes, the victim learns from the action and words of the courage and love of the new comrade that "divine hope can temper human grief."[12]

The comrade, as it were, has been there before, is not afraid to be there again, and thus has a sure and certain knowledge of the peace and redemption to come. It is especially important to note that such a gift is made possible by the friend's realization that it is not in our nature to know just what God is intending in the victim's situation. It is by avoiding the prideful boasts of the homespun theologian that something of the divine pathway is discovered and the divine goal is reached. Those estranged—if not simply by dint of the sin that separates any two people, then by the wall built by the shame of the victim and the fear of the friend—are reunited.

The second reason Farrer gives follows logically from this new fellowship. With reconciliation made, it is possible to carry out the severe moral duty of giving consolation. The new fellowship is indeed the foretaste of divine hope and promise and, more importantly, is the evidence that the final redemption won at the cross is certain. Homespun theodicy separates pain and promise by its all-knowing gaze, thereby providing a gratuitous promise, an accountable pain, or a consolation of mere words. To quote Farrer, it is by having a "faith in the working of a particular providence, not a detection of it," that we learn in small measure to construe the justice of God toward man.[13]

But no matter how cogent we might find Farrer's reasoning on these matters, there remains the difficult problem of how we are to understand it to be an intellectual and theoretical response as required by an exercise as mentally straining as theodicy. Surely a wise pastor or believing counselor could come up with the same advice, and there is no reason to suppose that a philosophical critic would not admire the convictions, motives, and resolutions that this advice would represent. But could this critic let it stand for a rational response to direct and pointed questions about the evil we find in the world? On Farrer's behalf, we must note that we have not yet addressed the question of the reason God should allow for pain and suffering at all — we have only seen how we should respond to it and offer consolation for it given that it does exist. But even at this stage of the enquiry there is room to wonder whether Farrer will be able to sustain an argument in this vein.

THE RELATION OF THEORY AND PRACTICE

We need not look far for evidence for worry. The first page of *Love Almighty and Ills Unlimited,* right where Farrer sets up his program, looks to be a direct contradiction of everything we have seen in this past discussion. We must cite it at length:

> Evil commonly strikes not as a problem, but as an outrage. Taken in the grip of misfortune, or appalled by the violence of malice, we cannot reason sanely about the balance of the world. Indeed, it is part of the problem of evil that its victim is rendered incapable of thought. So, if we are to start with the sufferer, there are two problems, the first practical, the second theoretical. First, he must recover the power of dispassionate vision; and second, he must exercise it on the place held by evil, including his own trouble, in the whole scheme of things. The practical problem is pastoral, medical, or psychological, and differs from case to case too widely to allow of much useful generalization. We are concerned with the theoretical problem only.[14]

In this opening paragraph Farrer appears to be saying that there is a practical part to theodicy and a theoretical part. The practical deals with those therapies that will bring the sufferer back to his or her senses; the theoretical deals with reasoning and argument. But if we look closely at the passage, we can see that this interpretation is not quite right. To be sure, Farrer states that in theodicy there is both practice and theory. He also says, however, that these two aspects are but parts of one final goal: bringing the sufferer back to the point where he or she can reason sanely about the balance of the world.

These two activities, then, are not independent exercises. By "theory" Farrer does not mean an autonomous and independent grid of philosophical reasoning; and by "practice" he does not mean the medical, pastoral, and psychological techniques we may use to regain the theoretical high ground for the patient. To refer again to the passage, theory is the act of focusing the "dispassionate vision" — once practice has regained it — "on the place held by evil, including his own trouble." In this sense, then, Farrer was being perfectly theoretical when, in the case we have just considered, he advised that suffering and pain are not simply there for our destruction. As the cross reveals, suffering is a pathway to redemption, and once we enter into suffering, either our own or that of another, we make our way to the goal of a balanced Christian construal of the workings of good and evil.

What leads to the hasty misinterpretation of this passage is the general assumption that "theory" or "reflection" is by definition a self-contained and independent activity to which we turn when practice breaks down. As Farrer described the notion, we think without question that theory is a sharpshooter who rides to the rescue when practical faith has a moment of crisis, and we are hard pressed to imagine that a person in the grip of grief would welcome the words "enter into and honor the suffering" as theory. Yet these words are as indispensable in restoring the habits of theodicy as is the medical procedure that heals the broken mind.

When Farrer said that God gives a Son, not explanations, he was insisting in the most radical way that we consider the faith to be what it undoubtedly is — a dealing with a living Deity and God's ways with us — and not as an ideology that can explain our plight better than such faith can. It is in theodicy that we most want to transform faith into a system of ideas that can explain to us why our journeys must at times be so intolerable, and so it is in theodicy above all other theological exercises that we must bear the stern voice of grace the most. There is theological reasoning and there are answers (and any reader of Farrer knows that he was a master of abstract philosophizing), but the reasoning must be what we can hear faith saying, or what we can help faith to say, or what we can say on behalf of faith. In a word, no independent path exists, no Saturday-morning sharpshooter who can say with any right or sound reason (as Farrer gave him voice): "[T]he One you ignorantly worship, Him I declare unto you."

It was not that Farrer was simply the partisan of faith. He denied the counsel of the thinker who thinks that common faith cannot be anything but a cover for error simply for sound reasons. An enquiry that sets out to see if any neutral case can be made of what believers mean by "God" would be like "fitting out an expedition" to see if there are really any such things as mermaids.[15] It is sheer folly to "discount the fact and forms of religious belief while raking the heavens for signs of a first cause."[16] If, then, we are to clarify the idea of God, we can begin with no better task than the one of clarifying what believers do in believing.

WHY NOT A WORLD FREE OF PAIN AND SUFFERING?

We have already looked at the way believers hold their belief in providence by responding to grace — not explanations — and by entering into the suffering of their fellows. We can develop this investigation of believers' reasons by asking a further — and, for theodicy, a central — question: Why should there be pain and suffering at all? If God is all-powerful, why does God not make a world that is free of pain?

Any careful thinker, whether believing or nonbelieving, can venture sound answers. A world free of pain would be one in which no parts ever make contact. No molecules would interact, no trees would fall, and no lightning would strike. All of these events are perilous to human life, but without the mutual contact that makes up a physical system, there would be no world of life at all. Pain, then, is not simply wanton destruction and agony. It signals us to avoid something making or about to make contact. The human nervous system, to put the point another way, provides for our well-being by reacting to malevolent contact just as the digestive system provides for our well-being by reacting to food.

THE PHILOSOPHER OF THE BELIEVER'S REASONS

But, as we have seen before, what the believer takes as providence, the nonbeliever sees to be simply the balance of natural forces, and we are right back at the homespun theodicy that confessed a providence in the young girl's death because she was now finally free of her pain. Does the believer have a reason that the philosopher of those reasons can help to bring out and clarify? Is there a cogency to and a justification for the belief that these forces balanced by physical contact and systems are signs of a working divine providence as well?

Of course there is. The believer holds "that all such forces are tools in the hands of a Master."[17] If the believer judges that pain is purposive, it is because he or she sees, implicitly or not, that all natural activities, without being lured off their natural path, give rise to the stable systems we call minerals, vegetables, and animals. Therefore, to call a constituent "natural" and to call it "providential" are one and the same thing. Blood cells act like blood cells, digestion occurs by natural chemical processes, and neurons fire in the brain; but with no observable interference, all of it gives rise to the functioning, say, of a human agent. To put it the other way round, when a person performs an action, say he or she swings a tennis racket, that action is nothing to the blood cells. They carry on as they naturally will, as will all processes in the general sweep of the tennis player's action.

We can strengthen this point by comparing a human artifact to a divine creation. No part of a house is present for its own purpose. Studs form the walls and the walls hold the roof. There is no "natural setting" for a wall or a stud. We can see that they have been fabricated and arranged because we can comprehend the overall design of the house. But in a creation, the constituent parts behave naturally and do not seem to have been fabricated and arranged. We can see that they are constituent parts because they give rise to a total structure, but unlike a wall, we cannot see the "fit"; we cannot see how a natural activity and a constituent part can be the same thing.

What is more, because we can see how the parts of a house fit together, we can infer the hand of a human builder. We can see that something made them fit. But with a creation we cannot obtain this same comprehensive grasp of structure and purpose. We are not able to see where the natural forces, because they are natural, are "bent" to make them "co-operate" with the other parts in making up the design. Nothing seems "forced" the way a wooden joint is forced. God makes the creation seamlessly and does not betray God's hand.

The believer who hears his or her reasons unearthed in this way will initially want to argue that he or she infers the hand of the Maker from the fact of the thing made, and thus will have a "proof" that God exists and a case that any rational mind must accept. The philosopher of the believer's reasons would caution the believer against attempting to make this move, however. To quote Farrer, "the perfection of the Creator's management of his creatures is shown by his ability to dispense with anything forced, anything adventitious, in his direction of them. Working in their own way they do his amazing will."[18]

Nowhere in the actual stream of the believer's reasons has the philosopher entertained a proof. Nowhere has he inferred God from the creation. Rather, he has simply reflected on the fact that the actions of the constituent parts do not have it in themselves to give rise to the final object, and in the midst of this reflection he has struck upon the idea of God. We first encountered this approach in the believer's claim that natural forces (those causing pain) are at the same time actions of God's providence.

This reflection on creation we have just discussed was meant to unearth the believer's reason behind this claim, and we began the question regarding the presence of pain to explain what Farrer meant by the theorizing involved in bringing the devastated but medically and psychologically healed believer back to the point where he or she can again envision the balance of good and evil in the world the way he or she could before the bout of suffering began. We have not arrived there yet, because we can further enquire after the reason that nature, now understood to be providentially involved in the making of the world and all its creatures, can be at the same time so destructive and, as it were, unmindful of human life and its flourishing.

A PHYSICAL UNIVERSE

We have already seen something of an answer to this question. A physical universe is one of real contact among the parts, some of which are detrimental to humanity. But falling trees and hurricanes are one thing; cancer cells are quite another. The force of the question is why, if nature is providential, should creations arise that are simply malignant? The answer is easy, but the lesson is hard. The question assumes that there are domains in which we can sort out the things in the world—good things and evil things, or benign things and malignant things. Such labeling expresses our likes and dislikes but is obviously not proper appellation.

To use one of Farrer's illustrations, a gardener will find jimson weed or crab grass detrimental to his or her designs and could perhaps think of it as evil. But in and of themselves these growths are just as natural and good as the finest rose and the greenest grass. By "evil," the gardener simply means that the plants wreak havoc in the garden and spoil the designs.[19] Plants are plants; they can grow to be roses, palmettos, or mushrooms, but they cannot grow to be evil. Evil is not a "way" for plants to be and to grow. We may not like some of them, but they remain parts of the creation.

Can we say the same of a cancer cell? Can we say that *this* agent of mass destruction requires a realm of its own and is quite appropriately "evil"? Unfortunately, we cannot. Like the plants, cells can be blood, brain, or skin, but they cannot be evil. Evil is not a way for cells to be. Accordingly, as difficult as it may be for our sufferer being led back to normalcy by the rope of "theory" to accept, a cancer cell in itself is a natural and healthy part of creation. If he or she has accepted the case that the creations of the world are composed of the activities of nature acting their part, then he or she cannot ask that it be removed. Even if he or she loses faith in a Creator in demanding that it be removed, he or she will be asking to rid the world of its actual ecology; in short, asking that there be no universe at all.

There is nothing in the nature of physical order that requires that creatures be immortal. In fact, the opposite is the case: Death is the norm. In Farrer's reckoning, if we are to survive death, we can do so only by a special gift. This gift, as we saw, moves us to enter into the pain and suffering of the world and to heal its victims as best we can, offering the only consolation we are able to give, that of fellow sufferer. If that is the way we lay hold of divine hope, as Farrer has said, then we can say, here on the natural level, that our hope for natural flourishing is seized by seeing that natural suffering is our natural lot, and falling to with help for and fellowship of our fellow creatures. If suffering is our lot as physical creatures, then aid and succor are every bit as natural. This activity is not a gratuitous "bringing of good out of evil." The model for it is God's own act of bringing life out of the infinite play of natural forces acting on their own. We too can act on our own; that is, we can be fully human, and thereby fit the hand of God's providence like a glove.

THEOLOGY RATIONAL AND REVEALED

When faced with the option of being either a rational (or natural) theologian or a revealed theologian, Farrer said that he was "hearty" enough to be both. [20] We have witnessed his heartiness in this essay by seeing how he was able to bridge the gap between what we have called justice-of-God theodicy and problem-of-evil theodicy. Farrer always felt that this distinction between knowing God by way of nature and knowing God by revelation was artificial and indeed so abstract that no common believer could possibly entertain it, let alone live by it. As we said earlier, the reasons for belief are those that we can find along the arc of the believer's actions in attending to God (whether or not they are actually conceptualized by the faithful). Early in *Love Almighty and Ills Unlimited*, Farrer expressed his frustration with the choice of rational or revealed that has so exercised modern theodicy:

> Philosophy herself will be wise to admit that our evidence for God is always the evidence of his activity, and most forcible where it touches us nearest. And where is that? No doubt the activity of the Creator comes home to us, when divine eternity is felt through the veil of perishable things. Yet men have never, in the mass, felt the Maker in his works, without at the same time finding their wills engaged with the action of a Saviour. . . . [Natural theology's] aim is not a selfless contemplation of natural fact. In identifying nature with God, it teaches that the springs of life are wholesome. It holds us out the hope that we may somehow wrap our roots round the fountain of existence. . . . Religious naturalism may conceal, but cannot eliminate the saving function of the godhead. . . . A theology which stops short at creation . . . handles a one-sided abstraction, which is not even the diagram of an actual belief.[21]

In following the believer's reasons as he or she attends to God's actions as they can be encountered by reason through nature, one finds the believer also witnessing a "turning" of God toward us in beneficence and love. There is certain joy in the bare knowledge of God. Modern theology has for so long split theologians into rationalist and revealed camps (or, in theodicy, into justice-of-God and problem-of-pain camps) that it seems certain that Farrer believed that we have lost this crucial aspect of holding the faith.

GOD'S "TURNING" TOWARD US

If the notion that the mere knowledge of God is a joy untellable has been lost, then we can retrieve it from a world in which it was commonplace. In his great *Commedia,* Dante followed a standard poetic simile that likened God to the sun. God blesses our existence as the sun sustains our natural being; but God also defeats our knowledge and contemplation as the sun's rays burn and destroy a steady gaze. But Dante added a twist that reveals the full splendor of the simile in a way that stock poetic devices cannot possibly achieve.

Dante's genius asked his reader to consider that the burning, broiling turmoil of the sun as we can catch it for but an instant looks indeed to be overpowering—but it also looks every bit as much engaged in a fitful attempt to *restrain* itself and thereby save our vision. This new twist works our minds into knowing what we are aware of in some reach of the mind: that God's power in nature is also a grace, or, as we said above, that in God's aseity there is also a "turning" toward us. This moving of the mind in poetry is what Farrer calls the unearthing of the believer's reason. Somewhere we have forgotten it.

If modern theologians know anything of Farrer, they know the last lines of his first book, *Finite and Infinite*. Written in 1943, it is a severe and challenging enquiry into rational theology, but it ends with these words:

> As I wrote this the German armies were occupying Paris after a campaign prodigal of blood and human distress. Rational theology will not tell us whether this has or has not been an irretrievable disaster to mankind and especially to the men who died. It is another matter if we believe that God Incarnate also died and rose from the dead. But rational theology knows that whether Paris stands or falls, whether men die or live, God is God, and so long as any spiritual creature survives, God is to be adored.[22]

Paris fell, but that is no threat to the vision of God's turning our way, of God's "restraint" in grace. Rational vision cannot promise that we are more than mortal creatures and that we will rise. It cannot even tell us whether after world wars we are not on a downhill collision course, which given our calamity we cannot stop. Farrer's theodicy meant to exercise restored vision on the point of our suffering. That can be done, as we have seen, by focusing on God's turning as it courses through natural activity. It would be the height of abstraction to think that it will not move us to enter into the suffering of modernity as the gift of the Son beckons us to do.

NOTES

1. Austin Farrer, *Finite and Infinite* (London: Dacre, 1943), vii.
2. Austin Farrer, *Faith and Speculation* (New York: New York University Press, 1967), 15.
3. Harold S. Kushner, *When Bad Things Happen to Good People* (New York: Avon, 1997).
4. Austin Farrer, *Love Almighty and Ills Unlimited* (Garden City, NY: Doubleday, 1961).
5. Austin Farrer, *Said or Sung* (London: World, 1960), 27–28.

6. Austin Farrer, "Providence, Mystery, and Evil," in *The Brink of Mystery* (ed. Charles C. Conti; London: SPCK, 1976), 6–7.
7. Austin Farrer, *Saving Belief* (New York: Morehouse-Barlow, 1964), 55.
8. Farrer, *Love Almighty and Ills Unlimited,* 146.
9. Ibid., 146–47.
10. Ibid., 147.
11. Austin Farrer, "Hopes on Earth and Hopes in Heaven," in *A Celebration of Faith* (ed. Leslie Houlden; London: Hodder & Stoughton, 1970), 118. Emphasis added.
12. Farrer, *Love Almighty and Ills Unlimited,* 150.
13. Ibid., 151.
14. Ibid., 11.
15. Farrer, *Finite and Infinite,* 3.
16. Farrer, *Faith and Speculation,* 1.
17. Farrer, *Love Almighty and Ills Unlimited,* 83.
18. Ibid., 87.
19. Ibid., 26–27.
20. Farrer, *Finite and Infinite,* 1.
21. Farrer, *Love Almighty and Ills Unlimited,* 16.
22. Farrer, *Finite and Infinite,* 300.

Chapter Five

FARRER ON FRIENDSHIP, SAINTHOOD, AND THE WILL OF GOD

David Hein

In the Oxford microcosm that was the world of C. S. Lewis and Austin Farrer, friendships flourished. Notwithstanding the rivalries and jealousies that all flesh, especially scholarly flesh, is heir to, the loose band of assorted characters with which both these men were associated appears to have produced more than its share of solid, even virtuous friendships as well as fresh thinking and imaginative writing about friendship.

For many of these friends, brought together in part by a common interest in making sense of Christian faith in the face of cultured indifferentists, the highest expression of human love was *caritas,* the non-preferential love displayed by the Good Samaritan toward the wounded stranger. But they probably would have agreed with the Oxonian John Henry Newman that the best preparation for loving the world at large is the cultivation of rightly ordered friendships, because "by trying to love our . . . friends, by submitting to their wishes, though contrary to our own, by bearing with their infirmities, by overcoming their occasional waywardness with kindness, by dwelling on their excellences, . . . we form in our hearts that root of charity, which, though small at first, may, like the mustard seed, at last even overshadow the earth."[1]

Friendship shapes character, for good or ill. Within a sound and steadfast friendship, such practices as kindness and mutual forbearance can make people not only happier and stronger but also more charitable. No one who has ever participated in a friendship of this quality can have failed to observe how one friend will at times provoke the other to greater self-understanding and to a more generous appreciation of life's possibilities.

One person in particular appears to have performed this function for Austin Farrer, who was challenged by and sometimes even perplexed on account of this friend. Farrer came to see a former seminary classmate as someone whose life and friendship were as joyfully human as they were profoundly theocentric. He noticed that this man embodied the virtue of friendship even as his words and actions blithely transgressed the virtue's theoretical limits. Hugh Lister's neighbor was his friend; his preferred coterie an open fellowship; his self-offering, prodigal.

EXEMPLAR: HUGH LISTER

"I knew a man once," Austin Farrer recalled, "but this is not the time for reminiscence, and you perhaps have not been so happy as to know living saints."[2] Invariably when Farrer made this kind of remark in his essays or sermons, as on this occasion in Pusey House Chapel, he had in mind an extraordinary individual he had first come to know as a fellow student at Cuddesdon Theological College: Hugh Evelyn Jackson Lister.[3]

Farrer would deal most fully with Lister's career in his Remembrance Day sermon of 1963, a sermon that is still widely known: "So many millions — my mind is numbed by the huge arithmetic of death. To gather and concentrate my thoughts, and yours, maybe I will tell the story of one man, than whom I never knew a better."[4] This time he mentioned Lister by name, and connected the sketch he furnished of his friend's life with two themes that were consistently at the center of his thought: sainthood and the will of God. To begin to flesh out our own understanding of these important themes in Farrer's theology, we will follow his lead and start with the example he provided.

Born in Aberdeen, Scotland, on May 15, 1901, Hugh Lister graduated from Lancing College (an English public school) and earned a BA in engineering from Cambridge University. As a member of the staff of the Great Western Railway, he worked in Swindon, Cardiff, and London, and lived for a time in the workmen's dormitories at Cardiff. Attaining a deeper awareness of the lives of these industrial workers transformed him. According to one of his biographers, his experience prompted him to enter "a period of extreme mental and spiritual conflict, which made him restless... and sent him headlong on long tramps" to think about what he should do with his life.[5]

Eventually he realized that he should dedicate himself to Christian service on behalf of the less-well-off members of British society, especially those individuals whose condition only increased their sense of alienation from the church. What he wanted to do was, as Farrer put it, to "devote his life to breaking the barrier between these men and their Redeemer."[6] Other Anglicans before him had carried on active social ministries in industrial centers; Lister would have been familiar with much of this activity as well as with the sacramental and practical theology that undergirded it.

With few exceptions, the most socially minded clergy were Anglo-Catholics, whose theology stressed not so much personal salvation and individual initiative as the corporate life of the Christian and collective responsibility. The historian Adrian Hastings ticks off the chief concerns of Anglo-Catholics in the 1920s and '30s: "Incarnation, sacraments, church and a revival of what was seen as the medieval socialist protection of the poor against the capitalist: that more and more was the heart of the Anglo-Catholic message in this its most lively and most influential period."[7] For these Anglo-Catholics, incense and elaborate furnishings were not the core of the faith but ways to convey a sense of the beauty and depth of the Christian vocation to a holy life of devotion and service.[8]

These essential Catholic themes were proclaimed by Frank Weston, the bishop of Zanzibar, in his stirring address to the Anglo-Catholic Congress of 1923. Lister may well have known these words and weighed their import for his own life. "You cannot claim to worship Jesus in the Tabernacle," Weston declared, "if you do not pity Jesus in the slum.... It is folly — it is madness — to suppose that you can worship Jesus in the Sacraments and Jesus on the Throne of glory, when you are sweating him in the souls and bodies of his children." When the bishop of Zanzibar addressed the thousands assembled in the Albert Hall in London and spoke of "step[ping] out ... in definite obedience ... to offer the Sacrifice of Christ's obedience," he had in mind not only the sacrifice at the altar: "You have got your Mass, you have got your Altar, you have begun to get your Tabernacle. Now go out into the highways and hedges ... and look for Jesus in the ragged, in the naked, in the oppressed and sweated.... "[9]

Turning his back on a promising career in engineering, Lister accepted a vocation to the priesthood of the Church of England and entered Cuddesdon, the theological college of the Anglo-Catholic establishment. Farrer remembered meeting him there: "When I came to my theological college I noticed a superb man, tall, strong, with keen eyes [and] ... the features of determination.... " When Lister studied, Farrer recalled, he did not read in a chair. Rather, "he put the chair on the desk and the book on the chair, and stood: he did not want to go to sleep," because, having pursued a career in another field, "he had much studying to make up." Possessing a character that regularly urged him toward the harder path, at Cuddesdon he displayed a tendency toward rigorous self-discipline that prompted concern among his teachers, who observed Hugh coming down to breakfast blue with cold after long periods of prayer and ice-cold baths.[10]

Following his ordination to the diaconate in 1929, Lister held a curacy at All Saints' Church in Poplar, a run-down section of the East End close to the London docks. In 1931, he resigned this post to accept an invitation to become one of the London secretaries of the Student Christian Movement, which meant that he served as an unofficial chaplain to Christian students in the colleges. Discussion among the staff of the movement revolved around social and political matters in relation to the Christian faith. In the early thirties a leading topic was the dole: Was it really enough to live on? Seeking to find out, Lister attempted to function on the meager sum supplied by unemployment insurance. The experiment proved ruinous to his health; in 1932, he contracted tuberculosis and landed in a sanatorium in Switzerland, where he served his fellow patients as chaplain.[11]

In 1934, Lister returned to England, and in the autumn of the following year he began his celebrated tenure in Hackney Wick, a "remarkable island of smelly factories and tiny houses" in the East End. For more than three years, as senior curate on the staff of St. Mary of Eton (the Eton College Mission), he performed the customary ministrations of an Anglican priest while devoting the lion's share of his fourteen-hour days to his duties as chairman of the local branch of the Transport and General Workers Union.[12]

Holding a view of God as the friend of innovators and artists, Lister came close to formulating an explicit theological rationale for the novel quality of his trade union involvement. He believed that becoming human requires persons to grow in freedom, but too often "we . . . talk as if the Christian life was only following the straight and narrow path already mapped out for us by God." Firmly grounded in his tradition, this priest felt free to explore how best to impart the meaning of Christianity to others. "I like to think of [God]," Lister said in a sermon in the spring of 1936, "not as a school teacher who has given the children something to copy as exactly as they can — but as the great artist who has given his pupils the chance of making a picture for themselves. God says to each one of us, 'Here is your life, here are your circumstances and endowments, now make the most beautiful thing of it you can. I am working with you—but I am not going to hold your hand.' "[13]

Believing that their living and working conditions were fostering a spirit of secularism among the people of his parish, Lister determined to aid them in their places of employment, helping them to organize—and to strike successfully—for better wages and shorter hours. As Farrer wrote of his friend: "For, he said, these people are oppressed; why should they listen to us until we get them justice? The people in that part were working, indeed, at sweated wages for prosperous masters; and they lacked a leader to organize them. He did it."[14]

When Lister began his work in Hackney Wick, he was regarded by the residents there as a naïf, "a pious interloper," in the words of a contemporary. Over time, his shyness dissipated, and his hesitant speaking style developed into "a racy and pointed one." He became a formidable branch chairman: organizing a paint factory and a rag firm; leading strikes at rubber, furniture, and waste supply companies; arranging transportation blockades; serving as cartoonist and satirist; and acting as amateur lawyer and tough bargainer, all for the good of the cause.[15]

"He hit as hard as he dared," wrote a local newspaper columnist after his death, "and he learned to be very daring. A libel action brought against him by one firm engaged in these disputes was abandoned, and the plaintiffs had to pay Lister's costs as well as their own. . . . " The same columnist recalled a British Union of Fascists' meeting at the Hackney Baths in 1937 when William Joyce (later known as Lord Haw-Haw) "inflamed the anti-Semitic passion of those days with a speech of gibes and sneers." Lister was one of "the very few in that crowded gathering with courage enough to challenge Joyce."[16]

Lister made friends with individual members of the Hackney branch of the British Communist Party, and he remained loyal to these relationships even when his friendship was no longer reciprocated and his Communist acquaintances ignored and betrayed him. When he defeated the party candidate for union branch chairman and the local Communists launched a vicious whispering campaign against him, calling him "anti-Semitic" and a "Fascist," he struck back against the party in speeches. Through it all, though, he never gave up on his friends among the Communists. After Lister was dead, a Communist acquaintance who had turned his back on him said that during this difficult period Lister had written him a letter in which he "did not attack me for what my Party was doing. He merely expressed his anxiety for our friendship, and hoped we would keep it alive whatever happened." But, he added regretfully, "I never replied to his letter."[17]

In Hackney Wick, Lister maintained an austere existence in two rooms of an old house he had bought. The spare rooms of this house, Farrer noticed when visiting his friend one day, "were occupied by thieves and wastrels, whom [Lister] had begged off the probation officer and had to live with him, to see if he could love them and drill them back into a regular life." On the occasion of this visit, Farrer said, Hugh

> scratched us up a snack; while he ate, he worked on, interjecting cheerful remarks, and taking me into the business. "Now," he said, "I'm sorry, I must turn you out," for there was a meeting of the Trades Union branch. It did not last long. "Now you can come in," he said, and introduced me to his trades ministry: of whom a few went away, but the most part stayed, and turned themselves, would you believe it, with the utmost simplicity, into a Bible class; and asked searching questions about the will of God for them in their situation.[18]

Throughout his priestly career, Lister saw a distinction but no gap between single-minded worship in the sanctuary and scrappy service for and amongst his fellows in a hostile world. Beginning each day with the eucharistic celebration at the Eton Mission, at midday he could be found standing outside the gates of a local factory, speaking and handing out leaflets.[19] Years afterward, those who remembered him spoke of what a "worldly" priest Hugh made and a moment later of what an "unworldly" person he was.

In a sermon at the Eton Mission in the autumn of 1937, Lister told his congregation, "We belong to one another, and not only to each other here [in church] but to the whole of Hackney Wick, and far beyond it. The people we despise, the people who have wronged us . . . we belong to them and they to us. And we know it, and they don't. And we have got to behave like that." A Christian is not primarily someone who prays long prayers and belongs to every guild and religious society. "The test of the Christian," he said, is "not whether he is a regular churchgoer, but whether he behaves as if he knows that his neighbour is loved by God as much as he is."[20]

Deeply patriotic, Lister backed military conscription in March 1939, when the draft was unpopular among his comrades in the labor movement, because he knew it to be the most efficient way to commence a necessary task: saving freedom and democracy by preventing the Nazis from conquering Great Britain.[21] Moreover, he decided, in his habitually straightforward manner, that he could best help men bear the trial of war by sharing this experience with them. He hoped to be an example and a companion to those who knew fear, suffered wounds, and faced death; and he believed that he could make a better job of it if he fought alongside them than he could otherwise.[22] So in the fall of 1939 he joined the regular army as an emergency commission second lieutenant in the Welsh Guards. Over the next several years, he not only honed his skills as an officer but also employed his engineering knowledge to improve the design of the Universal (Bren) Carrier, a light armored and tracked vehicle used to transport the Bren machine gun.[23]

At the end of June 1944, as a result of casualties his battalion had suffered shortly after landing in Normandy, Lister, now holding the rank of temporary major, moved up to take command of Support Company, in the 1st (infantry) Battalion. His platoons assisted the rifle companies by clearing the way through obstacles, by carrying out reconnaissance, and by providing the required guns and mortars before and during a battle. In an army that has since been criticized for demonstrating an insufficient quantity of flexibility and initiative, Lister consistently displayed imagination and sacrificial courage, as well as a determination to get the job done that could border on recklessness.[24]

His bravery was much in evidence at Le Bas Perrier, a town in the *bocage* country, on August 12, 1944. Ordered to form a firm base with Bren gun carriers and anti-tank guns to protect the command post, Lister did so while his company was subjected to intense artillery fire that caused many casualties. Sent by his commanding officer to find out what was happening with another company that was in difficulty, Lister reorganized the company under heavy fire and got it to its objective. When a road to two of the companies needed to be cleared so that anti-tank guns could be brought up and casualties evacuated, he achieved the necessary result. Praising Lister's "disregard for himself and tireless energy," his commanding officer said, "I could not have commanded my battalion without his assistance." For his heroic conduct at Le Bas Perrier Lister was awarded the Military Cross.[25]

Although heedless of his own safety, Lister never let his men get into any trouble if he could help it. "His only imperative," said Lieutenant Richard Mosse, who commanded Support Company's anti-tank platoon, "was that we were utterly responsible for the men under our command. Their lives and well-being depended on us and we must never fail them whatever the cost to us." Mosse remembered Lister's demeanor in battle:

"He was always quiet and peaceful however wild the action around him. The only time I ever saw him rattled was if any of his boys strayed into danger."[26] "You knew that he had thought everything through," Mosse said, "and if he asked you to do something it was the right thing to do." As a result, "everybody adored him and would simply do whatever he asked." Hugh was "slightly unworldly, and we trusted him completely." But he was also "a very unchurchy man. All the young officers would gather in his bivouac and drink calvados [applejack] and just chat. He was very good company."[27]

General (then Lieutenant) Peter Leuchars, who served with Lister in the Welsh Guards, recalled that Lister "was totally unlike the picture you might have of a Guards officer—*totally unlike.*" Never aloof, "he was much more like somebody who had risen from the ranks of a Guardsman, rather than an officer who had come in from Sandhurst. A very caring person, he'd take a great deal of trouble of going to base hospitals or forward casualty collecting stations. You know you meet an awful lot of people in life who you just forget. You never would forget about him."[28] Hugh could reach his men by speaking to them in the vernacular of the common soldier; many officers were unable to do that.

The high point of the Welsh Guards' activity in northwestern Europe came in early September 1944. Lieutenant Mosse recalled, "Hugh came in and said, 'We're going for Brussels.' We simply got on the main road that led from Douai to Brussels and drove flat out [for over ninety miles]."[29] Encountering little opposition, the Welsh Guards, with their fast Cromwell tanks in the lead, reached the Belgian capital as night was falling on September 3 and liberated the city.

Three days later, under orders to seize the crossings over the Albert Canal and the road system beyond it, the Guards Armoured Division continued their northeasterly advance. Hard fighting ensued, with the Germans putting up a spirited resistance. After forcing their way through Beeringen and Helchteren, the Welsh Guards met stiff opposition around Hechtel. In the center of this town, two roads intersected, one leading north to Eindhoven and the other east into Germany. At this important and strongly held crossroads, the Welsh Guards fought a protracted battle, and, on September 9, lost an officer whom the 1st Battalion diary called "truly great" and "irreplaceable."[30]

In his Remembrance Day sermon, Austin Farrer said that Hugh Lister was killed because "he would not let his men advance, until he had made his personal reconnaissance, to be sure that there were no machine-gun posts left behind by the retreating enemy, and missed by Allied observation. Well, there was a machine-gun post; Hugh Lister was shot, and so his men were not taken by surprise."[31] This poignant depiction of his friend's demise undoubtedly reflects all that Farrer knew about Lister's death. Although his spare account lacks some telling details, including the degree of foolhardiness present in Lister's habitual efforts to test enemy fire, Farrer's words accurately convey the self-sacrificial quality of Lister's conduct.[32] What Farrer recognized in the story of his friend's final moments was the same spirit of self-denial that was visible throughout his career.

Employing a bit of historical imagination, we can attempt to make out some of the influences on Lister's character, including an upbringing that would have given him a strong sense of noblesse oblige and an appreciation for martial valor. The walls of Lancing and Trinity would have provided Hugh with daily reminders of the heroic self-offerings of those who went before him. As an officer he might well have thought that this sacrifice was what he was made for: to risk his life for others, to be willing to be among the first to die. "One need not even think about being brave," he is said to have told his men, "if one throws oneself into the forefront of the battle with one's heart united to God."[33]

Lister's temperament—a taste for exacting self-discipline, for testing the limits of physical endurance—dovetailed with his religious outlook to produce a priest-soldier for whom martyrdom was anything but unthinkable. With his whole being he embraced, it seems, a sacramental interpretation of his life and vocation. This orientation would not have been unusual for any Anglo-Catholic whose social conscience was quickened and informed by eucharistic devotion. Indeed, Lister's experience in the Second World War may have enhanced, not hollowed out, his sacramental understanding. Even in the field this Welsh Guards major used to hold Communion services, which were always well attended, mostly by members of his own company.[34] As Austin Farrer commented, "There was no unreality in those [celebrations] when so thin a veil of safety stood between this world and the other."[35]

Lister would have experienced the Eucharist in a manner consistent with the theology of the church fathers: The Lord's Supper is the occasion of communion with Christ and with those who make up the Lord's body; the liturgy is an event that, in its dramatic summary of the way of the Christ, displays not only a symbol of faith but also a norm of conduct. Lister, therefore, would have understood *leitourgia* to be both an invitation to unite with Christ and a call to offer himself, in unity with the great high priest, in service to others.[36] He had told his labor colleagues in 1938 that by the power of Christ "ordinary persons like you and me" can perform "heroic" deeds, "which otherwise would be far beyond us."[37] For Lister, *leitourgia* was both an act of worship and a distinctive form of daily existence, the two sides held together through participation in and obedience to the way of Christ.

It is not hard to detect in the life of this priest a valiant effort to live in the pattern of Christ, to make the most of his calling in his own situation, to give himself without stint for all sorts and conditions of human beings. The quality of the man is mirrored in the responses of those who trusted him implicitly. One of them, Richard Mosse, was aware of "a presence about him that set him aside."[38] The best evidence for his saintliness, however, may be a character that would have compelled him to laugh at any suggestion of his special virtue.

FRIENDSHIP

Hugh Lister was a man whose "eyes," Farrer said, "were not on himself, they were turned elsewhere."[39] Among the outstanding characteristics of this priest, labor leader, and army officer, his lack of self-centeredness and his capacity to transcend the customary boundaries of class, role, and rank were crucial to Farrer's appreciation of him as an exemplar of Christian friendship. Whenever he spoke of friendship, Farrer made it clear that he perceived no real or enduring opposition between *philia,* Christianly understood, and *agape.*

The danger has often been remarked: In its exclusivist bent, its "in-crowd" familiarity, friendship represents a relationship that is morally inferior to *agape,* the universal, need-oriented love of the outsider that was enacted by Christ in his ministry and supremely displayed on the cross. Farrer would have been well aware of this particularizing tendency in *philia* — and of its deleterious consequences — among the Oxford students and dons he knew. And so he reminded his hearers and readers that at the end of his earthly career, Jesus gave to his friends his body and his blood in bread and wine, making his companions one with himself and sharers in his own destiny.[40] Thus persons who by grace participate in the friendship of Christ share his death and resurrection, his life and love. Christian friendship, then, drives the disciple to have regard not just for a small inner circle of appealing friends but also for those who reside in "the outer circle, most distant, hungry and dark," the out-group of the less privileged.[41]

Without at all sentimentalizing the image, Farrer extended the language of friendship to the relation of God and humanity. "God makes every one of us his friend, he sets us at his table, he shows us his kindness, he puts an infinite price upon our love." The "equalization" necessary to bring about a friendship between unequals is achieved by God's "dealing humanly with human creatures," "by [lifting] us to himself" and "conversing with us." In employing this richly analogical language in his devotional writings, Farrer was concerned to give his readers a powerful sense of God's loving-kindness and sovereign purposes. He was not intent on preserving the sorts of careful terminological distinctions among the various forms of love that professional ethicists would want to maintain. In these instances Farrer was using metaphors from the world of human *philia* in order to depict the priority, intensity, and extent of divine *agape,* which is itself the ground of true and lasting communion (or friendship) between God and human beings.[42]

By the gift of Christ, human beings are raised to life with God: "There is an equal friendship or association of the Father and the Son, into which the Son may bring us by living as man, and by making us the disciples and partners of his life."[43] Our adoption is effected by the work of Christ on the cross, where "love is almighty, and mercy irresistible," where "your creator lays down life, to make his enemies his friends."[44] In this encounter initiated by divine love lies the potential and lives the reality of all relationships of Christian friendship. "He who is the Way [is also] the everlasting Life of his friends."[45]

For Farrer and for Hugh Lister, the eucharistic celebration makes the divine way and life present to believers, binding them sacramentally to Christ.[46] But Farrer knew that ordinary Christians may not take away from this event all that it truly signifies. What he called "the grasp of faith on what the sacraments effect" may be uncertain. There may indeed be other occasions when faith apprehends — grasps more securely — what incorporation in Christ means: in meditation, in conversation, or in doing God's will. It "may be then that we make free with Christ, and Christ with us, giving us away to his friends."[47]

In the rarefied atmosphere of Farrer's poetic prose, the reader frequently becomes almost dizzy, and is therefore pleased to discover in his books so many examples drawn from the down-to-earth realm of human friendship. In portraying, for example, the heavenly, even godlike nature of friendship, the openness and easy exchange of give-and-take between friends, and the free mutuality between Jesus and the Father, Farrer told the story of the undergraduate who laments the loss of his bicycle. " 'Why don't you padlock it?' 'Padlock it! Then what are the chaps going to do who want to borrow it?' "[48]

Nowhere did Farrer develop this topic systematically, as other Christian writers have done. But he frequently returned to the language, customs, and problems of friendship; and in his philosophical theology, especially in *Faith and Speculation,* he explored analogies drawn from this social sphere.[49] In his own life he was a devoted friend to many, including the theologian Eric Mascall, the poet Martyn Skinner, the Benedictine monk and liturgical scholar Gregory Dix, the literary scholar and Christian apologist C. S. Lewis and his wife Joy, and the bishop of Oxford, Kenneth Kirk. And he was, allowing for some "equalization," a helpful ally and confidant of numerous students and graduates as well.

His advice to them about friendship and Christian community was candid and practical. In your own prayers, he would tell them, throw yourselves into your friends' deepest concerns.[50] Consider those whom "a superficial and callous social judgement holds . . . cheap." Resist the temptation "to let friendship be corrupted with ambition," leading you to curry favor only with the most popular and successful.[51] Make an effort to "look for the lonely or depressed character on the fringes of your acquaintance, and go out of your way a bit. . . . "[52] Come to the weekly Communion and share the bread of God at the eucharistic table, thereby helping to build up the Body of Christ and the faith of all.[53] Prayers, sacraments, scripture, works of practical kindness — these are the ordinary means, Farrer believed, that will help Christians realize what is already theirs: a relationship with Christ that becomes a companionship in love, a school of compassion, a transforming friendship.

When he recalled his friend Hugh Lister, Farrer dwelled on the life of someone who was an adept practitioner of Christian friendship. Throughout the postwar period he seemed haunted by the memory of his fallen colleague. Professor J. L. Houlden, who succeeded Farrer as chaplain of Trinity College, believes that after the Second World War, Oxford chaplains that had remained in the university during the war "felt rather humbled by ex-service returnees: conscience even sharper for friends who had been killed"; and he has surmised that Farrer was one of these chaplains.[54]

Appearing to acknowledge as much in one of his sermons, Farrer spoke of his "perplexity" when he looked back on those desperate months of 1939 and 1940 and saw himself "sheltered from battle and sudden death, while the man I thought the best man of my acquaintance" went to war. Many in the Church of England, he recalled, had looked to Lister to achieve the "miracle" of a significant ecclesiastical influence in the world of organized labor. "Like the disciples on the road to Emmaus, we thought it was he who should have redeemed our Israel." But history and Lister's nature decreed otherwise. Being the sort of man he was, "he got himself shot; just as Christ, being what he was, got himself crucified. Others of us, not being that sort of man, got ourselves a wider scope of further life, but not being that sort of man, we have not done anything very striking with it."[55]

One good work that Farrer urged other Christians to accomplish in their own lives he himself achieved in relation to Lister: to prize what is best in our friends, having "a special regard" for "what [in them] expresses the goodness and the beauty of God."[56] In Hugh Lister, Farrer believed that he had known a living saint. But it is clear that what Farrer meant by saintly character is not what conventional wisdom usually means by "sainthood."

SAINTHOOD

A social ethicist who worked with Lister in the Student Christian Movement in the 1930s has commented that his associate "could hardly [have been] more different from the stereotype of [a saint]."[57] With eyes cast heavenward or smiling on wretched humanity, the stereotypical saint is a lean, ascetic figure of benevolent mien; his or her hands are folded in prayer, lifted in blessing, or engaged in good works. In the contemporary imagination, the saint is a holy person supernaturally meek, pious, pure, and charitable — in brief, someone indeed very fine but probably not all that much fun to be around for any extended period.

C. S. Lewis might well have been referring to saintly types — to human beings who always suppress their own desires in order to live for others — when he said that you can tell the individuals these good souls serve so devotedly by the hunted look in their eyes.[58] Unquestionably, in the popular mind, saints are less exciting than heroes, far less titillating than celebrities, and no longer compelling as persons to emulate.[59]

In a recent novel, when an eccentric young healer named DJ GoodNews transforms a selfish and mean-spirited man into a moral saint, his wife, a physician who works in a London clinic for the indigent and conscientiously votes Labor, soon misses her husband's former self. Although Katie had been repelled by David's bitterness and anger, she finds herself after GoodNews's intervention wistful for her husband's familiar wit, however bilious and cynical; now she never laughs. The old David was more complicated and interesting than this new, angelic person who gives their son's computer to the poor and invites a homeless man to live with them. The lazy and sarcastic David was more tolerable than this sanctimonious moral crusader who cares about the plight of the weak and the suffering. Understandably, Katie longs for a life that includes not only a reasonable amount of social concern but also the pleasures of art, sex, and laughter.[60]

This fictional slant on sainthood parallels the skeptical treatment saints received in an article published in the *Journal of Philosophy* in 1982. In a provocative essay titled "Moral Saints," the author made it clear at the outset that she was glad that neither she nor anyone she cared about was a saint. She found moral sainthood to be a condition that she could not urge anyone to strive for, because it is neither rational nor good nor desirable for a person to try to be a moral saint. Indeed, in her view the absence of moral saints in our lives might be a "blessing." The moral saint may be "too good for his own well-being" and thus unable to realize the nonmoral virtues and interests that make for a well-rounded person.[61]

The moral saint who is spending all of his or her time taking care of the needs of the world, this philosopher held, will have no time or energy left to play an instrument or read a novel or enjoy a sport. No one of these nonmoral goods is essential to a happy life, of course, but a life that contained none of them would be "strangely barren." Other personal characteristics that we might relish in others, such as a slightly wicked sense of humor, the moral saint could not display, because to do so would cut "against the moral grain." The moral saint needs to be upbeat, not pessimistic; looking for the best in people, not pointing out flaws. Consequently, "although a moral saint might . . . enjoy a good episode of *Father Knows Best,* he may not in good conscience be able to laugh at a Marx Brothers movie or enjoy a play by George Bernard Shaw." Nor could the moral saint savor gourmet cooking, and the fine arts might be problematic as well. He or she "will have to be a very, very nice" sort of person: inoffensive, humorless, and dull.[62]

This is why the saint may not seem like the most invigorating company. The onlooker, our philosopher pointed out, appreciates the moral virtues being blended with "mischievousness" and a "sense of irony." Those sorts of saints that have no trouble forgoing a fishing trip or a romantic evening at a moment's notice in order to serve humanity seem seriously deficient in their capacity to experience joy in the created world.

Other saints, who truly love earthly pleasures but renounce them, appear to this philosopher to have "a pathological fear of damnation or an extreme form of self-hatred that interferes with [their] ability to enjoy the enjoyable in life." She worried that those who pursue morality with single-minded devotion — or those who similarly serve "a certain kind of religious ideal" — run the risk of losing their own selves.[63] The author nodded approvingly at George Orwell's comments that "sainthood is . . . a thing that human beings must avoid" and that being a saint and being a human being do not seem to go together.[64]

Comprehending the life of Hugh Lister within the categories provided by this philosopher would be a difficult assignment. Referring to him as a saint, Farrer also characterized him as "a heroic, hearty, enjoying sort of man."[65] We can easily see that, like many other saints, he lived a life that was not "out of this world" or barren but "massively real."[66] On the pleasures of Lister's company we have the testimony not only of a Christian theologian but of hard men who struggled with him in Hackney and fought with him in France. If they did not find him bland or humorless, neither did the Communists and factory owners find him inoffensive. To fit Hugh Lister into the terms of this philosopher's scheme we would need to adapt the method of an ancient heresiarch and impose on our subject a Nestorian-like division into two selves: To the saintly self would belong the Lister who led a class in Bible study; to the appetitive man would belong the Lister who sipped calvados with friends.

We have learned enough of Lister's story to know that any kind of artificial juxtaposition will not work. His life was all of a piece, indivisible: He discovered strength in self-denial, found his personal identity in communion with others, and realized freedom in divine service. He "just cared for the will of God," Farrer said, "as other men care for the girl they love or, more likely, for themselves. . . . We know we are supposed to love God, and we go through various exercises in the hope of doing it; the saints just do it."[67]

Lister was no copybook saint. Indeed, to Farrer, that phrase would have been an outright oxymoron, because each saint possesses an integrity that makes possible spontaneity and a unity of thought and action. A veteran ecumenist who knew Lister in the 1930s said that "the most striking thing about him was undoubtedly his disconcerting directness both of speech and action." Most people, he observed, hesitate to speak up about something that's true — and are even more reluctant to point out that some widely believed notion is false. "Hugh," on the other hand, "never had any compunction about proclaiming truth or denouncing falsehood." People always knew where he stood. "But, even more disconcerting, if he saw a thing to be right, he went and did it. There was no havering about him. . . . " To his companions, Lister's manner could be productively unsettling. "To be with him was to be challenged at the deepest level of thought and action, and all the more sharply because this effect was entirely unconscious and unstudied."[68]

To Farrer, also, the saints are disturbing friends. They challenge us to question our lukewarm attitudes and indifferent habits and to confront anew the meaning and truth of our religion. They help us to see our duties, and they provide a guide for our conduct; together with Christ they support and carry us. When we fall short in our efforts to follow the divine will, they teach us repentance. Most of all, they focus our attention on the will of God as, in Farrer's lyrical phrasing, "the bread of my hunger and the water of my thirst."[69] In the lives of the saints, we see a demonstration of the "real connection" between "religious symbols" and "everyday realities."[70] In their own centered existences, the saints provide "evidence" of the meaningfulness of religious truth claims.[71]

The most godlike part of a human being, Farrer said, is not an individual's body or inherited aptitudes and instincts but his or her free will.[72] In the saints' deliberate activity, in the exercise of their wills, they reveal what it means to live in obedience to God's kingly rule. "I should be a fool indeed," Farrer remarked, "if I took my godly actions and thoughts (supposing I have any which deserve the epithet) as providing a disclosure of God equal to the disclosure he made in the lives and the minds of heroic saints."[73] For discovering and fulfilling God's purposes, "the spirituality of the ordinary believer is a negligible equipment compared with that of the saint."[74]

By starting with our own lives and conducting our own experiments—that is, by exercising our free wills in response to God's grace and command—those of us who are not saints can gain some sense of God and of God's purposes. Then, with this "slender clue" in hand, we can discover more about God in the careers of the saints, whose embracing of the divine will is so much stronger and more consistent than our own. We learn from them as we attempt to look at existence through their eyes.[75] Farrer thought that the experiences of the saints are more revealing of God not only because saints fulfill the divine will more completely but also because the vocations laid upon them more clearly point to the larger pattern of God's purposes than do the comparatively ordinary tasks that God lays upon less-exceptional men and women.[76]

Mindful, then, of what God has done for and in us, we take up the golden thread of our own experience and follow it as it runs through the lives of the saints, the study of whom should be even more fruitful of insights.[77] Farrer, who always read the life of a saint when he went on retreat, did not urge Christians to pay heed to the saints because he believed that the divine agency at work in them reveals itself in paranormal phenomena or in knowledge accessible only to a spiritual elite.[78] He bade us examine saints' biographies not because God's action in their careers takes the form of spectacular miracles or mystical raptures but because the lives of saints (canonized or not) are more abundantly revealing of God's intention and work in loving and healing a fallen world.[79]

For both the saints and the rest of us, the "equipment" we use to know God is not the methods we would use in a scientific laboratory, where we test and learn about natural phenomena by dividing them up and applying our instruments. We learn about God, Farrer said, by "humble obedience" and by patiently waiting upon God's will. "What is received on authority must be proved in action."[80]

But in her or his own efforts to live a godly life, the Christian would be prudent never to jettison that "authority," which includes the wisdom and the practices of the saints over centuries. While scientists may be able to exclude outside influences from their experiments, the believer "has no such assurance of excluding folly and sin from his attempt at co-operation with Divine Grace." Even as we feel gratitude for what God appears to have done for us and our communities, we must continue to learn from and be corrected by the experiences and perspectives of the saints, "extend[ing] experiment by proxy." In this way we go on hoping to find clues to "a labyrinth of spiritual history." Participating in the communion of saints, we continue to search in our own time and place for the fitting response to the divine will.[81] What suggestions did Farrer provide to aid us in discerning the will of God?

THE WILL OF GOD

Farrer has given us, it should be said at the outset, no infallible methods for testing our conclusions, no means of certain wisdom. Even in the case of Hugh Lister, Farrer said in a British Broadcasting Corporation talk in 1952, none of the answers to the crucial questions his friend faced was to be found in a cosmic rule book. Should someone with Hugh's excellent training in engineering — expertise that might be used in all sorts of ways to benefit humankind — put aside his education and experience in order to answer what he takes to be a divine call to the ordained ministry? Should he risk his life by working in a slum, when he might engage in worthwhile endeavors elsewhere? Should he become chairman of a trade union and lead a labor strike? Would he be more useful to the Allied effort by remaining in weapons design or by leading an infantry support company? Should a priest serve as a combatant, taking part in the shedding of blood? None of these dilemmas was susceptible of easy resolution, but Farrer was confident that his friend approached each question in an attitude of self-abnegation and moral seriousness and in a frame of mind disposed to discovering as best he could the will of God for him in his situation.[82]

One equation Farrer did not accept was that between psychological health and spiritual well-being. Making important choices on the basis of what would bring the deepest personal contentment or make one feel most in harmony with the music of the spheres was not a decision-making process that Farrer could endorse. Doing the will of God is not the same as finding peace of mind and increased vitality: Those conditions, however good and desirable, could well elude the doer of God's will. Farrer remarked that if a psychologist told him that the way to stay sane and achieve happiness was to take life easier and develop his hobbies, then he would have to reply as follows: I appreciate your concern, but I must pursue my calling, though it entails risks to my mental stability. Other things being equal, we should do what protects our health, but other things, he said, are not always equal — as indeed they were not for Hugh Lister.[83]

Another notion that Farrer rejected was the pious view that everything is to be accepted as in some sense given by the Almighty. No, God's will is made known in "facts," which comprise our own set of opportunities and problems, and in "leadings," which help us to determine how to deal with those facts. Often, if we are attentive to divine leadings, we can see that we must change the facts, not submit to them. "Nothing forces God's will on me more plainly than your unhappiness or than my sin." Our duty then does not consist in always yielding to existing conditions in nature or society as divine dispensations. "Christ," Farrer pointed out, "came to transform the world, not to conform to it; and the transformation was to be physical as well as moral."[84]

The assistance we obtain comes in the form of divine leadings, through the inspiration to be found in the words and example of Christ and the prophets, in the careers of the saints, in our own life of prayer and reading of scripture, and in our participation in the sacraments and examination of conscience. By these means "we seek to touch the living movements of God's present creative work," and we endeavor to discover the roles proper to us as instruments of God's purpose. Divine leadings prompt us first of all to recognize that the other person is as real as ourselves. "God's will is my neighbour's good, and to see it I must look at my neighbour," Farrer said. "What is God sustaining, what is he making or perfecting in that person? And what does his work there demand on my part?"[85]

Farrer referred to Jesus' parable of Dives and Lazarus, found in Luke 16:19–31. In his life on earth, Dives, a rich man, had always ignored Lazarus, a poor man covered with sores; he refused even to give Lazarus the scraps from his table. When both died, Dives was sent to torment in Hades, and Lazarus was carried away by angels to be with Abraham. Take pity on me, the rich man beseeched Abraham, and send Lazarus to dip his finger in water and cool my tongue to mitigate my agony! But Dives cried to no avail, as there was a great gulf fixed between him and Lazarus, and the rich man had received good things during his lifetime while the poor man suffered and dogs licked his sores.

And so Farrer commented, "If Dives wants to find the will of God, let him look at Lazarus. How much longer are his sores to go untended or his hunger unfed?" In other words, often the will of God is not a deeply buried secret but a call perceptible in our immediate environment, if our senses are properly tuned to receive it.[86] "If we are to share the will of God," Farrer said, "it must be in the form of love. We must look first with [God's] eyes, then care with his heart." To see Lazarus, Dives needed for a moment to step out of his own constricting circle of self-regard and widen his angle of vision. "We must go out of the world into God, but only so that we may stand out of our own light, and see things in the clearness of that uncreated beam" which is Christ.[87]

To perceive his or her duty in the light of Christ, the believer has the assistance of the whole Christian tradition. God speaks to individual women and men, but God "does not," Farrer pointed out, "interpret himself only by speaking in the single [Bible] reader's mind." God also speaks "in the Church, the whole organized body of Christian minds; we are not alone, we have the mind of Christendom, the Catholic Faith, to guide us."[88] Why is it not enough simply to have faith and to be good? Christians sometimes ask. Why must we also go to church every week? One important reason, Farrer would reply, is to provide this repeated opportunity for acquaintance with the mind of Christ: "Worship is not to be substituted for practical virtue, no; but practical virtue finds its orientation in a life of worship."[89] Farrer may have heard and certainly would have agreed with one of the speakers at the Second Anglo-Catholic Summer School of Sociology, who said in 1926 that the sacraments declare what God's purpose for us is: They are "standing witnesses to the will of God for humanity," and that will is not the saving of souls in isolation from others but the building up of the city of God.[90]

Farrer believed that the crucial revelatory images that express "the thought of Christ" are present in scripture and reinforced in worship. One of the most important of these "dominant images," he said in *The Glass of Vision,* may be found in the "supernatural revelation" contained in the account of the Last Supper. Christ "displayed, in the action of the supper, the infinitely complex and fertile image of sacrifice and communion, of expiation and covenant."[91]

When this dramatic and complex image is re-presented in the celebration of the Eucharist, then worship should help to overcome the natural problems all of us have when our sight is blocked and our wills hobbled by inadequate imaginations. "For, if our difficulty is one of imagination, that we cannot imagine and feel and live our identification with Christ, is it not," Farrer asked, "one purpose of the sacrament to make such identification visible and palpable?"[92]

More important than the celebration of sacraments is the life of practical obedience to God's commands, but insofar as our model for that service is Christ, then the Eucharist has an essential role to play in Christian formation. The Holy Communion, Farrer said, should not be thought of as merely one aspect of Christianity, one rite among others: "it just is our religion, sacramentally enacted." In the Eucharist the whole Christian life is summed up. "For the whole of our religion is summed up in Christ, and the sacrament presents Christ, his birth, death, resurrection, and his present existence. . . . "[93]

Always, for Farrer, in order for Dives to see Lazarus, Dives needs to sacrifice his own selfish will and care for the will of God. In the Eucharist we receive the body that accomplished its purpose by being nailed to a cross. "You are to become this body," Farrer said; "you are to be nailed: nailed to Christ's sacrificial will." Thus Christ's resurrection is ours, but so also is his death. And his sacrifice was not accomplished in one afternoon but throughout his life: "Christ's passion was no more than the last expression of what he had done all his life. He had set his body aside whenever its demands conflicted with man's need or God's will, and so he had rehearsed his death continually; not morbidly, but with joy and self-forgetfulness."[94]

For us as for Dives, discerning the will of God requires us to relax our self-absorption and to risk expanding our circle of friends. Just a few days before he died, in the last sermon he preached, Farrer remarked that in our daily lives our glimpses of God's purposes may seem trifling and inconsequential. But even in this mortal life, he said, God enables us somewhat to overcome our self-concern and to perceive God's own desires. "Even today, when we pray, the hand of God does somewhat put aside that accursed looking-glass, which each of us holds before him, and which shows each of us our own face." Only in the next life, however, will our vision be fully transformed. In the language of judgment and redemption Farrer presented a vision of the Christian life realized. "Only the day of judgement will strike the glass for ever from our hands and leave us nowhere reflected but in the pupils of the eyes of God." On that day "we shall be cured of our self love, and shall love . . . the face of God." Then, "passing from the great Begetter to what is begotten by him, we shall see his likeness in his creatures, in angels and in blessed saints: returning at long last the love that has been lavished on us. . . ."[95]

To pray, then, is to surrender for a time our clamant selves, to seek the will of God, and perhaps thereby to gain a foretaste of eternal life. To pray is to enjoy a friendship with Christ. But how to pray? Clear a set period of time for it, the always practical Farrer advised the members of his student congregation; keep these minutes clear and remain quiet until the clock strikes. When your mind wanders, return to your prayer. Farrer told them that he might begin by reading some verses of scripture or a list of his friends' names, or he might recall what his life was supposed to be about or remind himself of the attributes of God. Most of all, he said, he must give his thoughts to God, trusting that God would enlighten him. Prayer may be dry and unamusing, he acknowledged, but it is necessary if the Christian would know God's will.[96]

To confront God's will, Farrer said, means bringing to God the tangled skein of my own desires in order to "be pulled together into something more real, and something far more simple." So I bring to God my bundle of choices and desires and attitudes, which, Farrer noted, are sortable into good, bad, and indifferent. The bad choices I may have tried to forget, but with a little effort I can remember yesterday's conduct, examine my conscience, repent, and seek amendment of life. My good desires are not good enough; I can pray for greater strength and purity of will. I can remember to give thanks to God for blessings, for joys and happiness.

My attitudes that are indifferent I cannot leave out of my prayer, for they are most of what I am. "Talk to God," Farrer urged his congregation, "about the things that really concern you," and let these matters also "find their place, and learn their true proportion, in relation to God's holy will."[97]

Pray for others: The worthiest part of each of us, Farrer remarked, comprises concerns for and attachments to other people. "Praying for your fellows is not something different from bringing yourself before God: for your concerns for them are half your heart, and you would be a better man, if they were far more than half of it." In prayer we fix our eyes on God and our neighbor, and it is in this reorientation of the self that we find ourselves. "The more you look outwards, the more you will be yourself. For love is the substance of character, and love self-forgetfulness." Intercession for others means that we bring our own hearts into congruence with God's will for others, and the influence that God has placed in us will flow outward in support of our friends' happiness and virtue. "Mind," Farrer believed, "does everywhere flow into mind." There is likely to be a purity to our intercessory prayer that will not be an ingredient in our prayers for ourselves. "When, in the sight of God, you wish well to another, can even the Spirit of God himself," Farrer asked, "get a knife's edge between your wish and his own will?"[98]

CONCLUSION

Austin Farrer's most important contribution to contemporary Christian spirituality is his consistent emphasis on the primacy of will and action, both human and divine. We may not know who we are, we may not even be who we think we are, but we can become the persons we ought to be by doing, by seeking and obeying the divine will for us.[99] Incorporating a strong emphasis on agency and a roster of exemplars on the order of Hugh Lister, Farrer's spiritual theology is a bracing tonic. It stimulates the body of believers to overcome the harm caused by detaching the interior life from external observance, by separating the private, meditative self and the public actor, and by privileging "spirituality" over religion.[100]

For Farrer the spiritual life is not merely spiritual; it is an eminently practical, indeed a bodily and communal affair, in which in order to know God and to know ourselves we must exercise our actual, personal relation with God.[101] "Belief in God," he said, "is essentially a practical and passionate belief."[102] To know God we have to do more than contemplate the divine, and certainly we must do more than indulge our spiritual feelings. "Emotion," Farrer observed, "can be misplaced to an almost indefinite extent; the doing, not the feeling, is the empirical test."[103] One of Farrer's basic principles is that we can have "no thought about any reality about which we can do nothing but think."[104] Therefore, to engage with God the human mind is dependent on the interaction of God and the human will.[105]

When Farrer reflected on the human mind engaging with God, he spoke of God not as the Ground of Being or Ultimate Reality but as sovereign and holy Will. To Farrer, God is supreme agent: unconditioned, everlasting will.[106] We know God by actively embracing the divine will. "Coinciding with God's action in one's own life," wrote the bishop of Oxford Richard Harries in a recent discussion of Farrer, "and knowing that there is an action of God to coincide with are inextricably bound together."[107]

What are the practical results of obedience to the will of God? Trusting obedience, the correspondence of the human will with the divine, is itself a gift of grace; therefore, Farrer spoke of the fruits received when "grace triumphs" and we "love the love and will the will of God." Incorporate in Christ with the saints, believers enjoy the benefits of "continual repentance"; we are forgiven and accepted. Grace gives us good desires and expels many desires that are evil. We are able to carry out duties we dislike, to find ourselves in our callings, and to pray for those whom we had once regarded with indifference.[108]

To be justified and sanctified, the fruits of grace: blessed assurance. But what about the many times when knowledge of that assurance escapes us, and we perceive nothing resembling an alignment of our wills with God's will? What are we to make of those days when we exercise our wills as conscientiously as we are able but divinity is still absent, like the hidden God of R. S. Thomas's poems?

Or we have made choices and they have turned out badly, and we know our hearts and minds well enough to see why they did. We look back months or years afterwards and can recognize where we went wrong, the ways in which vanity, impatience, insecurity, or sheer heedlessness played a role in what we did or failed to do. As we ruminate on poor decisions and missed opportunities, our awareness of the relentless passage of time deepens our sense of sorrow and regret. Overburdened, we may feel "continually overtaken by time, and by remorse"; and this mode of existence, Farrer said, is "a pattern of damnation."[109]

In the event, our heart condemns itself; and if we were to look into our inner selves and see ourselves as clearly as God sees us, then we might, as Farrer remarked, "condemn ourselves to worse than stoning."[110] But then St. John declares, "God is greater than our heart." And "[God] knows," Farrer commented, "not our heart only, but all things," especially "his own heart. He knows that he has loved us with an everlasting love, and will not let us go."[111]

What else? When Jesus died on the cross, Farrer said, his conscious mind probably had little to do with thoughts of the world's redemption, so occupied was it with enduring the physical pain. But God saw Jesus' conscious thoughts as accidents; underneath them the Father could see "the current of Christ's will steadily running in its set direction." God knew that Christ, in his deepest self, "was praying for the salvation of mankind with the whole weight of his sacrifice."

With us, Farrer observed, just the reverse occurs. The prayers and good thoughts we have are superficial, while the main current of our selfish will flows on underneath. Once again, our wills and God's seem hardly to converge at all; and our hearts, if they do not condemn us, feel isolated and impoverished. But our prayer, weak as it is, is not alone. "The prayer which saves the world," Farrer wrote, is prayed by Christ and the saints; with this prayer they pray for our "happiness, prosperity, and peace." In the sacrament of the Lord's Supper, our feeble petitions are joined with their mighty prayer: "by the virtue of this sacrament our prayer and theirs is one."[112]

In the end, then, Farrer's is a practical approach to religion and life but never a do-it-yourself kind of spirituality. Bereft of the noble company of martyrs and apostles, the believer could scarcely be a Christian at all. On its own, the will that the Christian possesses is a mean instrument for accomplishing any good. Therefore Farrer always stressed the virtue of humility and the saintly character of repentance, rather than naked striving and spiritual achievement. And so he would have the penitent Christian feel not remorse but hope, and pray:

> I missed this or that call from a fellow-being, I followed my pride, or my pleasure, I did not do as you, my Lord, would have done. But you have let me fall into these errors to show me my heart, and you in your mercy, will use them for my discipline, and turn them to account in the designs of your loving kindness. You have undertaken my life, and you will bring it to good. While we are yours, we shall never be overtaken by darkness; work out in us the

purpose of your perfect will and bring us to that day, which will marry us to joy, and ring every peal in all the city of heaven.[113]

NOTES

1. John Henry Newman, *Parochial and Plain Sermons* (8 vols.; London: Rivingtons, 1868), 2:55.
2. Austin Farrer, *Said or Sung* (London: Faith, 1960), 88.
3. "Austin Farrer and I share a fire," Lister wrote to his mother one Sunday morning. "I am sitting in his room just now. It is nice to have him at Cuddesdon." Hugh Lister to Sybil Palgrave Lister, holograph manuscript, no date; in packet of letters marked "Cuddesdon," Hugh Lister Papers, in the custody of Rev. William Pryor, Oxford, England (hereinafter cited as Lister Papers).
4. Austin Farrer, "Remembrance Day: On Hugh Lister," in *The Brink of Mystery* (ed. Charles C. Conti; London: SPCK, 1976), 115.
5. Eric Fenn, "Introducing Hugh Lister," in Alice Cameron, *In Pursuit of Justice: The Story of Hugh Lister and His Friends in Hackney Wick* (London: SCM, 1946), 11.
6. Farrer, "Remembrance Day," 116.
7. Adrian Hastings, *A History of English Christianity, 1920–1990* (London: SCM, 1991), 174.
8. Peter Doll, review of Nigel Yates, *Anglican Ritualism in Victorian Britain, 1830–1910, Anglican and Episcopal History* 70 (June 2001): 257.
9. Frank Weston, "Our Present Duty," in *Report of the Anglo-Catholic Congress* (London: Society of SS. Peter and Paul, 1923), 183, 185–86.
10. Farrer, "Remembrance Day," 116; Fenn, "Introducing Hugh Lister," 11. From Cuddesdon Theological College, Hugh — paraphrasing a writer he agreed with — wrote his mother that "Suffering is useful when it de-occupies us with ourselves, not the reverse." Undated holograph manuscript, in packet of Cuddesdon letters, Lister Papers.
11. Fenn, "Introducing Hugh Lister," 12.
12. Millicent Rose, *The East End of London* (London: Cresset, 1951), 143 (quotation); *Crockford's Clerical Directory for 1939* (London: Oxford University Press, 1939), 825.
13. Hugh Lister, sermon on Matt 21:28, St. Augustine's Church, Lent I 1936, typescript, p. 6, Lister Papers; also quoted in Cameron, *In Pursuit of Justice,* 127.
14. Farrer, "Remembrance Day," 116.
15. "Hugh Lister of Hackney Wick," *Hackney Gazette,* August 21, 1946 (quotation); Cameron, *In Pursuit of Justice.*
16. "Hugh Lister of Hackney Wick."
17. Charles Henry Darke, *The Communist Technique in Britain* (London: Collins, 1953), 119. Hugh Lister's thoughts on the relationship between Communism and Christianity may be found in a six-page typed manuscript in the Lister Papers (the first page contains the heading "Communist Arguments against Religion").
18. Farrer, "Remembrance Day," 117.

19. Cameron, *In Pursuit of Justice,* 26. "These three aspects [of Lister's life and work] really merge and reinforce one another—the trade union brotherhood, the hospitality for the homeless, and the religious inspiration of the leader, make something which is a center of life and hope in that part of London." Alice Cameron, "Memorandum on H. E. Lister's Experiment at Hackney Wick," November 1937, carbon typescript, Lister Papers.

20. Hugh Lister, sermon, Eton Mission, October 3, 1937, holograph manuscript, Lister Papers. In July 1941, Lister wrote, "[I]f there is one thing I want specially to find is true, it is that God is not a religious maniac." "What It Means to Be a Christian in the Army," July 1941, two-page typescript, Lister Papers.

21. Cameron, *In Pursuit of Justice,* chap. 9. In the Lister Papers, see the following documents: Hugh Lister, letter to the *Times,* October 7, 1938, carbon typescript; "Conscription and the Unions: An Open Letter from a Few Members of the Rank and File," April 1939, printed leaflet; "Conscription and the Unions: A Personal Explanation," April 1939, printed leaflet; "Conscription and the Unions: Latest Developments," April 28, 1939, printed flyer; "Conscription and the Labour Movement: An Open Letter to Mr. Attlee, from a Few Members of the Rank and File," May 10, 1939, mimeographed typescript; "An Appeal for Funds: Conscription and National Unity," May 24, 1939, printed flyer.

22. Cameron, *In Pursuit of Justice,* 184. Perhaps Lister was familiar with the observation that, in the First World War, Anglican chaplains were only too happy to obey orders to stay well back of the front lines and thereby avoid risking their lives. "If the regimental chaplains," Robert Graves remarked, "had shown one tenth the courage, endurance, and other human qualities that the regimental doctors showed, we agreed, the British Expeditionary Force might well have started a religious revival. But they had not." The result, Graves said, was that "Anglican chaplains were remarkably out of touch with their troops," and failed to win the respect of the fighting men. *Good-bye to All That: An Autobiography* (London: Cape, 1929), 242, 243.

23. See the items concerning this vehicle — photographs, manuals, etc. — in the Lister Papers; see also in the same collection, in the letters to his mother dated October 26, 1941, and November 9, 1941, Lister's discussion of his work on the carrier's design.

24. See Max Hastings, *Overlord: D-Day and the Battle for Normandy* (New York: Simon & Schuster, 1984), 146–51.

25. Official citation, Headquarters Welsh Guards, Wellington Barracks, London. A carbon copy of the original recommendation by his commanding officer is in the Lister Papers.

26. Richard Mosse, letter to the author, December 23, 1998.

27. Richard Mosse, interview with the author, Bognor Regis, West Sussex, June 5, 1999.

28. Peter Leuchars, interview with the author, London, June 9, 1999. In a letter to his mother dated August 23, 1940, Lister stated, "I am much more an 'Other Ranks' at heart." Holograph manuscript, Lister Papers.

29. Interview with the author.

30. Laurence Rosse and E. R. Hill, *The Story of the Guards Armoured Division* (London: Bles, 1956), 104–22; L. F. Ellis, *Welsh Guards at War* (1946; repr., London:

London Stamp Exchange, 1990), 65–68, 216–26 (quotation, 221); G. L. Verney, *The Guards Armoured Division* (London: Hutchinson, 1955), 94–95.

31. Farrer, "Remembrance Day," 118.

32. The degree of detail in the information available to Farrer is indicated by the paucity of facts provided in the biography of Lister published almost two years after the tragic event. Alice Cameron's *In Pursuit of Justice* states only that "[Lister] was shot down by a machine-gun when engaged on a reconnaissance" (189). For an account of Lister's death that incorporates the recollections of his contemporaries, including fellow officers in the Welsh Guards, see David Hein, "Hugh Lister (1901–44): A Modern Saint?" *Theology* 103 (September–October 2000): 339–46.

33. Lister, quoted in Cameron, *In Pursuit of Justice,* 189.

34. Peter Leuchars, letter to the author, October 25, 1998.

35. Farrer, "Remembrance Day," 118.

36. M. Pellegrino, "Liturgy and Fathers," *Encyclopedia of the Early Church* (2 vols.; New York: Oxford University Press, 1992), 1:494–95.

37. Lister, quoted in Cameron, *In Pursuit of Justice,* 123.

38. Interview with the author.

39. Farrer, "Remembrance Day," 118.

40. Austin Farrer, *Lord I Believe: Suggestions for Turning the Creed into Prayer* (Cambridge, MA: Cowley, 1989), 60. See also Austin Farrer, *The Brink of Mystery* (ed. Charles C. Conti; London: SPCK, 1976), 83.

41. Farrer, *The Brink of Mystery,* 55.

42. Farrer, *Lord I Believe,* 18, 19. In his theological approach to *philia* and *agape,* Farrer once again reveals his spiritual and intellectual kinship with Augustine and Aquinas. Among the many recent treatments of Christian friendship, *Love Disconsoled* (Cambridge: Cambridge University Press, 1999), by Timothy P. Jackson, is one of the more judicious; see esp. 79–88.

43. Austin Farrer, *Saving Belief: A Discussion of Essentials* (1964; repr., Harrisburg, PA: Morehouse, 1994), 85.

44. Farrer, *Lord I Believe,* 57.

45. Ibid., 78. See Gilbert Meilaender, *The Taste for the Other: The Social and Ethical Thought of C. S. Lewis* (Grand Rapids, MI: Eerdmans, 1978), 159–78.

46. Austin Farrer, *The Crown of the Year: Weekly Paragraphs for the Holy Sacrament* (London: Dacre, 1952), 9.

47. Farrer, *Lord I Believe,* 49.

48. Farrer, *The Brink of Mystery,* 169. See also his *A Celebration of Faith* (London: Hodder & Stoughton, 1972), 206.

49. See William McFetridge Wilson, "A Proof of the Faith: Austin Farrer's Case for Theism" (PhD diss., University of Virginia, 1983), 146–47; J. N. Morris, "Religious Experience in the Philosophical Theology of Austin Farrer," *Journal of Theological Studies,* n.s., 45 (October 1994): 578; and Edward Hugh Henderson, "Valuing in Knowing God: An Interpretation of Austin Farrer's Religious Epistemology," *Modern Theology* 1 (April 1985): 165–82.

50. Farrer, *The Crown of the Year,* 20.

51. Farrer, *Words for Life* (ed. Charles Conti and Leslie Houlden; London: SPCK, 1993), 64.

52. Farrer, *The Brink of Mystery,* 79.

53. Farrer, *Words for Life,* 65.

54. J. L. Houlden to John Davies, May 18, 1998 (used by permission); J. L. Houlden, letter to the author, June 3, 1998. Farrer occasionally saw his friend Hugh Lister even during the war years. On March 22, 1943, while staying at Cowley Barracks in Oxford, Lister wrote to his mother that "On Sunday I went to Austin F for tea. . . . He was at his best, & told me about his Bible doings. I really do think he makes it seem quite sensible! I long to see his book [either *The Glass of Vision* (1948) or *A Rebirth of Images: The Making of St. John's Apocalypse* (1949)]." Lister Papers.

55. Farrer, *A Celebration of Faith,* 82, 83.

56. Ibid., 76.

57. Ronald Preston, letter, *Theology* 104 (January–February 2001): 40.

58. C. S. Lewis, *The Screwtape Letters* (New York: Touchstone, 1996), 96.

59. See Alan Wolfe, *Moral Freedom* (New York: Norton, 2001), 190.

60. Nick Hornby, *How to Be Good* (New York: Riverhead, 2001).

61. Susan Wolf, "Moral Saints," *Journal of Philosophy* 79 (August 1982): 419–21. Cf. Robert Merrihew Adams, "Saints," *Journal of Philosophy* 81 (July 1984): 392–401.

62. Wolf, "Moral Saints," 421–23.

63. Ibid., 423–24.

64. Ibid., 436n4.

65. Farrer, "Remembrance Day," 118.

66. Farrer, *A Celebration of Faith,* 199.

67. Farrer, "Remembrance Day," 118.

68. Fenn, "Introducing Hugh Lister," 12–13. See Robert L. Wilken, "The Lives of the Saints and the Pursuit of Virtue," *First Things* 8 (December 1990): 45–51.

"There was no havering about him": In response to a request from J. H. Oldham, the senior statesman of international Protestantism, for an essay to be published in the *Christian News-Letter,* Hugh Lister penned some notes in which he deprecated the tendency among some Christians to succumb to "an over-dose of reflection," which is a "form of self-hypnotism." Lister felt that "the debate as to whether or not this war is worth fighting seems to be too much like that to deserve a vast amount of patience. Thank God we have got our Christian Pacifists, and the men who for any reason of conscience have the courage to stand aside from the popular clamour. But the fact that we thank God for them does not mean that we ourselves are condemned to an eternal weighing of the pros and cons." Draft of a letter to J. H. Oldham, three-page holograph manuscript, no date (probably late 1939 or early 1940), Lister Papers; J. H. Oldham to H. E. Lister, October 14, 1939, typescript, Lister Papers.

See also Lister's draft of an article for the Student Christian Movement: "What It Means to Be a Christian in the Army," July 1941, two-page typescript, Lister Papers.

69. Farrer, "Remembrance Day," 118.

70. Farrer, *A Celebration of Faith,* 29.

71. Farrer, *Said or Sung,* 139. See John H. Whittaker, "Kierkegaard on the Concept of Authority," *International Journal for Philosophy of Religion* 46 (October 1999): 88.

72. Austin Farrer, *God Is Not Dead* (New York: Morehouse-Barlow, 1966), 101.

73. Ibid., 117.

74. Austin Farrer, "Revelation," in *Faith and Logic* (ed. B. G. Mitchell; London: Allen & Unwin, 1957), 90.

75. Farrer, *God Is Not Dead,* 117.

76. Ibid., 118.

77. Farrer, *Said or Sung,* 88.

78. Diogenes Allen, "Faith and the Recognition of God's Activity," in *Divine Action: Studies Inspired by the Philosophical Theology of Austin Farrer* (ed. Brian Hebblethwaite and Edward Henderson; Edinburgh: T & T Clark, 1990), 202.

79. Philip Curtis, *A Hawk among Sparrows: A Biography of Austin Farrer* (London: SPCK, 1985), 143; Allen, "Faith and the Recognition of God's Activity," 202. Allen writes: "We can all see that the saints love their neighbors to an impressive extent and that Christ does so paradigmatically. If no one loved his or her neighbour, it would be utterly implausible to claim that there is a grace or a divine activity at work in people and in Christ. But God's sanctifying work in me as an individual is insignificant as evidence, not because it is private, but because it is so paltry. Were it greater in me, then my life would be joined to that of the saints and Christ and play with them the evidential role Farrer assigns to them . . . " (202–3).

80. Farrer, "Revelation," 90.

81. Ibid.

82. Austin Farrer, "The Righteous God II," BBC talk, autumn term 1952, Farrer Papers, Bodleian Library, Oxford University (photocopy from E. H. Henderson), 5–6. Lister himself addressed what he called "the art of making up our minds" in a twenty-two-page holograph manuscript (untitled and undated), Lister Papers.

83. Farrer, "The Righteous God II," 2. See Farrer, *Saving Belief,* 77–78.

84. Farrer, *A Celebration of Faith,* 124, 126.

85. Ibid., 126; Farrer, *God Is Not Dead,* 114. See Austin Farrer, "Inspiration by the Spirit," in *The End of Man* (ed. Charles C. Conti; London: SPCK, 1973), 62–66.

86. Farrer, *God Is Not Dead,* 114 (quotation), 115.

87. Farrer, *A Celebration of Faith,* 135.

88. Austin Farrer, *Interpretation and Belief* (ed. Charles C. Conti; London: SPCK, 1976), 11.

89. Austin Farrer, *Faith and Speculation* (Edinburgh: T & T Clark, 1988), 9.

90. Dudley Symon, "The Nature of the Sacraments," in *The Social Teaching of the Sacraments, being the Report of the Second Anglo-Catholic Summer School of Sociology, held at Keble College, Oxford, July 1926* (ed. Maurice B. Reckitt; London: Society of SS. Peter and Paul, 1927), 27.

91. Austin Farrer, *The Glass of Vision* (London: Dacre, 1948), 42.

92. Farrer, *The Brink of Mystery,* 4.

93. Farrer, *A Celebration of Faith,* 184.

94. Farrer, *The Crown of the Year,* 24, 25.

95. Farrer, *A Celebration of Faith,* 122.

96. Ibid., 141, 207, 212.

97. Ibid., 142–43.

98. Ibid., 143–44.

99. Gilbert Meilaender, "Divine Summons," *Christian Century* 117, no. 30 (November 1, 2000): 1112.

100. Owen C. Thomas, "Interiority and Christian Spirituality," *Journal of Religion* 80 (January 2000): 41–60.

101. Farrer, *Faith and Speculation,* 22.

102. Austin Farrer, *Love Almighty and Ills Unlimited* (London: Fontana, 1966), 11.

103. Farrer, *Faith and Speculation,* 28. See Brian Hebblethwaite, "The Experiential Verification of Religious Belief in the Theology of Austin Farrer," in *For God and Clarity: New Essays in Honor of Austin Farrer* (ed. Jeffrey C. Eaton and Ann Loades; Allison Park, PA: Pickwick, 1983), 167.

104. Farrer, *Faith and Speculation,* 22.

105. Ibid., 22, 70.

106. Farrer, *God Is Not Dead,* 92; Farrer, *Faith and Speculation,* 167.

107. Richard Harries, " 'We Know on Our Knees,' " in Hebblethwaite and Henderson, *Divine Action,* 28.

108. Farrer, *Said or Sung,* 109–10.

109. Farrer, *A Celebration of Faith,* 191.

110. Farrer, *Words for Life,* 39.

111. Ibid., 39.

112. Farrer, *The Crown of the Year,* 33.

113. Farrer, *A Celebration of Faith,* 192.

Chapter Six

FARRER'S SCRIPTURAL DIVINITY

Charles Hefling

When Austin Farrer chose the subtitle for *A Rebirth of Images,* his first full-length work in biblical studies, he provided a key to everything he wrote in that field. In this case, he wrote on the book of Revelation, but more exactly his subject matter was the composition of that book. Thus, he called his study *The Making of St. John's Apocalypse.* The key is "making." As no one knew better than Farrer, a "maker" is by derivation a poet, just as a poem, in Greek, is a thing made, and by studying the "making" of Revelation he was studying the process that gave birth to the book he called "the one great poem which the first Christian age produced."[1] How the making was done, how the poem came into being in the mind of the poet—that is what he set out to understand, using methods of investigation that had something in common with those of literary criticism. And he applied the same methods to other New Testament books as well, in the conviction that they too, in their own way, are poetic works.

What methods? A poem, like any piece of writing, comes to exist because its writer's mind operates in a certain way. Where the "making" of poetry is concerned, however, the operation is unpredictable and the product unique, inasmuch as poetic thinking is imaginative rather than logical. Only after the poem has been made, therefore, can the workings of a poet's mind be understood; and the only way to understand them is to repeat them, as it were, by retracing the imaginative process of making through a sympathetic exercise of one's own imagination. Such, in brief, was Farrer's approach to biblical interpretation—or "scriptural divinity," as he sometimes called it. He endeavored to reconstruct what the writers of the New Testament constructed, or, in his own phrase, to think their thoughts after them.

In *The Glass of Vision,* possibly his best book and certainly his most fascinating, Farrer discusses at length the kinship of scripture and poetry as results of the same sort of "making." In this chapter I will try to suggest something of what he discovered when he turned from theory to practice and applied his ideas to the exegesis of the New Testament text. Since every instance of "making" is different, generalizations will take us only so far, and we will have to examine a specific instance. The sample I have included is Farrer's reading of the Sermon on the Mount. Before we can get to that, however, some further introduction is necessary, and it may as well begin with a concession and a caution.

The concession: Scriptural divinity is not the side of Farrer's many-sided genius for which he is most esteemed, and it probably never will be. Even his most enthusiastic admirers are apt to moderate their enthusiasm when it comes to assessing his biblical studies. Was Farrer a brilliant philosophical theologian? Yes, indeed. An eloquent and powerful preacher? Yes again. An original and illuminating interpreter of scripture? Well.... Certainly his writings on the Bible are extraordinary, and they are original in the sense that they are neither derivative nor commonplace. There is nothing else quite like them. Yet their originality is such as to be a liability as well. What Farrer wrote about the New Testament was peculiar, not to say idiosyncratic, when he wrote it, and since then neither his unorthodox method nor his unorthodox conclusions seem to have commended themselves to the community of New Testament scholars. True, the march of scholarship has taken new and surprising directions since Farrer wrote, but if he were to join it today, he would still be out of step.

That, of course, does not mean that he is wrong. He might be a voice of sanity crying out in an exegetical wilderness, a prophet without honor among his own professional colleagues. Be that as it may, his work stands outside the circle of commonly accepted ways to interpret biblical texts. This does mean that nonspecialists can read it without mastering a lot of in-house technicalities, but it also means that readers who have any acquaintance with standard-brand scholarship will be that much more puzzled by the Farrer brand. Things might be easier all around if he had pointed out exactly where and why he was parting company with established schools and movements. Certainly he could have done so. He kept abreast of what other scholars were writing. But his own pages, unlike theirs, never carry a fringe of footnotes that advertise his erudition.

In a word, Farrer does not fit. There is no way to place him on a map of interpretative positions or to introduce him from a familiar viewpoint. I will do my best to describe and even to commend his scriptural divinity, but at the end of the day you can only read what he wrote and, in keeping with his own method, endeavor to think his thoughts after him. The endeavor is well worth the effort, but an effort it is. That is the caution. Understanding Farrer's biblical studies demands as much care and concentration as understanding his philosophical theology. *Reading* what he wrote about scripture is not difficult; far from it. Never does he perpetrate the kind of word-clotted Germanic sentences that seem to be the biblical scholar's stock in trade. Yet even the least technical of his book-length studies, a second commentary on Revelation that he wrote for a popular series, was pronounced too long, too difficult, and too speculative for publication. In reply, Farrer observed dryly, "How one is to write anything to the purpose about the Revelation on a level of greater facility, brevity, and common agreement, I cannot conceive."[2] The difficulty in this little commentary is due not to Farrer's exposition, which could hardly be clearer, but to the text on which he comments. Revelation is not, by anyone's reckoning, a book with a straightforward meaning.

"But that," you might be saying, "is neither here nor there. No doubt Revelation is a mysterious book, hard to interpret, a poem if you like; but it is also a special case. The other New Testament books, the gospels surely, are another matter." Are they? Farrer did not think so. To be sure, the Gospel of Matthew, say, is not a poem in quite the same way the Apocalypse is. But its "making" was not all that different, and it certainly was not simple. Its author's thinking was formal, symbolic, and in many respects strange. To rethink his thoughts is not the easy matter it might at first seem to be.

That the gospels did have authors, who did think, and whose thinking was anything but naïve — that, in brief, was the idea on which Farrer took his stand, and the idea he wrote much of his scriptural divinity to substantiate. It was also the idea that set him at odds with other scholars. St. Matthew and St. Mark — Farrer always used the traditional names for the evangelists — were not, as conventional wisdom had it, transcribers or compilers. They were "makers" who made whole books and made them *as* wholes. They exercised their own mental capacities of wit, intelligence, discernment, and above all, imagination; and the books that resulted can be understood only by entering imaginatively into the mental making that made them. Farrer thus had good reason to warn readers of his Revelation commentary that they cannot dip into it here and there, or skip the introduction, and expect to learn anything worth learning about what its author meant. The meaning is in the details, and it emerges only in the progressively unfolding pattern of the whole book. To summarize this commentary, then, even if that were possible, would defeat its purpose. And the same is true, for the same reasons, of Farrer's arguments about other books of the New Testament.

I have admitted that Farrer's interpretation of the New Testament is unconventional, and I have warned that understanding it takes work. For both these reasons, anyone who would write about it briefly, but not superficially, is at a disadvantage from the start. Faced with this problem, Farrer's biographer Philip Curtis decided to hand over the task to Michael Goulder, a New Testament scholar self-confessedly biased in Farrer's favor, whose solution was to select three seminal insights, one concerned with Revelation, one from Farrer's analysis of symbolic patterning in Mark, and one from his assault on the so-called "Q hypothesis."[3] In choosing this strategy, Goulder evidently had in mind the wholesale neglect of Farrer's work on the part of academic interpreters. His chapter in the biography aims to salvage what can be salvaged, and by doing so, to blunt the edge of the objection that Farrer invariably let his speculative brilliance get the better of judicious scholarship. The strategy I have adopted here is different.

In what follows, I will leave the professional exegetes to their own devices. They have their reward. My first assumption will be that readers are most likely to be interested in Farrer's scriptural divinity *as* divinity — that is, as bearing somehow on Christian belief and practice. Farrer himself would be the last person to segregate religious meaning from questions about the "making" of particular books, for reasons I will discuss later. A second assumption here will be that readers are more likely to be interested in what Farrer has to say about the gospels than in his views on the Revelation to John, although that is arguably the book he analyzes most brilliantly. Hence my choice of Farrer's analysis of the Sermon on the Mount, which is a fairly characteristic and more or less self-contained argument. But we have not quite finished with Revelation, even so.

MAKING LITTLE INTO MUCH

For Farrer the book of Revelation is the most striking instance of imaginative and poetic ways of thinking, but not by any means the only instance. Now one way to describe the making of Revelation, as he analyzes it, would be to say that the author has made little into much.

Nearly the whole book is an elaborate expansion of an older and much shorter text. If other New Testament authors indeed thought in similar ways, we might expect their books to be similar in this regard. Do we, then, find that little has been made into much in somewhat the same way? We do. But that is to anticipate. I need to make more explicit what I mean by "little into much."

In Revelation, the "little" is the gospel passage commonly referred to as Jesus' apocalyptic discourse. From this brief text, Revelation takes not only its theme but also the broad strokes of its outline. What St. John wrote is a meditation or commentary that develops the theme, and fills the outline, using imagery familiar to him (and to his first readers) from the Old Testament and certain other ancient Jewish writings. All this material he transformed, however; in Farrer's excellent phrase, there was a "rebirth of images," and the result is a formally intricate composition that grows line by line, paragraph by paragraph, out of the vision of the exalted Christ with which Revelation begins. And the fact that it grows in just the way it does, sprouting just these branches, these symbolic elaborations, these patterns of association, Farrer attributes to the imaginative mind of its maker.

Without going further into Farrer's interpretation, the point to note is that it is an interpretation which sees St. John not only as a poet but also as the creative or originative agency that explains the existence of most of what Revelation contains. Since the book is, in fact, a poem, that is what we should expect. Poems do originate in the minds of poets, who do turn little into much. But, to return to the question posed earlier, how far is the same thing true of the minds of the evangelists? Have they too made much out of little, and if so, how much out of how little? Take the Gospel of Matthew, for example. Everyone acknowledges that its writer borrowed much of what he wrote from a written source that still survives, namely the Gospel of Mark. That he had another source, which does not survive, has long been a basic tenet of mainline scholarship. This source, known as "Q," together with the Gospel of Mark, supplied between them just about everything the Gospel of Matthew contains. Such was, and still is, the scholarly consensus. Farrer demurred.

The scholarly consensus, he never tired of pointing out, begs a question. *If* the writer of Matthew was a more or less mechanical compiler of existing texts, then it is quite logical to hold that there must have been a text for him to draw on for the passages he added to the ones he drew from Mark. If he was *not,* however — if he was a genuine author and indeed a "maker" — then the expansion of Mark might well have been of his own making.[4] Of these two possibilities, Farrer considered that the first is less economical and, more importantly, that the second has far stronger support in the text of Matthew as it stands. His argument is that we have only to see what St. Matthew was doing, by retracing the steps his imagination followed as he wrote, to realize that what he wrote needs no other explanation. But what we will realize, otherwise stated, is that St. Matthew was doing something much like what the author of Revelation did. Each of them was unfolding the Christian gospel as it was known to him in written form, and taking from the Old Testament both the manner and the matter of the elaboration. As the report of Jesus' apocalyptic sayings stands to the book of Revelation, so the whole Gospel of Mark stands to the Gospel of Matthew. In each case, although the proportion is different, little has been made into much by one author's making.

The proportion of little to much is not the only difference, of course. St. Matthew did not set out to write a vision of heaven or the future but an account of earthly events. Accordingly, he did his making under one control that did not apply to the making of Revelation. It does not follow, however, that the imaginative process was different *as* imaginative. Like the poet of the Apocalypse, the gospel writers felt themselves obliged "to set forth the image of Christ as what the Spirit now shows it essentially to have been, rather than as what it could have been seen at the time to be."[5] The Gospel of Matthew sets forth the image of Christ "shown" to one mind, one imagination — St. Matthew's — and to meet that mind at work was Farrer's goal. If we wish to see how he reached it, only a specific example will do.

ST. MATTHEW AS "MAKER"

How did the Gospel of Matthew, a sequence of words, come to exist? That, it should be clear, is the sort of question we need to ask in order to take Farrer's scriptural divinity with the seriousness it deserves. We may suppose that someone, at some time, first wrote down the text we have. Call this person St. Matthew, as Farrer did, without prejudice to the question whether the gospel writer was or was not the same as anyone named in the text. What, then, was St. Matthew *doing* as he wrote, and more particularly as he wrote the section we now call the Sermon on the Mount? How did he move from one sentence to the next?

Since St. Matthew left no methodological report, any answer to such a question will necessarily be conjectural. We have to infer, from the result of a process, what the process was like. And the explanation we construct will inevitably be psychological. That is, it will be the reconstruction of a *mental* process, the acts of thinking that first put the words we have into the order we have them in. Such an explanation, as Farrer puts it, "is plausible if it can plausibly answer the question, 'What did the author intend?' And the plausibility will depend on our being able to see the author intending what is attributed to him."[6]

Now, "to see the author intending" is a metaphor. Interpretation is not an ocular event. What the metaphor refers to is the one criterion Farrer acknowledges for judging whether an exegetical hypothesis is correct. By way of illustration, consider a few of the explanations of the Sermon on the Mount that do *not* meet this requirement. First, there is what might be called the eyewitness hypothesis. St. Matthew was present when Jesus delivered the Sermon on the Mount; some time afterwards, he wrote down what he remembered hearing. On this hypothesis, his intention was simply to record his own experience. But while we may perhaps believe, on other grounds, that such was the evangelist's intention, there is nothing in the text itself that lets us "see" it. The same defect appears in the various hypotheses put forward by classical form criticism. St. Matthew, we are told, had available to him certain sources, perhaps written documents, which have since vanished. His intention, in this case, would have been to hand on the material handed on to him, without changing it significantly. But again, the text of the Sermon on the Mount as it stands gives no supporting evidence; quite the contrary, as we shall see. Yet a third possibility, now somewhat unfashionable, is the hypothesis of verbal inspiration. The Holy Spirit gave St. Matthew word-for-word instructions for writing. The evangelist moved his pen, but beyond that, he cannot be said to have had much intention of his own at all. None of these three explanations is an impossibility. Any of them *may* be correct. But none of them is plausible in Farrer's sense of the word. They cannot be confirmed by what we can "see" of the sermon *coming* into being as the embodiment in written words of an intended project.

None of the three, to put the point another way, makes St. Matthew an author, much less a poet. They all propose that for the most part he was mentally passive — that his mind functioned as a sort of conduit for transferring the form and content of the Sermon on the Mount from somewhere else onto the pages he wrote. Possibly so, but Farrer thinks otherwise. His assessment of St. Matthew's pages is that they are evidence for mental activity. They manifest the workings of a highly formal mind, which is to say a highly *formative* mind, similar in that respect to the mind of St. John. The very first page is a case in point. The Gospel of Matthew opens with a genealogy that turns out to be just the kind of exercise in numerological symbolism that we find again and again in Revelation. After this, admittedly, numbers are much less conspicuous. Still, the narrative that begins when the genealogy ends is no less formally structured, albeit in other ways. St. Matthew's intention went beyond just telling a story. He wrote his book according to a "grand design" that determines, in large part, the placement and the meaning of smaller-scale components. The narrative that opens in chapter 2 is not put together only, and sometimes not even mainly, by the chronological sequence of the episodes narrated. "Certain incidents, being the turning-points of the history, keep their true historical positions. For the rest we must be in large measure content not to know what followed what,"[7] because sequence is subsumed within a set of symbolic patterns that are "typological."

Since Farrer has been pigeonholed as a typological exegete, and typology has been the subject of acrimonious debate, we had better pause to take note of what he thought about it.[8] Nobody doubts that there is *some* typology in the New Testament. The prophet Elijah, for example, is mentioned in all the gospels as a prefiguration or foreshadowing — that is, a type — of John the Baptist; and the Baptist, conversely, appears on the scene as another or a new Elijah. In general, typology is a kind of comparative symbolism, imaginative rather than logical, which expresses the meaning of something or someone (in this case John the Baptist) in terms of something or someone whose significance is already familiar (in this case Elijah). Sherlock Holmes was thinking along such lines when he declared that Dr. Moriarty was the Napoleon of crime, and people who call Boston the Athens of America are likewise speaking typologically.

Farrer reasoned that where there are obvious instances of typological correspondence, there are likely to be others that are more cryptic. Perhaps they were plain to first-century readers, but in any case we no longer recognize them without exegetical help. His critics complain that the typology Farrer claims to be helping us recognize was largely the product of his own imagination, like faces seen in the clouds, not anything the original writer meant. This is not the place to debate the justice of the complaint, except to point out that typological thinking *is* imaginative. To suppose that it is a single, well-defined technique, the sort of thing that can be decoded using a step-by-step recipe, is to misunderstand it from the outset. There are no criteria for detecting typological symbolism that are "objective" in the sense that they bypass the interpreter's own mind. If St. Matthew's thinking was imaginative — as, at times, it assuredly was — then the only way to think his thoughts after him is to exercise one's own imagination, as Farrer assuredly did. Accordingly, the best plan, I think, will be to lay out part of Farrer's argument and let it stand on its own merits.

To return, then, to the question at hand: What is the typological design that gives a shape to the Gospel of Matthew as a whole? We can best consider it by starting from the purpose for which that whole was presumably written. St. Matthew is writing to convey to his readers a gospel, the "good news" enacted in Jesus. To proclaim this gospel and to communicate Jesus' significance are the same thing. But the "news," however new, has to do with God — otherwise, why proclaim it? — and so it has to be communicated in terms of what "God" already means. For St. Matthew and his earliest readers, "God" could only mean the God of Israel. To narrate Israel's origin and destiny was at the same time to describe God's relationship and dealings with God's people. St. Matthew, believing that in Jesus the same God was dealing with men and women in a new way, narrated this news imaginatively, and much of the imagery he uses is such as to show that Jesus was a new Israel. The primary image in his book is Israel itself, God's "son," the type of Jesus the Son of God.

This Israel-typology shows itself in two main ways, one narrative, the other formal and structural, which shade over into each other. On the narrative side, the Gospel of Matthew sets up parallels between certain events in the life of Jesus and certain stories about Israel's past. These stories, however, not only described events; they constituted a "biography" that defined or identified Israel. Not only the stories but also the writings that record them could themselves be regarded as embodying Israel's corporate identity. What it meant to be Israel had been set down in the five books of scripture attributed to Moses, Genesis through Deuteronomy, or in "Moses" for short. So "Moses" was not only the source of stories and narrative images that St. Matthew used typologically; it was itself the model for an overall structure. To put it the other way around, not only do incidents involving Jesus echo stories written in "Moses," but the design of the whole Gospel of Matthew reflects the formal configuration of "Moses" as a written text. What St. Matthew wrote about Jesus, the new Israel, was itself to be seen as a new "Moses."

Let us take this last point first. It has long been recognized that the Gospel of Matthew is divided into fairly well-marked segments. Some interpreters have argued that there are five of these, to symbolize the five Mosaic books. Although this argument never won general acceptance, Farrer thought its basic insight was sound, and offered an improved version. For one thing, he points out, we cannot infer that St. Matthew intended to write a new "Moses" if all we have is a number. By itself, quintuplicity might symbolize all sorts of things besides the fivefold Law. We need in addition to be able to find a section of the Gospel of Matthew that calls Genesis to mind, followed by a section with overtones of Exodus, and so on. Just such a series of typological correspondences does appear, when Farrer points it out, although he acknowledges that the correspondence grows fainter the further we read, as though St. Matthew's adherence to his "grand design" loosened as he went along.[9]

As for the evidence that lets us "see" St. Matthew's intention to write a new "Moses," I can only give a few samples. One unmistakable clue appears at the very outset. Translation obscures the fact, but the first verse is a title: "Book of *genesis* of Jesus Christ." And what follows is a genealogy very much like those that appear so frequently in the first book of the Bible. This first "book" of the Matthean "Moses" extends through the narratives of Jesus' infancy. As if to underscore the point, St. Matthew begins the familiar Christmas story in chapter 2 by writing, "Now the genesis of Jesus Christ was on this wise," and ends it by quoting the words "*out of Egypt* have I called my son," as if to announce that his "book of *exodus*" is about to start. Since this second "book" includes the Sermon on the Mount, we may be excused from following the series further, and concentrate on St. Matthew's "Exodus."

THE SERMON ON THE MOUNT

By the time the reader of the Gospel of Matthew arrives at the sermon in chapter 5, it has been set in a context of allusions to the Exodus narrative. The plainest of these clues is the setting. At the heart of the canonical book of Exodus is a long passage consisting of divine instruction delivered from a mountain (Exod 20–23). The book of Deuteronomy repeats the instruction, in the form of an address given by Moses that is even more plainly a "sermon from Sinai." If there is any doubt that between this mountain discourse and Jesus' mountain discourse the parallel is deliberate, we have only to recall that when the Sermon on the Mount begins, St. Matthew has already told us how Jesus, like Israel, went down to Egypt and returned; how at his baptism he passed through the waters, as Israel did at the Red Sea; and how, like Israel, he met with temptation in the wilderness—an episode to which I will return below. Any reader thoroughly familiar (as Matthew's readers were) with the story told in Exodus and retold in Deuteronomy might well anticipate that what would come next is what does: an extended announcement of directives for living as God's people, delivered in a sermon and at a mountain.

Within the "grand design" of Matthew, then, Moses' discourse at Sinai serves as a type of Jesus' address to the multitude. There was no need for St. Matthew to say so in as many words; the topography combined with allusions to a familiar narrative — Egypt, exodus, wilderness — make his intention plain enough. Nor is the typological correspondence of the two sermons limited to the similarity of their contexts. They are similarly structured. Moses' discourse begins with a list, the Decalogue, and goes on to comment and expand on its prescriptions at length. Jesus' discourse likewise begins with a list, the eight Beatitudes, and likewise goes on to comment. This last point brings us to Farrer's main thesis: The Sermon on the Mount is an expository sermon on a stated text, namely the Beatitudes. His argument for this interpretation will concern us below. First, it should be pointed out that Farrer does not think St. Matthew's meaning is that the Beatitudes are a new Decalogue, Christ's law, if law is understood in contrast with gospel. While the structure of the Sermon on the Mount reflects an Israel–Jesus typology, that is not the only typology St. Matthew works with. The character of the sermon's teaching is prepared for by another one, in which the type of Jesus is John the Baptist.

John and Jesus both preach a message of repentance. Both draw crowds to hear them. John, seeing the Pharisees and Sadducees coming for baptism, pronounces excoriation: "You brood of vipers!" Jesus, however, seeing another crowd, pronounces blessing: the Beatitudes. This antithesis of condemnation and blessing has, in turn, its own model in "Moses," where Farrer finds the solution to a small but interesting riddle. Why does the list at the beginning of the Sermon on the Mount have the number of items it has? We might expect to find ten, if St. Matthew was indeed working out a symbolic parallel with the "sermon at Sinai." But while the Beatitudes, as a list, do correspond to the Decalogue, their number alludes to a passage in Deuteronomy where a series of curses for disobedience to God's commandments is followed by a paragraph that sets out "all the blessings" for obedience. John the Baptist's speech to the "brood of vipers" corresponds to these curses; the Beatitudes correspond to the paragraph of blessings. "By the simple (and rabbinic) method of counting the occurrences of 'blessed,' 'blessing,' 'bless' " in Deut 27:1–8, Farrer observes that "we can bring 'all the blessings' promised in verse 2 out as eight in number."[10]

That is by the way, although it is typical of Farrer's approach. More important than the number is the organization of the Beatitudes. They are not eight miscellaneous blessings, assembled more or less at random, but a single prose-poem, unified by verbal resonances and thematic associations. Formally, Farrer discerns within the poem an opening three-line stanza, followed by two stanzas of two lines each. Then comes a refrain line that ends, as the first line does, with "theirs is the kingdom of heaven." Even in English, it is possible to test the artistic rightness of this analysis. Give serious thought to how the Beatitudes can best be read aloud, or listen to them spoken effectively (as the liturgical gospel on All Saints' Day, for example), and you may well agree with Farrer's artistic judgment. The sixth and seventh beatitudes, about peacemakers and the pure in heart, "want" to be said together, so as to bring out the rhythmic parallel of "see God" with "sons of God." Much the same is true of the fourth and fifth. On the other hand, a pause seems to be demanded after the first three beatitudes, since the fourth, about those who hunger and thirst for righteousness, shifts both rhythm and theme.

The eighth beatitude, with its echo of the first in a promise of the kingdom to those who are persecuted for righteousness' sake, marks a conclusion, and the next verse shifts plainly to what is plainly commentary. The teaching is applied to those who have just heard it taught: "Blessed are *you* when men persecute you." But as I have mentioned, on Farrer's interpretation, commentary does not end there. It continues through to the end of the sermon. Nor does he mean "commentary" in a loose or general sense. A commentary properly so called expounds each part of a given text in an orderly, systematic way, and the sermon does just that, although the fact is a little obscured in that St. Matthew does not follow the Red Queen's advice to begin at the beginning, go on to the end, and stop. As we have seen, he begins at the end, with the last beatitude in the list. Having done so, he continues to work his way backwards. His commentary takes up the second of the two-line stanzas, then the two-line stanza that precedes it, and finally the three-line stanza with which the Beatitudes open. Formally speaking, the structure of the commentary is "chiastic": Like the Greek letter *chi,* written X, it adds a second stroke to the first, but in the opposite direction. If the text to be explained runs *a–b–c–d,* an explanation in chiastic form would proceed in the order *D–C–B–A*. To us it seems odd to comment on a text in any order besides its own, but St. Matthew's readers would have found nothing unusual in reversing the order. The ancient formal device of chiastic sequence was part and parcel of early Christian imagination; Farrer shows it being used again and again in the book of Revelation, and elsewhere in the Gospel of Matthew too.

To show, however, that the Sermon on the Mount is such a commentary as I have described, the connections between its contents, taken in (reverse) order, and the text it comments on, the Beatitudes, would have to be shown in detail. As I pointed out earlier, it is with the cumulative detail of Farrer's analysis that his interpretive conclusions stand or fall. But the nuances of his own commentary on St. Matthew's commentary are more than a short commentary of mine can show. I have already had to leave out a good many of the threads he weaves into his argument that the Beatitudes themselves are a unity, not a mélange. It is impossible here to reproduce the richness of his discussion of the rest of the sermon. At most I can suggest the overall relations of whole and parts. For conveying such structural features, Farrer was partial to charts and tables, and since in this case he did not provide one, though he might have done so, I have done it for him on the following page. The reader will do well to have a Bible open at Matthew 5, to fill in what the chart omits.

The left-hand column lists the eight Beatitudes in reverse order, that is, the order in which the rest of the sermon expounds them. The right-hand column lines up some of the correspondences that link the topics of the individual blessings, grouped in stanzas as Farrer groups them, with the themes and phrases of the commentary. The three main divisions in the right-hand column have the names Farrer gives them. The division itself is not very controversial, although there are other ways to outline the sermon. The interesting question is how exactly it aligns with the first column.

At first, the match of item with item seems as if it is going to be quite close. Beatitudes 8, 7, and 6 do correspond to the first three topics of the commentary. The eighth was mentioned above; persecution for the sake of righteousness is the unifying theme. The seventh beatitude speaks of peacemakers, and the comment (1) specifies a peacemaking above and beyond what the Decalogue requires. Likewise, the comment (2) on the commandment against adultery sets out what true purity of

The Sermon on the Mount
as a Commentary on the Beatitudes

	BEATITUDES		COMMENTARY	
	REFRAIN LINE			
8	persecuted	*kingdom of heaven*	disciples as persecuted; disciples' character and conduct	
	THIRD STANZA		(SIX) LEGAL ANTITHESES (Matthew 5:21–30)	
7	peacemakers	*sons of God*	(1) killing (5:21)	(6) hatred of enemy (5:43)
				(5) retaliation (5:38)
6	pure in heart	*see God*	(2) adultery (5:27)	
			(3) divorce (5:31)	(4) swearing (5:33)
	SECOND STANZA		THREE PIOUS WORKS (Matthew 6:1–18)	
5	merciful	*obtain mercy*	(1) almsgiving (6:2–4)	
			remission of debts	
			(2) prayer (6:5–8)	
			The Lord's Prayer (6:9–15)	
4	hunger, thirst	*be satisfied*	(3) fasting (6:16–18)	
	FIRST STANZA		DISSUASION FROM WORLDLINESS (Matthew 6:19–7:12)	
3	meek	*inherit the earth*		
2	mourners	*consolation*		
1	poor in spirit	*kingdom of heaven*		

heart, which gains the sixth blessing, consists in. Then there is a digression of sorts. By what is surely a natural transition, the sermon turns to a topic related to adultery, namely (3) divorce, and the permission to divorce given in "Moses" is canceled. Then come three further practices — (4) swearing, (5) "an eye for an eye," (6) hatred of enemies — which likewise seem to be allowed, even recommended, according to what was "said to the men of old," and in each case permission is again canceled. The transitions here are intelligible enough. The expanded prohibition of adultery (2), which itself comments on the beatitude about purity, is linked by the teaching on divorce (3) with a further triad of legal antitheses (4, 5, 6). The whole list of six grows out of the first two, which build on the third stanza of Beatitudes; the final antithesis brings the series back to the theme of its first item, namely peacemaking; and the injunction to "be perfect, as your heavenly *Father* is perfect" returns to the corresponding (seventh) beatitude's promise that peacemakers will be called *sons* of God.

So far, so good. We turn to the next section of the sermon, which begins with chapter 6, and find that there is still correspondence at the outset. Compared with the section of legal antitheses, however, the section concerned with "three pious works" corresponds less closely. Like the section on legal antitheses, it branches into other topics, but here the digression leads further away from the parallel (second) stanza of the Beatitudes. That stanza promises blessing to those who hunger and thirst for righteousness and to the merciful. Chiastic ordering still prevails in the commentary, in that mercy is taken up first.

To see the correspondence, we need to know that "mercy" was commonly used as a synonym for almsgiving, in much the same way that we use "charity" today. Moving down the left-hand column, the fourth beatitude had spoken of hunger and thirst, words that suggest fasting, and before long fasting is discussed in the sermon. The connection is not merely verbal. In St. Matthew's milieu, someone who in spirit longed for righteousness and someone whose devotion took the form of bodily fasting would not have been thought of as doing entirely different things, though our own tendency to segregate the spiritual and the physical might lead us to think so. Fasting was a form of intercession as well as a form of asceticism (a point that will return below). Moreover, fasting together with prayer and almsgiving or "mercy" made up a traditional triad of pious works, and Farrer suggests that St. Matthew was associating this triad, as a unit, with the two beatitudes of the second stanza, also taken as a unit. That explains why, between the two pious works that most clearly parallel the two beatitudes (the fifth and fourth) of the second stanza, the commentary inserts a discussion of prayer, which in turn leads to a quotation of the Lord's Prayer.

When the commentary reaches the first stanza, the correspondence is broader, and I have not attempted to show it on my chart. Farrer maintains that this final part of the sermon, which he calls a dissuasion from worldliness, is a continuous whole, not a miscellany, despite what seem to be abrupt transitions. There are no lists, however, such as appear in the two previous parts, and the line-by-line method appears to have been abandoned. Nevertheless, it has the same overall purpose. "The Beatitudes being just so many promises of divine reward, the business of the Sermon is to show how they are to be secured," and that is what the final part continues to show. "The accumulation of heavenly reward is incompatible with the pursuit of earthly accumulation; one cannot serve God and mammon."[11] Those who do not secure this world's rewards—those who do receive the kingdom, the consolation, the inheritance—are those whom the first three beatitudes single out. Farrer thus finds it incontestable that in its dissuasion from worldliness the sermon is in line with the opening stanza of Beatitudes. At the same time, he observes that this final section of commentary derives as much from the Lord's Prayer, in the immediately previous section, as it does from the first stanza of Beatitudes further back. And he admits that, especially toward the end, this section is the least successful of the three as judged by literary or artistic standards.

THE GOSPEL OF MATTHEW AND THE MIND OF CHRIST

Such, in brief, is St. Matthew's commentary as Farrer analyzes it. Obviously, it does not consist of eight well-marked parts, one for each beatitude. Nor does it announce itself in the manner of preachers who begin by saying, "My text is taken from. . . . " Nowhere is the structure of the sermon merely mechanical. It allows of digressions and subsidiary lists. On the other hand, it is not haphazard either. There is no doubt that everything that follows the Beatitudes depends on them for its order and its content. Or at least there is no doubt for Farrer himself. Others, whether professional exegetes or not, have had their misgivings. How much of his argument is carried by genuine insight into what St. Matthew was thinking and how much by Farrer's own fancy, reinforced with his acknowledged skill at winsome paraphrase and rhetorical suggestion? In the example I have been discussing, the combination of many lines of argument—far more of them than I have mentioned—makes it hard to think he is altogether wrong. Deciding how far he is right depends on "seeing" the intention he sees, and at the end of the day, it is a decision his readers have to make for themselves. Even if we are convinced only tentatively, however, or only by the main lines of Farrer's case, it still carries some notable implications, and it will be more profitable here to take note of these than to deal with potential objections.

Most notable, perhaps, are implications that have to do with the "historical Jesus" debate, as raucous now as it was in Farrer's day. Readers will have noticed that my report on Farrer's treatment of the Sermon on the Mount did not report anything he says about its Preacher. That is because he says very little. Christ is mentioned, of course. But Farrer concentrates on the making of the sermon, and the gist of his analysis is that it was made by St. Matthew and by no one else, at least as regards its order or internal arrangement or form.

What about the content, then? It was not taken from the Gospel of Mark. No such content is there to be taken. But St. Matthew did not take it from some other source, such as the shadowy Q, either. It was suggested, called for, brought to mind by the Beatitudes with which the sermon opens. It grew out of them in an intelligible way, as the visions in the book of Revelation grew out of the depiction of Christ in glory with which St. John's book opens. The notion that the sermon "must" have existed, ready-made, in some such form as Q is supposed to have been, is not impossible. But in the first place, it is not necessary. In the second, it leaves out the factor that for Farrer is decisive — the writer's mind. And in the third, it cannot draw support from the sermon itself, as Farrer's analysis can and does. If we grant, however, the implausibility of St. Matthew's having copied the teaching of the Sermon on the Mount from an older document, it will likely occur to us to ask whether he made use of *any* source. The argument that makes Q superfluous can readily be turned into an argument to the effect that not just the structure or the phrasing but the very ideas expressed in the sermon originated in the mind of St. Matthew. In other words, it is a short step to the conclusion that Jesus never preached such a discourse as the Sermon on the Mount. The maker of the Gospel of Matthew, making little into much, made it up.

That step Farrer himself does not take. "Being, as I trust I may call myself, a believing Christian," he writes, "I take the Sermon on the Mount to be a tissue of Christ's spiritual teaching." Nevertheless, according to his own analysis, "the tissue was woven in one piece throughout by the Evangelist himself," on a framework that situates it typologically and patterns it thematically.[12] Even the Lord's Prayer? On *a priori* grounds, if any passage in the sermon is *likely* to be a quotation from an older source, the Lord's Prayer is. In itself, however, it consists of phrases all of which have antecedents in Jewish usage, and the fact that they were chosen and arranged in the way that appears in the sermon can be explained quite plausibly, along much the same lines we have already sampled, by their context and placement within a commentary on the Beatitudes. Farrer leaves the question open, but we are given the impression that his own answer would have been that, as likely as not, the Lord's Prayer owes as much to St. Matthew as the rest of the sermon does.[13]

By itself, obviously, ascribing the whole sermon to St. Matthew does not settle the main question — whether the Gospel of Matthew gives us "historical" information about Jesus. An argument for St. Matthew's veracity might accept Farrer's analysis of the sermon but insist that what he has analyzed is, after all, a speech and not a narrative. Presumably, on this argument, we may trust St. Matthew to have known what sort of speech would appropriately convey the substance of Jesus' teaching. Moreover, even if he did compose the sermon, St. Matthew was not, by ancient standards, any less a historian for that. Thucydides is well known for having put into his history speeches that, as he tells us, he composed so as to fit appropriately with the occasion he was describing. All this is true enough. But St. Matthew's poetic imagination did not exercise itself only on what he portrays Jesus saying. It shaped the narrative that portrays Jesus' actions as well. There is no space here for an extended example, but a brief one may serve to illustrate the point. We have only to turn back a page from the Beatitudes to the narrative of Jesus' three temptations.

Here once more we find a case of little turned into much. St. Matthew read in the Gospel of Mark a two-verse account of Jesus' being driven by the Spirit into the wilderness for forty days and tempted by Satan (Mark 1:12–13). His own account fills half a chapter. Tradition has assigned this much-expanded version of the story to the first Sunday in Lent, and it has been expounded in many devotional writings. Farrer himself wrote such a book, *The Triple Victory,* which, though not perhaps a scholarly work, does exemplify much the same approach we have already sampled. As we might expect, it lays out the imaginative process by which St. Matthew expanded St. Mark's two verses.

At the outset of *The Triple Victory*, Farrer declares it "utterly pointless to discuss what evidence St. Matthew had for the detail he supplies." The evangelist "is at no pains to reveal his sources, whereas he does all he can to make his meaning plain."[14] Among other things, St. Matthew builds the temptation episode into the same Moses typology discussed above. Two of the details he adds to Mark's account — that Jesus *fasted* and that his fast went on for forty days *and forty nights* — are significant in this regard. They bring the story into a typological correspondence with fasting that Moses undertook on two occasions. He fasted on behalf of Israel, to intercede and atone for their unfaithfulness — first, for their mistrust about sustenance, bread (Exod 16) and water (Exod 17), and for their putting God to the test; later, for their apostasy in worshiping the golden calf. In St. Matthew's story, the same three things — bread, tempting God, and false worship — are put before Jesus by Satan. The parallel is plain enough, and Farrer is hardly the first to notice it. His point is that St. Matthew *meant* it to be noticed: He put it there. Nor does the correspondence between Jesus' temptations and Israel's lapses stand alone. The first of Moses' two fasts appears in chapter 9 of Deuteronomy. The first of the three quotations with which Jesus answers the devil comes from the previous chapter — "Not by bread alone" (Deut 8:3). The next is a couple of chapters back — "Thou shalt not tempt the Lord" (Deut 6:16). Just above it is the third — "The Lord shalt thou serve" (Deut 6:13), which combines in Matthew with the greatest Deuteronomic text of all, "Hear, O Israel: the LORD thy God is ONE LORD" (Deut 6:4), to yield "him shalt thou serve ALONE."

There is no need to follow Farrer's interpretation further. Its direction will be clear enough, given what we have seen of his methods as applied to the Sermon on the Mount. Here too the accent falls on "making" and the evidence for it appears in formal and symbolic relations of parts to each other and to larger units of meaning. Here too the most comprehensive unit is a typology of Moses, in this case standing in and interceding for Israel, in correspondence with the new Israel and new Moses that is Jesus. Here too the associations of particular words and images — fasting, forty days and nights, bread, temptation — have been woven into a literary fabric that is all of a piece. Here too St. Matthew did the weaving. And here too the question whether he also spun the thread is left open. Farrer is quite sure about the mental route that St. Matthew took as he worked backward through the book of Deuteronomy from Moses' fast in chapter 9 to "Hear, O Israel" at the beginning of chapter 6. But whether St. Matthew's was the first mind to take that route he declines to say. "The Christian is free to believe that the mind of Jesus had been that way before; 'This' he may have said to his disciples 'is the path along which the Tempter drove me' — making a thoroughly Jewish and scriptural interpretation of his experience."[15] Jesus *may* have said something of the sort. That is as far as Farrer will go.

I have been pressing the "historical Jesus" question because, on the one hand, no thoughtful reader of the gospels today can be wholly oblivious of it, and on the other hand, because Farrer's literary approach seemingly leads to very skeptical answers. Goulder remarks that "bishops wished that Farrer would leave the Bible alone and return to philosophy where he was a redoubtable defender of the faith: cycles and paracycles and numerology in the Gospels could only serve to undercut the historicity of Jesus."[16] But with all respect to the bishops, whoever they were, that depends on what you mean by Jesus' "historicity."

The first point to note in this regard is that there is nothing to suggest that Farrer's own faith was disturbed by his studies in the making of the gospels, and everything to suggest that his theology remained thoroughly orthodox throughout his life. He does not ignore the question his own scriptural divinity raises. In *The Glass of Vision* he faces it squarely, acknowledging that unless he thought himself honestly led to recognize in Christ's historical teaching the seeds of Christian doctrine, he would cease to believe. "I cannot take these things simply from St. Peter and St. Paul" — or, he might have added, from St. Matthew. Nevertheless, he continues, he can accept their comment as "the absolutely necessary guide to what I may recover of the Lord's own oracles."[17] At the same time, it would seem that between dominical "seed" and later apostolic growth there is no sharp line to be drawn; or, if there is, Farrer himself never draws it. He does tell us in no uncertain terms how such a line should *not* be drawn. In an unusually outspoken essay, he declares himself disgusted with

> the inconclusiveness and the irresponsibility of supposedly scientific New Testament scholarship or supposedly neutral historical investigation of Christian origins. Great systems of organized and co-operative folly take the field and establish themselves as the academic orthodoxy of the day. To the detached observer, the theological or philosophical bias animating much of this work is obvious; sometimes the *parti pris* is unconscious, sometimes it is openly professed. There is no such thing as a neutral or purely scientific study of Christian origins....[18]

Elsewhere Farrer explains why there can be no "neutral" standpoint from which to retrieve a Jesus whose "historicity" is uncontaminated by anything that early Christians thought or felt about him. The reason is that "according to the canons of a sound historical procedure, we cannot establish what happened, we cannot establish the bare historical facts, without a personal understanding of Christ"[19] — as remarkable a statement, in its way, as Farrer ever wrote. Sound *historical* procedure requires a *personal* understanding of Christ. How much neater and more "scientific" it would be if we could first determine what St. Matthew thought on his own, then subtract that contribution from the book he wrote, and assign what is left over to the action of Christ on *his* own. But that is just what we cannot do. We have no way to get clear about

St. Matthew's mind, as distinct from Christ's actions, unless we already know what sort of thing Christ could or could not, would or would not, have said and done — unless, that is, we have already found the very thing we are setting out to find.

Farrer's example is the Palm Sunday gospel of Jesus riding an ass in triumphal procession into Jerusalem. This happened, St. Matthew says, to fulfill what Zechariah prophesied about Zion's king. Shall we say that Jesus, being weary, actually did ride, but that the procession is a pious exaggeration? Or that the whole episode was made up in order to supply the "fulfillment" of a messianic prophecy? Or, perhaps, that Jesus himself deliberately enacted the prophet's words? Well, *could* he have done that? "Only as we answer this question, shall we decide whether he sent for the ass and headed the triumph, or not."[20] How we do answer it will depend on how we understand Christ, and in the last account, the understanding will not be scientific but personal. "We know . . . what Christ is, by knowing what he has made of us: and we know what he has made of us, by knowing what he is."[21]

Farrer offers these methodological observations in a sermon that has as its text St. Paul's statement that "we have the mind of Christ" (1 Cor 2:16). It is a passage Farrer took very seriously. I have focused in this chapter on St. Matthew's mind, and on Farrer's extraordinary ability to enter that mind and think as St. Matthew may have thought. But he would add, turning from exegesis as such to scriptural divinity, that St. Matthew's mind was not St. Matthew's and his alone. It was the mind of Christ, and that in no mere figure of speech. Sometimes Farrer puts this in terms of revelation, sometimes inspiration, sometimes the indwelling of the Holy Spirit. Whatever theological terms he uses, the point is the same. We can understand other people only insofar as we share in what they are and enter into their personal being. So that if Christ is to be understood personally, and Christ was divine, then no purely "natural" endowment will suffice for understanding him. Without a "supernatural" gift, St. Matthew could not have known what he was writing about, and without some measure of the same gift, we cannot know it either: "[A]part from a claim, however modest, to a divine gift, the Christian can say nothing rational about the fact that he believes. . . . If the Gospel is credible to him it is that some touch of the supernatural presence which the Gospel describes acts in his mind."[22]

The discussion could be carried further by turning to Farrer's philosophical theology, and specifically to his argument that there is no "causal joint" between the natural and the supernatural, no line where one leaves off and the other takes over. For present purposes, I will only note that one application of this general principle is Farrer's unwillingness to specify a point where the "historicity" of Jesus gives way to St. Matthew's imagination. If Jesus' actions were the actions of someone who was a man and only a man, then the human mind they disclosed was only a human mind, his alone and not St. Matthew's. But if they were the actions of the Son of God, and if, as Farrer maintains, "to *be* the Son was to *know* the Father,"[23] then they are actions that disclose a mind truly and entirely human yet truly divine also. In that case, what it was to be the Son of God was not something that only Jesus himself could know. St. Matthew too could have the mind of Christ, and, Farrer would say, he did. Only insofar as he did have it could he write his book, according to Farrer's "canons of sound historical procedure." And his act of writing it was not separate from the historicity of Jesus. It was part of the historicity of Jesus.

All this flies in the face of what most of us, probably, have been told about how historical "objectivity" is achieved. But we cannot have it both ways. If we set aside the doctrine of the Incarnation until it has been "objectively" established by (say) the Jesus Seminar, then we rule it out in advance. Otherwise, it is a case of in for a penny, in for a pound: If we do accept the Incarnation as Farrer construes it, we have no reason to rule out in advance the extension of Christ's mind either to his evangelist or to ourselves. "The work of revelation, like the whole work of Christ, is the work of the mystical Christ, who embraces both Head and members."[24]

SCRIPTURE AND DIVINITY

Odd though it often is and difficult though it can sometimes be, Farrer's scriptural divinity belongs to a seamless whole. Pursue it in one direction, and it leads to what he thought about theological truths that are specifically Christian: the Incarnation, the Trinity, nature and grace, revelation. Pursue it in another direction, and it leads to matters that are more philosophical, indeed metaphysical: his understanding of the relation of finite and infinite, the essence of personhood, and the freedom of the will. Pursue it in yet another, and it leads to what is rather vaguely called spirituality. However intricate the patterns he examines, and however abstruse the typology, Farrer never loses sight of the fact that the texts he is analyzing are scripture and that God, in the words of the

Collect in the *Book of Common Prayer,* has "caused all holy scriptures to be written for our learning."

A book like *The Triple Victory* shows how we may, as the Collect goes on, "hear them, read, mark, learn, and inwardly digest them," precisely by thinking their writers' thoughts. Farrer brings all his erudition to bear, unobtrusively, on finding out what those thoughts were — in this case, what St. Matthew meant. What he *wrote* about the temptations "may for all we know rest on Christ's description of his early experiences; or, to take the opposite extreme, it may be St. Matthew's dramatization in a single scene of trials which beset Jesus throughout his ministry. . . . On either view, . . . the temptation-narrative promises to cast a unique light on the heart and mind of Jesus."[25] For just that reason, it casts light also on the hearts and minds of Christians — on their temptations, not insofar as these are moral difficulties such as beset everyone, religious or not, but as the typical temptations of God's sons and daughters.

It is the same with Farrer's discussion of the Sermon on the Mount. It is exegesis, it is literary analysis, it is scholarship; and it is *lectio divina,* divine reading, no less meditative for all its learnedness. Still, as I have observed more than once, it is in the details of the New Testament that Farrer finds its meaning, and so it is only by their detailed exposition that his own writings will promote an inward digestion of scripture. This chapter stands at a further remove. If it encourages anyone to search out some of Farrer's scriptural divinity and work through it firsthand, it will have done all it can do.

NOTES

1. Austin Farrer, *A Rebirth of Images: The Making of St. John's Apocalypse* (London: Dacre, 1949; Boston: Beacon, 1963; Gloucester, MA: Peter Smith, 1970), 6.

2. Austin Farrer, *The Revelation of St. John the Divine: Commentary on the English Text* (Oxford: Oxford University Press, 1964), v. This is the book Farrer wrote, although it had to be published separately.

3. Goulder's essay is chap. 11, "Farrer the Biblical Scholar," in Philip Curtis, *A Hawk among Sparrows: A Biography of Austin Farrer* (London: SPCK, 1985), 192–212. Readers for whom the phrase "Q hypothesis" is mysterious will find some explanation below.

4. Farrer's most extended discussion of his argument is "On Dispensing with Q," in *Studies in the Gospels: Essays in Memory of R. H. Lightfoot* (ed. D. E. Nineham; Oxford: Blackwell, 1955), 55–88. In the interests of brevity, I have passed over the bigger question that, in Farrer's opinion, defenders of Q beg — namely, what the author of the Gospel of *Luke* was doing. The Q hypothesis was originally

framed to explain how the Gospels of Matthew and Luke could have as much in common as they have, *on the assumption* that St. Luke could not have read what St. Matthew wrote. That St. Luke did read it is the heart of Farrer's position; his argument, discussed below, that the Gospel of Matthew can be explained without recourse to any source besides the Gospel of Mark is important, but only a part of the case against Q.

5. Farrer, *A Rebirth of Images*, 16. Farrer is referring to St. Mark in particular, but he would certainly allow that his point can be generalized.

6. Austin Farrer, *Saint Matthew and Saint Mark* (2nd ed.; London: Dacre, 1966), 192.

7. Austin Farrer, introduction to *The Core of the Bible: Arranged by Austin Farrer from the Authorized King James Version* (New York: Harper, 1957), 10. This book was published in England as *A Short Bible.* Farrer's introduction is by far the best popular statement of his position on scripture as a whole, and it is to be regretted that it is not more widely known.

8. The most succinct statement of his views is another neglected piece: "Important Hypotheses Reconsidered," *Expository Times* 67 (May 1956): 228–31.

9. Moreover, counting the segments by their content ends up with six, not five, which further weakens Farrer's argument. For reasons that will be mentioned later, however, the weakness does not affect his "Moses" typology insofar as it bears on the Sermon on the Mount.

10. Farrer, *Saint Matthew and Saint Mark,* 163n.

11. Ibid., 171.

12. Ibid., 178.

13. Austin Farrer, *The Triple Victory: Christ's Temptations according to Saint Matthew* (London: Faith; New York: Morehouse-Barlow, 1965), 111; also Farrer, *Saint Matthew and Saint Mark,* 170n.

14. Farrer, *The Triple Victory,* 10, 12.

15. Ibid., 16.

16. Goulder, "Farrer the Biblical Scholar," 193.

17. Austin Farrer, *The Glass of Vision* (London: Dacre, 1948), 41.

18. "Infallibility and Historical Revelation," in Austin Farrer, *Interpretation and Belief* (ed. Charles C. Conti; London: SPCK, 1976), 151–64, at 162.

19. Austin Farrer, "A University Sermon" (the Hulsean sermon, preached November 14, 1948), Appendix 1 in Curtis, *A Hawk among Sparrows,* 232–39, at 236.

20. Ibid., 237.

21. Ibid., 239.

22. Austin Farrer, "Revelation," in *Faith and Logic: Oxford Essays in Philosophical Theology* (ed. Basil Mitchell; London: Allen & Unwin, 1957), 84–107, at 104.

23. "Very God and Very Man," in Farrer, *Interpretation and Belief,* 136.

24. Farrer, *The Glass of Vision,* 41.

25. Farrer, *The Triple Victory,* 11.

Chapter Seven

FARRER'S PREACHING

"SOME TASTE OF THE THINGS WE DESCRIBE"

O. C. Edwards and David Hein

Austin Farrer preached a high doctrine of the priestly calling. Referring to the Christian apostle, bishop, or priest, he asked, "Has not Christ promised to bless the preaching of his word, and the ministry of his sacraments? Confess to me and you shall be absolved, listen to me with faith and you shall hear God speak."[1] And on another occasion, after describing the ideal priest as "a walking sacrament," he told his audience that the priest "must keep the congregation supplied with its staple diet: he must keep giving them some word from God."[2] At other times, however, Farrer was capable of expressing a clear awareness of the limitations of preaching: "I do not need to tell you that all preaching is folly: no one can speak worthily of divine themes."[3]

This chapter will offer a historical and critical perspective on Farrer as a preacher and attempt to throw some light on the distinctive features of his sermons. It will also indicate how his sermons might be employed as sources within the conscientious Christian's own spiritual life. Readers may recall the moment in *Absolute Truths,* one of Susan Howatch's Church of England novels, when Bishop Charles Ashworth needs shoring up following a difficult confession he has made. The wise spiritual director Jonathan Darrow advises him not to " 'attempt to read any new books; stick to the old favourites. A sermon a day by Austin Farrer will do you far more good than the latest volume from some learned German theologian.' "[4] The authors of this chapter see no reason to restrict the range of beneficiaries to fictional prelates.

THE OCCASIONS OF FARRER'S PREACHING

For the most part, the occasions of Farrer's preaching were related to his duties in the Oxford colleges in which he spent his ministry after his curacy. Every Sunday in term-time, he preached a one-paragraph sermon at the early Eucharist. These "Farrergraphs," as they were called, represent his way of conforming to the rubric in the 1662 rite that called for a sermon — a rubric that he obeyed at early services more scrupulously than did most priests of his day.

The three terms of the Oxford academic year were each eight weeks in length. With the exception of the "long vac" of summer, vacations of six weeks separated these academic terms. Because at Christmas and on other important occasions Oxford students were away on vacation, Farrer did not always have the opportunity to preach these brief sermons in his college chapel. In order to round out a set of these paragraphs for the full year, he provided some additional sermons to cover major events in the liturgical calendar. In 1952, he published a collection of these paragraphs as *The Crown of the Year: Weekly Paragraphs for the Holy Sacrament.*

Farrer also preached sermons at college for the Sunday Evensong services. Evensong sermons were of two orders. For four Sunday Evensongs of each term, he preached short addresses, which were usually based on scripture. Forty of these sermons were published posthumously as *Words for Life* (1993). They are midway in length between the Farrergraphs and his full-scale sermons: Each is approximately two small printed pages in length.

At the other four Sunday Evensongs each term, Farrer divided his labors with visiting clergy: He preached two full-scale sermons each term, and visitors preached two. Of course, on various Sundays and holy days during the year, Farrer, much in demand as a preacher, ventured beyond his own college chapel to hold forth in the pulpits of other churches, both within the city of Oxford and elsewhere in England (and, rarely, abroad).

From his full-length sermons preached in these different venues come the four principal collections of his sermons: *Said or Sung* (1960), *A Celebration of Faith* (1970), *The End of Man* (1973), and *The Brink of Mystery* (1976). The average length of these sermons is three-and-a-half longish printed pages. Read aloud at a moderate pace, each sermon would have taken approximately fourteen minutes to deliver. From the sermons included in these four books, the theologian Leslie Houlden culled and edited a new collection published in 1991 as *Austin Farrer: The Essential Sermons*. Much of the analysis that follows will focus on the sermons in this volume.

The publication of sermons in books changes the messages from oral into written communication and presupposes an audience of the world at large rather than a congregation of the gathered faithful. While good sermons have a general applicability that often makes publishing them worthwhile, reading them in cold print can obscure the transaction with the live congregation that the sermon's author originally had in mind. Knowing the occasion on which a sermon was preached invariably assists the reader's effort to understand its purpose. Unfortunately, in the case of Farrer's sermons, the author and his editors have not always left clear indications of the occasions for which these sermons were first written.

Taking a representative sample, the fifty-two sermons in Houlden's 1991 collection, we note that fifteen are reported to have been preached at Trinity College, where Farrer served as chaplain for twenty-five years, and eight at Keble College, where he was warden from 1960 until his death in 1968. For ten of the others, no place is stated; but internal evidence, such as the preacher's reference to himself as "your chaplain," indicates that at least two of these sermons (nos. 22 and 30) were products of Farrer's years at Trinity. Regrettably, no setting is indicated for a sermon with a rare reference to women in the congregation (no. 44).

Not all of these fifty-two sermons were delivered in the preacher's own college. Seven were for Pusey House, an Anglo-Catholic theological college, and thus principally directed toward men seeking ordination. Several of these sermons were parts of ongoing series on particular topics. Three sermons were for Christ Church, which was both a college chapel and the cathedral of the Diocese of Oxford; two of these were Christmas sermons. Two others were for the university church, St. Mary the Virgin, although whether they were formal university sermons is not stated.

Of the other sermons, one was preached at the church of the Cowley Fathers in Oxford; one was preached at Little St. Mary's, an Anglo-Catholic parish in the university section of Cambridge; and one was preached at a church where a priest was saying his first mass. Two were preached in London: one at St. George's, Bloomsbury, and the other for the Guild of Mercers in their chapel. This collection also includes a sermon given on an old endowment, the Hulsean, at the university church of Cambridge, Great St. Mary's. And another sermon (no. 50) was part of a service that was broadcast by the BBC from a parish near Oxford.

For most of these sermons we are not told the year in which they were preached, their text (if any), their date in the church year, or even the liturgical event of which they were a part. The lack of these data makes it difficult to form a complete picture of how Farrer went about the task of sermon preparation.

BEGINNING WITH A "BIT OF REALITY"

Most information about his preparation comes from the sermons themselves. Many of them open with a focus on what one student of the art of preaching refers to as a "luminous bit of reality." Like a playwright, the preacher "selects a portion of the creation and unfolds it," works hard to develop this piece of reality in a consistent and accurate manner, and then tries "to excite the audience to perceive more and more meaning in it."[5] In his sermons Farrer often invites his congregation to think about some aspect of ordinary life — a "bit of reality" — in such a way that his listeners will be drawn to contemplate the larger issues that he wanted them to reflect upon.

Thus, for example, he bids them consider two ways of being aware of the attributes of paintings. The dealer in art supplies has a certain kind of knowledge appropriate to his work; the artist has a familiarity that is proper to hers. Farrer establishes this distinction in order to bring out the difference between a scientist's approach to the universe and a theologian's understanding of creation. The scientist, like the supplier of artists' materials, will have an unrivaled knowledge of the physical properties but will have not a "syllable to say" about "what the Creator's will intends and achieves."[6]

In a similar fashion, Farrer begins a sermon by speaking of the peculiar wisdom of a man with whom he once shared a plot of ground on which they raised vegetables. His fellow gardener, Farrer recalls, had the benefit of having "received an agricultural, I a merely cultural, education." Farrer's experienced colleague not only knew "when to plant and where to sow"; he also applied a wisdom apparently gleaned from hoary maxims.

The contradictory nature of these gardening proverbs thwarted Farrer's desire to gain a similar wisdom: "[A]ll horticultural actions whatsoever," he learned, "could be proverbially justified." And, most unhelpfully, this knowledgeable gardener could not say how he knew which proverb he should rely on in a particular instance. But what he planted grew and flourished. Slowly Farrer perceived the underlying principle at work: "[H]is wisdom did not lie in the maxims he cited, but in the art of steering a course between the marks which, as it were, the maxims set up."[7]

That's all in just the first paragraph of this sermon. Having engaged the listener's interest with this story from the philosopher's own experience in getting his hands dirty and being confounded in the process, Farrer plows a deeper furrow, uncovering truths about the Christian's relationship with God. How does God assure us of God's presence and life within us? Not by any one means only; but as the Christian attends to the witness of the saints, partakes of the sacraments, reflects on the meaning of Christ's words and works, and lives a life of practical obedience, he or she will begin to perceive the presence of grace.

In another sermon, Farrer talks about a magnifying glass and the work it performs in igniting tinder. "The fire is kindled by no business of ours, no preparing or striking of matches on our part, but by sunlight falling through the burning-glass of faith." The sunlight is nothing other than the light of grace — that is, "nothing but Jesus Christ, God and man, burning his way through the wall of the heart."[8]

In a sermon titled "All Souls' Examination," before he takes up the serious theme of human sin and divine forgiveness, Farrer mentions his youthful belief that "fellows of All Souls [an Oxford college] were selected by a simple test: they were given cherry pie to eat." Those candidates who spat out the stones "were disqualified for boorishness"; those who swallowed the stones were disqualified "for smoothness." The real contest "lay between those who, with various degrees of elegance, got the cherries into their throats and the stones into their spoons."

Such an amusing opening gambit by their preacher must have tempted most of Farrer's student congregants to listen a bit more attentively, wondering where their chaplain would move next in his discourse. He goes on to mention an actual examination set by the All Souls examiners: a paper dealing with the subject of sin. But this choice of an exam question was scarcely any better than the ordeal by cherry pie, Farrer remarks, because "sin is not a subject, not, that is, a subject by itself; it is simply the negative aspect of my relation to God" — and the preacher-theologian is on his way.[9]

Having started his hearers thinking, Farrer would lead them through a series of ideas and images in which he developed his thought by association rather than by woodenly working his way down a rigidly logical set of points. Leslie Houlden alludes to this style of movement when he writes that although Farrer's "sermons often began with an amusing story or striking image, they would flow on into deep waters where not every hearer could easily follow and their course could be sinuous."[10] Avoiding what has come to be called the "deductive" method of sermon development, Farrer employed a more conversational flow of thought. He did not try to batter listeners with argument but rather enticed them with the lure of intriguing vignettes and perceptions expressed in well-crafted language. This technique anticipated what David Buttrick was later to refer to as sermons that develop by "moves" rather than by points.[11]

To cite another example: In "The Day's Work," Farrer begins by speaking of his aunts' somewhat disturbing practice of parceling out the facial features of their nieces and nephews among various ancestors. Thus young Austin's right eyebrow turns out to be "the property of cousin Hannah Maria," a puzzling assignment of provenance given his cousin's "collateral" relationship to him. By the time his aunts have finished dividing him up, Austin is no more than "a ragshop of patches . . . synthetic to the last drop." In a like manner, the mature Farrer asserts, do biblical scholars assign the themes of New Testament literature. They especially love to dissect the Fourth Gospel, attributing John's ideas not to his inspired mind or to his own experience but to Jewish rabbis, Greek philosophers, and the Essenes.[12]

But here in John 9, observes Farrer, in this account of Jesus healing the man born blind, the evangelist John realistically reports a simple fact; and "the ideas in the chapter are all irrelevances, pushed in by people who cannot face the impact of facts, but cloud them over with words and theories." The disciples begin the theorizing by asking if blindness in this case was divine punishment for sins that God had foreseen that the blind man would commit. Or, they ask, was the blindness divine punishment for the sins of this man's forebears? Neither, says Jesus; and he steps forward to associate the will of God with the act of healing. But no sooner is the man healed than confusion breaks out: Was this the man who had been blind? Can a sinful man who does not keep the Sabbath have healed him?

In our own day, too, Farrer notes, the perversity of human beings is such that they will not see "the work of Christ . . . in healing sores and making saints." Instead, disunion rules, as Christians quarrel over doctrine and polity. Such ecclesiastical debates have their place, but, "in the end, [we can] commend the doctrines and institutions of religion by nothing else but this, that they are channels [that] convey . . . the efficacious grace of Christ."

And, unlike Christ, people are often blind to the opportunities in their midst to do good. Instead of feeling annoyed by someone else's trouble or discouraged by a person's faithlessness, Christians might see such an occasion as "an opportunity the heart of God covets." We do well to remember, "[H]e has appointed me, with whatever capacity I have, to be his instrument."

Farrer concludes by suggesting spiritual practices that enable sight and better equip us to act in the world: "Above all, we are blind: blindfold in our prejudice, blinkered by our preoccupations, drugged in our self regard.... And... God longs to open our eyes." The cure for our blindness is "to practise looking through the eyes of Christ." We carry out this practice in "the contemplative art of prayer, when, invoking [Christ's] aid, we turn over quietly what we know of God or have just read in the Scriptures." Contemplating the meaning of a text such as this passage from the ninth chapter of John, we "try to see our lives and our neighbours in the light of [God's gracious activity], and what we have seen, to love and to adore."[13]

THE SOURCES OF FARRER'S PREACHING

While the foregoing is a good example of a Farrer sermon, it is in one important respect atypical. Most of the sermons in the Houlden collection are not so clearly based on a reading from the lectionary. More representative of the entire corpus is a sermon titled "Conscience" (no. 29), which Farrer preached at Pusey House during the Michaelmas term of 1966.[14] This sermon is essentially a lecture on the Christian's conscience as a witness to God. Its two biblical references are brief and largely incidental to the whole.

Although this sermon may be an extreme example, it is by no means unique. Few of Farrer's sermons so plainly grow out of reflection on an appointed reading as does "The Day's Work." While a reader could try to figure out whether any of the biblical references in a given sermon was the text on which Farrer based that sermon, he or she would seldom achieve certainty. If a student of Farrer's sermons went on to match the identified text with an appointed Evensong lection for a Sunday in the 1662 prayer book calendar and thus discovered the liturgical date on which Farrer preached his sermon, this effort would rarely prove worthwhile, because his sermons contain little reference to the church year.

In offering his own view of the task of the preacher, the biblical scholar Reginald Fuller is careful to hold Word and sacrament together: The purpose of liturgical preaching is "to extract from the scripture readings the essential core and content of the gospel" and then "to penetrate behind the day's pericope [lesson from scripture] to the proclamation of the central act [of God's redemption in Jesus Christ] which it contains." In this way, "the central act of God can be made the material for recital in the prayer of thanksgiving [in the Communion service]."[15] This approach enhances the worshiper's grasp of the fundamental unity of the Christian *kerygma*.[16] That Farrer was thoroughly familiar with this homiletical method is evident from his work in "Four Bible Sermons," a series he preached at Pusey House Chapel in 1963 on Sexagesima (the old name for the second Sunday before Lent), Quinquagesima (the Sunday before Lent), Lent 1, and Lent 2.[17]

His opening sentences in the first sermon make it clear that he recognized the hazards of the prescribed method: "Our assignment is to preach Bible sermons, in exposition of the set liturgy. The Catholic-minded preacher" — like Farrer — "is expected to comment on the inspired wisdom of the Church" in selecting liturgical texts. "Such a line of approach is not always convincing," however, because sometimes the scripture choices either individually or in combination with one another seem to make little sense, and the preacher feels constrained rather than liberated by his texts. Farrer remarks that in selecting this day's readings, "the Church (that mysterious lady) appears to have bandaged her eyes, and pulled today's portions out of a chance lot thrown into an old hat; and what is worse, to have torn one of them in half in extracting it, so that the lesson begins somewhere in the middle of the story."[18]

In any case, Farrer proceeds to preach on the passage he says begins in the middle of the story. He first comments, "It's a sore trial for a subdeacon [who would have read this epistle, 2 Cor 11:19–31, at a solemn high mass] to stand and shoot the opening line, 'Ye suffer fools gladly, seeing ye yourselves are wise.' " Those who struggle to understand Paul's meaning in this sentence have a difficult time of it. Indeed, Farrer observes, "they can't have a clue, unless they have looked up the full text beforehand." And even "if they have looked it up, they probably still haven't a clue. What can it be about?"[19]

Of course Farrer goes on to explain this text and to apply its meaning to the lives of his listeners. In other words, he does what a liturgical preacher today would do. The point is that Farrer could preach liturgical homilies but generally chose not to do so. A minority of his sermons are efforts to help his congregation to understand their lives in the light of passages of scripture that he interprets to them.

One of the authors of the present chapter found the joy he experienced in reading these sermons to be somewhat surprising, because most of them do not fit his own definition of a sermon, a formula he proposed in a homiletics textbook that he wrote over twenty years ago. After noting that a "sermon is a speech delivered in a Christian assembly for worship by an authorized person," he points out that a sermon "applies some point of doctrine, usually drawn from a biblical passage, to the lives of the members of the congregation with the purpose of moving them . . . to accept that application and to act on the basis of it."[20]

Farrer's sermons fail to fit this definition because most of them do not obviously draw their points of doctrine from scripture. While his theological points are certainly consistent with and informed by biblical teaching, usually they are not explicitly based on a passage of holy writ. In their essential form, then, most of his sermons are, to employ the jargon, neither *expository* — that is, based on a passage of scripture such as a lection, which is explicated and applied to listeners' lives — nor *textual* — based on just one biblical verse — but *topical.*

Farrer's topics, however, are invariably matters of lasting ethical or theological interest rather than engaging topics taken from the day's newspaper. What he said in his preface to *Saving Belief* applies almost equally as well to his sermons: "There is nothing in these pages about nuclear bombs, artificial insemination, free love, world government, Church reunion, or the restyling of public worship. Those who seek after news may save their pains."[21] Indeed, his choice of perennially relevant subjects accounts in part for the lasting value and appeal of his sermons.[22]

An American theologian makes a similar point about the sources and subjects of Farrer's sermons, but he states the matter somewhat differently: "Farrer often preaches on scriptural texts," but he preaches "*through* them rather than *about* them."[23] He derives "central Christian themes" from "unexpected lectionary assignments." Thus the story of Elisha and the widow's pot of oil (2 Kgs 4:1–7) leads to a discussion of "the difference between forms of worship and the Spirit who fills these forms," and thence to a treatment of the Christian believer as a member of Christ's body, and finally to the preacher's own suggestions regarding prayer. The story in 1 Sam 28 about Saul and the witch of Endor prompts Farrer to talk about God as the universal Cause, about discovering the divine will, and about the meaning of Christ's passion and resurrection.[24]

FARRER'S SERMONS IN HISTORICAL PERSPECTIVE

The style and content of Farrer's sermons stand in sharp contrast to the form and focus of sermons by ancient and medieval Christian authors. By the twentieth century, Anglican preaching had moved far past both the expository form of the patristic homily and the textual form of the "thematic" sermon (whose text was known as a *thema*) of the high Middle Ages. Nevertheless, a listener to Farrer's homilies may at times hear echoes of his distant predecessors.

Farrer was a learned student of the church fathers and an adroit interpreter of the biblical literature, even if most of his sermons were not explicitly aimed at expounding scripture. And, while he did not follow the medieval friars' practice of dividing and subdividing sermons into points that were proved by citing biblical, patristic, and classical authorities, he was frequently in the habit of providing sermon illustrations: narrative examples known as *exempla*.[25] His sermons resemble medieval English preaching in their use of such exempla as saints' lives and humorous anecdotes. Farrer had his own list of holy but human saints, heroes, and martyrs, whom he regularly set forth as models worthy of imitation. And, as was shown in our earlier examples, he relished dipping into a treasure chest of droll and pointed stories, some of which, as in the Middle Ages, involve family members. Unlike the medieval mendicants, however, he typically used these stories to introduce rather than to expand on the main points of his sermon.[26]

We can also see that in some important respects Farrer's sermons bear affinities with the homilies of one of his most celebrated antecessors, the Anglican divine Richard Hooker (1554–1600). Both men appealed to the intellectual and moral faculties of their hearers, not merely to their emotions. Both employed a highly literate style capable of conveying matters of theological subtlety. Lacking prophetic zeal and exciting modes of delivery, both sought to persuade through reason. Both focused on themes that were foundational and practical, such as the generosity of God's grace and the capacity of the Lord's Supper to strengthen faith. Both men preached sermons that were nourished by their authors' deep reservoirs of spirituality and devotion to the church and its sacraments.[27] For each theologian, *participation* — what Hooker referred to as "that mutuall inward hold which Christ hath of us and wee of him" — was a key concept.[28] Lastly, what has been said of Hooker could also be said of Farrer: He supplied "far too much solid meat in every one of his sermons to be easily digested by his listeners."[29]

Without intending to draw any clear lines of inheritance, we might also note that in his kindly spirit, gentle humor, and learned style, as well as in his use of catchy openings and striking images, Farrer resembles the eminent preacher Jeremy Taylor (1613–67), one of the Caroline Divines. Taylor, writes one student of English preaching, "taught that theological roots must bear ethical fruits."[30] Both men emphasized the practical unity of sound theology, sacramental piety, and faithful obedience. Both reckoned seriously with the concept of holy living as an orientation of the human will to the will of God, which is concretely revealed in the incarnate Word.[31] For both Taylor and Farrer, the life of Christian faith and practice is lived in relation to the eternal love of God in the Trinity.[32] An influence on later Anglicanism through his writings and through the example of his own lived faith, Taylor served in particular as an important model of Anglican identity for the leaders of the nineteenth-century Oxford Movement.[33]

As we have seen, it was rarely Farrer's primary homiletical purpose to engage in the sustained exposition of sacred scripture. Much of the reason for this fact is historical. In the seventeenth and eighteenth centuries, largely under the influence of John Tillotson (1630–94), archbishop of Canterbury, Anglican sermons began to look more like the essays written by Joseph Addison (1672–1719), Richard Steele (1672–1729), and Samuel Johnson (1709–84). After 1700 and continuing into Farrer's own day, within much of English preaching the essay was the dominant sermonic form.

As time went on, the substance of these sermons grew more varied. Later preachers would continue to deliver essay-type sermons without also copying the reductionistic rationalism and moralism of Tillotson and his eighteenth-century followers. While it is true that Farrer's sermons often develop theological topics within an essay form, there is nothing arid or only incidentally Christian about his pulpit essays. An orthodox preacher who faced contemporary challenges with both wit and devotion, Farrer was able to achieve a variety of interesting ends while working within a form that stressed the literate exploration of ideas.

That he was able to accomplish these ends so effectively is largely attributable to his own unique gifts. In preaching, as in much else, he was sui generis, and his distinctive approach to Christian philosophy is a recognizable element not only of his hard-to-classify theology but also of his extraordinary sermons. But shaping influences are still discernible in his work. Indeed, we would be remiss if we failed to recall that, between the departure of Tillotson and his long-winded, flat-footed followers and the arrival of Austin Farrer, there appeared on the English pulpit scene both the evangelicals and the Tractarians.[34]

Descended from the evangelicals by birth — his father was a Baptist minister: a preacher of the gospel — Farrer was a Catholic who maintained an unusual reverence for the preached Word.[35] His sermons do not neglect the Reformers' central theme of human beings' sinfulness and their need of Christ's grace. Related to the Tractarians by his own choice, Farrer poured his energies into crafting sermons that engaged the hearer's mind and heart in a fresh consideration of the possibilities of Christian living. The warden of a college named for John Keble (1792–1866), he preached that, as one student of the Oxford Movement has phrased it, "the sacramental life nourished the sacrificial life."[36]

FARRER'S PREACHING IN ITS TWENTIETH-CENTURY CONTEXT

The church historian Horton Davies has identified several functions of preaching, each of which he sees as characteristic of a particular homiletical type in the first two-thirds of the twentieth century. Considered in the light of Davies' typology, the overwhelming majority of Farrer's sermons appear to fall within the apologetical, moral, and devotional categories.

The aim of apologetical preaching, says Davies, is "to remove the errors and doubts that stand as barriers to belief." Apologetical preachers try to show that the Christian gospel is congruent with reason; they might attempt to "demonstrate that the Gospel as transforming truth fulfils man's nature and destiny."[37] Well-known apologetical preachers of the twentieth-century Church of England were W. R. Inge, H. Hensley Henson, and C. S. Lewis.[38] Able and eager to defend Christian doctrine in the face of intellectual assaults upon its claims, Farrer engaged, for example, in the science-versus-religion controversy still alive in that more positivistic age. Preaching with both candor and empathy, he often gave a far more sophisticated defense of the faith than probably most of his hearers would have thought possible. His sermons alerted students to the fact that just because they had heard about Christianity all their lives did not mean they really understood it.

The purpose of moral or ethical preaching — a type represented in some of the most famous statements of the episcopal leaders William

Temple and George K. A. Bell—is "to help [persons] to rediscover [the truth] that their near or remote neighbours of every class are brothers [and sisters] in Christ."[39] Farrer's sermons frequently have to do with the Christian life, and they include astute discussions of both ethical behavior and ascetic discipline. "His sermons on particular virtues and vices—pride, responsibility to friends, candor, caprice, chastity, Lenten duty, money, commitment—are anything but vague," a theological commentator writes. "They are disquietingly specific in their rebukes and their prescriptions alike."[40]

Devotional preaching, Davies says, ought "to teach the holy love of God so as to elicit the response of adoration." In the early years of the twentieth century, the English Congregational minister J. H. Jowett was an outstanding practitioner of this variety of preaching.[41] A strong devotional emphasis is characteristic of virtually all of Farrer's pulpit efforts. God's loving and sovereign will — active in creating and sustaining, in forgiving and sanctifying—is a persistent leitmotif in all the genres within which Farrer worked. The last sentences of a Farrer sermon often express this theme of God's holy love and our proper response by building toward a traditional ascription to the Trinity.

As a recent author has noted, however, "even [this] Trinitarian doxology is no afterthought; it is woven into the sermon and is one of [Farrer's] means of leaving his congregation in heaven as well as on earth."[42] At the conclusion of "The Painter's Colours," for instance, Farrer speaks of God as the Painter, in whom we "shall not deeply and honestly believe until we are willing to be liquid colours under his brush; and how little do we even pray for that, let alone live it!" This union of creaturely wills with the will of God is what heaven is: "a life in which the very countenance of God is constantly and visibly portrayed in the changing colours of his creatures' lives." In heaven "the blessed by their whole existence set forth the manifold mastery of God: and by their lives as well as with their lips ascribe as is most justly due to God the Father, Son and Holy Ghost, one deity in three persons, all might, dominion, majesty and praise, through ages everlasting."[43] In his final sentences, the preacher, by taking his hearers to heaven, gives them a richer appreciation of the possibilities of life on earth.

By catching up his listeners in this manner, by leaving them "in heaven as well as on earth," Farrer repeatedly conveys a sense of their participation by grace in the life of the Trinity and of God's condescension to share the life of God's creatures. "For God identifies himself unrestrictedly with every one of his creatures," Farrer writes; "he thinks and knows them from within, his creative thought is expressed in their very being; for else, how should they exist?" God's creation is not a long ago, faraway masterstroke but an ongoing achievement: It is "a coming down from heaven, an indwelling of his creatures; his heart goes with them. . . . " Farrer's devotional sermons typically include powerful assertions of his incarnationalist theology: "Above all, God becomes human in men; he is met in our neighbour, he speaks in the depth of our heart; not because the heart of our heart is other than we, but because it is our very self, the self God makes, wills and directs. . . . "[44]

In reference to Farrer's actual practice as a preacher, Davies' homiletical categories turn out to be anything but watertight compartments; indeed, the functions they delineate frequently overlap. Given Farrer's habitual manner of interweaving theology and spirituality, philosophy and ethics, it is not surprising that the stream of his pulpit oratory should overflow the banks of our taxonomies. His sermons reflect his belief that theism must be both lived and thought, with each activity informing the other.[45] As one recent commentator on Farrer has pointed out, "[His] unified theological vision requires that prayer and doctrine, rational and ascetic theology, never be separated."[46]

We gain a sharper awareness of the sort of preacher Farrer was when we note what kind he was not. Unlike the Anglican evangelical rector John Stott, he was not, predominantly, an "expository" preacher. Unlike the Methodist Leslie Weatherhead, he was not a "psychological" preacher who tried to show how Christian faith addressed human beings' frustrations and anxieties. Of course Farrer also focused on such themes as guilt and confession, the healing power of God's grace, and the restoration of community through forgiveness and new hope; but his preaching was not overtly therapeutic or beholden to psychological language and practices.[47]

Unlike such widely known Anglican priests as Dick Sheppard and "Woodbine Willie" (Geoffrey Studdert Kennedy), Farrer was not a "charismatic" preacher who conveyed his spiritual message largely through the power of his own radiant personality. An Anglo-Catholic, he read his sermons verbatim from a prepared text with little modulation of his voice and with few accompanying gestures; thus, he emphasized not the subjectivity of the preacher but the objectivity of the Word encountered in sacred doctrine and holy sacrament. Nor was Farrer, who was said to take little notice of the world that lay between Oxford and the cosmos, a Social Gospel preacher. Unlike the Anglican bishop

Trevor Huddleston, he rarely preached sermons that addressed issues of large-scale social injustice.[48]

FARRER'S SERMONS AS ADVANCED, INVIGORATING, AND STILL-VALUABLE CATECHESIS

Preaching profound sermons on the core features of what he called "our holy faith," Farrer practiced a pulpit art whose intent was essentially catechetical. Addressing an audience that was typically composed of young male undergraduates, whose rudimentary faith was in danger of erosion in what was already a largely secular society, he wished to express to them as accurately and imaginatively as he could the basic ingredients of the Christian faith. Representing a tradition that was under attack within his own university community, Farrer could demonstrate to his young listeners — and to any dons who happened to be in attendance — that, indeed, the Christian perspective made more sense and provided a better empirical fit than secular interpretations of reality. Thus Farrer's sermons may perhaps best be characterized as advanced catechesis — albeit catechesis of an unusually winsome and invigorating kind.

In her novel *Absolute Truths*, Susan Howatch not only has Jonathan Darrow recommend a sermon a day by Austin Farrer; she also uses quotations from Farrer's sermons as epigraphs for her chapters. Moreover, in her foreword to the Library of Anglican Spirituality series that she edited — a series that includes Farrer's *Saving Belief: A Discussion of Essentials* — Howatch remarks that although "much theology dates," the kind that "survive[s] the passing decades" is the kind that provides "for the intelligent reader . . . first-class expositions of classic Christian doctrine."[49] In these various ways does Howatch indicate that Farrer's advanced catechesis might hold much of value not only for Oxford undergraduates and mid-twentieth-century Anglican clergy but also for Christians in the new millennium.[50]

Darrow's advice suggests that Bishop Ashworth might dip into a collection of Farrer's sermons at random and receive the same benefit that he would from a more considered choice. Certainly the lack of indexes in the collections of Farrer's sermons makes a haphazard procedure a virtual necessity. Fortunately, almost all of these sermons bear reading a second or third time, and so the reader will not find it difficult to gain a sense of a sermon's subject the first time through and then to mark the text in such a way that the sermon will be readily accessible when fortifying words on such topics as "grace," "the communion of saints," "prayer," and "the divine creativity" are required.

Many of Farrer's sermons include references to scripture. The reader might, as a practice within his or her own spiritual life, search out these verses in the Bible and meditate on their meaning before—and after—perusing what Farrer makes of the same passage. A reader might also stop after Farrer gives him or her a taste of a "bit of reality" at the beginning of a sermon, halting long enough to consider where the preacher might go from there. Following this last suggestion will usually provide a lesson in dealing with frustration, as Farrer's homiletical moves are typically unpredictable even by aficionados.

In every instance, the spiritual reader would do well to contemplate what a particular sermon discloses about God's attributes and acts, about fellow creatures and our responsibilities toward them, and about the reader's own life lived within this triadic relationship of God, self, and other. The reader should ask not only, "What should I think?" and, "What can I believe?" but also, "What should I do?" Before drawing this chapter to a close, let us enjoy a final glimpse of Farrer's pulpit art and look at four of his most interesting homilies, all of which are in *The Essential Sermons*. Each tells us a bit about his homiletical practice, and together they provide an introduction to the form of spiritual life that his preaching outlines for us.

One reason that his sermons still work as well as they do is that we often have the same questions and doubts that his Oxford students had roughly half a century ago. In his apologetical writings, Farrer addresses these quandaries. His "Faith and Crutches," a sermon he preached in the chapel of Keble College, functions as a kind of pastoral prolegomenon to apologetics. He knows that most of his listeners grew up supposing that Doubting Thomas was a poor role model because of his lack of faith. But Farrer helps them not only to understand Thomas in a new light but also to perceive how they might follow this disciple's practice to their own spiritual benefit. Thomas said that he would not believe unless he was given empirical evidence: "[U]nless I see and touch, I shall not believe." Farrer points out that this statement was neither refusal nor boast but confession, as if Thomas was admitting, "That's the sort of man I am."

In speaking forthrightly, Thomas "could hardly have done better." Certainly he would not have improved his situation if he had lied, pretending to be someone he wasn't. For the rest of us also, Farrer says, we would do well not to come to Christ in our prayers and "tell him a pack of lies. Shall we pretend all sorts of noble sentiments we do not have: pretend to believe in him as firmly as we believe our own existence, pretend to care for his holy will as warmly and constantly as we care for our own comforts and ambitions?" No. We could not deceive Christ; we could only deceive ourselves. Instead, "we will confess ourselves as we are, and know that he will treat us on our level, and according to our need, as he did Thomas. . . . "[51]

This sermon reveals not only its author's ingenuity but also his recognition of the first task of the Christian apologist: to deal sympathetically with those who have doubts about the faith, meeting these individuals at their actual starting points. And it counsels all of us to present ourselves as we are, rather than attempting to foist on God what Susan Howatch would call "glittering images" of ourselves.

To his congregation in the Trinity College Chapel, Farrer preached a sermon on the famous parable of "the pearl of great price," which speaks of a merchant who sold all he had to buy this one pearl (Matt 13:45–46). An imaginative exegete as well as an able priest, Farrer says that we, "in our unconscious egotism," may well have been reading this parable "the wrong way round." In this sermon, which we might classify as a devotional homily, Farrer likens the kingdom of heaven to "the Divine King" and the pearl to human beings. That is the surprise: "You are the pearl of great price." And so this parable describes not our quest for God but "the King of Heaven's quest for us." The proper response to this King is not only praise and thanksgiving but also loving service. "Why then should I remember God, and serve God, day and night? Because he is all that is worth having to me; and because I am infinitely desired by his love."[52] In his startling sentence "*You* are the pearl of great price," Farrer memorably delivers to his listeners a striking image of God's loving-kindness and of their own desirability in God's eyes. In this sermon, he provides ample reasons for rendering praise to God and service to God's creatures.

Farrer's sermon "The Legacy" contains not only lyrical prose but also clear ethical content. The legacy that the evangelist John says the dying Christ bestowed upon his followers was breath, blood, and water. This threefold legacy is alive in the church as the sacramental gifts present in confirmation, communion, and baptism. In this sermon Farrer quickly turns to his central question, What is it to be alive in the Spirit? In dealing with this topic, he directly takes up the subject of spiritual-mindedness: What does it mean to be "inspired"? In his answer, he gives his listeners a "spiritual man," whom he calls "Angelicus."

As is inevitably the case with Farrer, his example contains important insights. Angelicus is not "spiritual" in the sense of being prone to displays of zeal; he is characterized by "self-forgetfulness." His strongest concerns are not about himself; and as a friend he cares at least as much for "the most tedious people, if they happened to be in any sort of worry or to need bolstering up," as he does for the more appealing types. "What God loves is lovely to him; he's up and after it." He is "inspired," though this term does not point to any mental superpowers. Angelicus has "a free concern for God's will," but "it's the same old heart-strings thrumming away, even when they are playing a divine music." The inspired life manifests itself in godly deeds, not in displays of special powers, and is realizable through the presence of Christ dwelling within.[53] In this sermon as in many others, Farrer provides concrete and therefore helpful examples of the contours and content of a Christian life. Practical in his approach, he makes it clear that the spiritual life is expressed in everyday acts of faithful devotion and loving sacrifice.

Finally, the last sermon in the Houlden collection, "A Grasp of the Hand," has much of value to say about power in general and specifically about the power of preaching. In our own day, people not only lust after the influence that derives from huge financial success and after the well-being they think accompanies social achievement; they also play with extraordinary new means of technological and scientific power. Human beings' "self-determining power," Farrer observes, is both "heavenly" and "satanic." We have so misused power that we are prone to mistrust even God's wholly beneficent sovereignty: "[W]e are made incapable of loving the government of God himself or feeling the caress of an almighty kindness." God's omnipotence overwhelms us; we, who are mere specks of dust in the universe, feel that we could not matter to God, and so "we miss the heart of love" and seek to establish our own security.

But, Farrer avers in this Christmas sermon, "Mary holds her finger out, and a divine hand closes on it. The maker of the world is born a begging child.... We will not lift our hands to pull the love of God down to us, but he lifts his hands to pull human compassion down upon his cradle." In this way "the weakness of God proves stronger than men, and the folly of God proves wiser than men." Love is God's most powerful instrument "for accomplishing those tasks he cares most dearly to perform; and this is how he brings his love to bear on human pride; by weakness not by strength, by need and not by bounty."

While the power of God may overwhelm and perplex us, the weakness of God is all around us. By his birth at Bethlehem, "the son of God makes all mankind his own.... All men's weakness speaks for [Christ's] humiliation. Christ is every sufferer, every child; whatever hand pulls at us is the hand which clutched at Mary, and would have clutched at the friends standing round his cross, if they had not been nailed." Although Farrer was not a Social Gospel preacher, his theology does offer a strong foundation for a Christian social ethic.[54]

Christ left, Farrer continues, two human deputies, or substitutes, for himself in this world: the deputies of his power and the deputies of his weakness. His apostolic ministers are the deputies of his power: "They speak his word, they pronounce his pardon, they give his body and his blood." The "little and the needy" are the deputies of his weakness. Farrer points out that "neither sort of deputies represent Christ by virtue of their merits." The clergy's infirmities always hinder their preaching, "and yet faith can hear through all their folly the voice of Jesus."

Through the inspiration of the Spirit, we receive Christ through both these human deputies. "But more endearing, more revealing, more present to us at all times, are the deputies of his weakness." These deputies confront us in the hungry, in the thirsty, in the stranger, and in the naked and imprisoned. As a deputy of God's power, Farrer sees his task as continually pointing to the compelling witness of the deputies of God's weakness: "In these then is very God to be found, and everlasting life; and we can turn our back on idols." The strength of the Christian preacher is that in spite of his or her own weakness, God can inspire the listener to heed the call of the stranger.

At Christmas "the love of God is born into the world, so strongly armed with weakness that it must prevail." And so Farrer concludes his sermon preached in Christ Church Cathedral in Oxford:

> Love is nowhere more truly omnipotent than in the manger; in the speechless child we adore the Word who made the worlds, the Son of the everlasting God, the express image of uncreated glory; to whom now, therefore, with the Father and the Holy Ghost, in three Persons one love, one light, one God, be ascribed, as is most justly due, all might, dominion, majesty and power, henceforth and for ever.[55]

In this sermon the language of devotion mixes with prescriptions of moral duty, and the underlying apologetical matter has to do with the paradoxical reasonableness of Farrer's claims about power. Davies pointed out that an apologetical preacher might attempt to "demonstrate that the Gospel as transforming truth fulfils man's nature and destiny."[56]

The ultimate apologetical question concerns Christianity's fittingness as a way of life. This way entails a transformation in our valuation of worldly understandings of power. How do we find lasting satisfaction and happiness?

Farrer's unfashionable answer would speak of dying to our own selfish will, of the shattering of pride and self-sufficiency, and of divine strength manifest in human weakness. Of course he had no illusions about the difficulties that preachers face in reaching their listeners with a message about Love Almighty: "There are no limits to the self-bestowing love of God," he declares in one of his Farrergraphs for the Eucharist. And surely, "no truth is more common on our lips than this": Christians regularly speak of God's infinite love. But, Farrer says, no truth is "more distant from our hearts."[57]

CONCLUSION

One of the most impressive features of Farrer's preaching is what he had to say about Christian living. Here his proclamation is both freshly insightful and consistently traditional. He is insistent upon a disciplined life of prayer. He expresses his belief in the value of auricular confession. And he teaches the intercession of the saints. What Houlden said of his doctrine holds true for his ascetical theology: "[I]t often had a Catholic hue which might seem sectional in its appeal, especially as it was a very special Catholic hue—firmly non-Roman, even anti-Roman, unmistakably Anglican and Oxford Anglican at that."[58]

The practical quality of Farrer's sermons is deeply appealing. They are essentially calls to holiness. What makes this feature of his sermons most attractive is the utter sincerity with which their author bids his auditors consider the Christian way of life. This quality of his sermons accounts for this chapter's subtitle, which comes from one of his remarks about preaching: "It is useless to preach unless we can claim some taste of the things we describe; just enough taste of them to interpret what we hear from the saints, or see in them."[59] The most compelling aspect of Farrer's sermons is his evident taste of the things he described.

NOTES

1. *Austin Farrer: The Essential Sermons* (ed. Leslie Houlden; Cambridge, MA: Cowley, 1991), 14; hereinafter cited as *The Essential Sermons*. The authors are grateful to Dr. James Dunkly, of the theological library at the University of the South, in Sewanee, Tennessee, for his expert bibliographical assistance, and to Professor Flora A. Keshgegian, of the Episcopal Theological Seminary of the Southwest, in Austin, Texas, for her constructive comments on this chapter.

2. Ibid., 103.

3. Ibid., 136.

4. Susan Howatch, *Absolute Truths* (New York: Knopf, 1995), 411.

5. Clement Welsh, *Preaching in a New Key: Studies in the Psychology of Thinking and Listening* (Philadelphia: United Church Press, 1974), 108.

6. *The Essential Sermons,* 1.

7. Ibid., 5.

8. Ibid., 20.

9. Ibid., 27.

10. Leslie Houlden, Introduction to *Austin Farrer: The Essential Sermons,* ix.

11. David Buttrick, *Homiletic: Moves and Structures* (Philadelphia: Fortress, 1987), 23–24.

12. According to the lectionary of the 1662 Book of Common Prayer, Farrer took his sermon text from the second lesson of the evening service of November 25.

13. *The Essential Sermons,* 109–12.

14. Michaelmas is the fall term, which begins near the feast of St. Michael and All Angels on September 29.

15. Reginald H. Fuller, *What Is Liturgical Preaching?* (London: SCM, 1957), 22.

16. Ibid., 23.

17. The publisher Mowbray included this series in a 1963 volume titled *Bible Sermons.*

18. Austin Farrer, *The Brink of Mystery* (ed. Charles C. Conti; London: SPCK, 1976), 22.

19. Ibid.

20. O. C. Edwards Jr., *Elements of Homiletic: A Method for Preparing to Preach* (New York: Pueblo, 1982), 7.

21. Austin Farrer, *Saving Belief: A Discussion of Essentials* (1964; repr., Harrisburg, PA: Morehouse, 1994), xiv.

22. See O. C. Edwards Jr., "What, if Anything, Is Anglican Preaching?" *Sewanee Theological Review* 41 (Pentecost 1998): 216.

23. Charles C. Hefling Jr., *Jacob's Ladder: Theology and Spirituality in the Thought of Austin Farrer* (Cambridge, MA: Cowley, 1979), 5. Emphasis added. Another student of Farrer's preaching has observed that his sermons are never "overloaded with heavy biblical quotation, and indeed on occasions biblical material appears to be used merely for its image-value, or as one might use any literary figure." Farrer's selection of material from the Bible turns out to be "fairly limited, with certain phrases [particularly from 1 Cor 2:9, 1 John 3:2, Rom 11:34, and 2 Cor 2:16] often repeated." Farrer also has favorite words that he uses: He "is keen to use terms like 'glory' and 'light' and so naturally enough the Prologue of John's Gospel

is a popular quarry for quotations." Stephen Platten, "Diaphanous Thought: Spirituality and Theology in the Work of Austin Farrer," *Anglican Theological Review* 69 (January 1987): 48, 49.

24. Hefling, *Jacob's Ladder,* 5–6. Farrer's sermon based on 2 Kgs 4:1–7, "Spirit and Form," is in *The Brink of Mystery,* 70–73. His sermon based on 1 Sam 28, "The Witch of Endor," is in Austin Farrer, *The End of Man* (Grand Rapids, MI: Eerdmans, 1974), 140–43.

25. Edwards, "What, if Anything, Is Anglican Preaching?" 216–17.

26. G. R. Owst, *Literature and Pulpit in Medieval England* (New York: Barnes & Noble, 1961), chaps. 3 and 4. See Hefling, *Jacob's Ladder,* 6–9.

27. Horton Davies, *Worship and Theology in England: From Cranmer to Hooker, 1534–1603* (Princeton, NJ: Princeton University Press, 1970), 249–54; Philip B. Secor, *Richard Hooker: Prophet of Anglicanism* (Toronto: Anglican Book Centre, 1999), 118; John E. Booty, "Richard Hooker," in *The Spirit of Anglicanism: Hooker, Maurice, Temple* (ed. William J. Wolf; Wilton, CT: Morehouse-Barlow, 1979), 2–3, 17–20, 40–42.

28. Quoted in Booty, "Richard Hooker," 17. See Platten, "Diaphanous Thought," 35–41.

29. Davies, *Worship and Theology in England: From Cranmer to Hooker,* 253.

30. Horton Davies, *Worship and Theology in England: From Andrewes to Baxter and Fox, 1603–1690* (Princeton, NJ: Princeton University Press, 1975), 157–61 (quotation, 160).

31. David Scott, "Jeremy Taylor," in *The SPCK Handbook of Anglican Theologians* (ed. Alister McGrath; London: SPCK, 1998), 210. On Taylor's preaching, see also James Thayer Addison, "Jeremy Taylor: Preacher and Pastor," *Historical Magazine of the Protestant Episcopal Church* 21 (March 1952): 164–69. Addison describes Taylor as a practical preacher who was "always suspicious of mere piety as an escape from duty" (168).

32. Scott, "Jeremy Taylor," 212.

33. Ibid., 210. Both men also emphasized the theme of Christian friendship. Our friendships in this world are imperfect, Taylor said, and but the "beginnings of a celestial friendship, by which we shall love every one as much as they can be loved." Jeremy Taylor, "A Discourse on the Nature and Offices of Friendship," in *The Whole Works of the Right Rev. Jeremy Taylor* (10 vols.; London: Longman, 1854), 1:73.

34. J. W. C. Wand, *Anglicanism in History and Today* (New York: Nelson, 1962), 203–4.

35. Platten, "Diaphanous Thought," 46n79.

36. Horton Davies, *Worship and Theology in England: From Watts and Wesley to Maurice, 1690–1850* (Princeton, NJ: Princeton University Press, 1961), 269. See Geoffrey Rowell, "John Keble and the High Church Tradition," in *The Vision Glorious: Themes and Personalities of the Catholic Revival in Anglicanism* (New York: Oxford University Press, 1983), 21–42; and three sermons by Austin Farrer: "John Keble" and "Simple Sanctity," in *The Brink of Mystery,* 149–51, 152–54, and "Keble and His College," in *The End of Man,* 153–57.

37. Horton Davies, *Worship and Theology in England: The Ecumenical Century, 1900–1965* (Princeton, NJ: Princeton University Press, 1965), 212.

38. Ibid., 213.
39. Horton Davies, *Varieties of English Preaching, 1900–1960* (London: SCM, 1963), 32.
40. Hefling, *Jacob's Ladder,* 10.
41. Davies, *Varieties of English Preaching,* 31.
42. Platten, "Diaphanous Thought," 47.
43. *The Essential Sermons,* 4; see also pp. 8 and 92.
44. Ibid., 91–92. See Platten, "Diaphanous Thought," 35–36, 40–41.
45. Austin Farrer, *Faith and Speculation* (Edinburgh: T & T Clark, 1967), 130.
46. Platten, "Diaphanous Thought," 31.
47. Davies, *Varieties of English Preaching,* 194–95, 138–63.
48. Davies, *Worship and Theology in England: The Ecumenical Century,* chap. 6; Davies, *Varieties of English Preaching,* chap. 4. "Using the word broadly, [Farrer] had no *political* interests. It was difficult to get him to take seriously the organized activities of any body intermediate between the college and the cosmos." Basil Mitchell, "Austin Marsden Farrer," in Austin Farrer, *A Celebration of Faith* (ed. Leslie Houlden; London: Hodder & Stoughton, 1970), 14.
49. Susan Howatch, Foreword to *Saving Belief,* v, vi.
50. "Austin Farrer deserves to be read today," declares Howatch, "by all those interested in truth, tradition and twentieth-century spirituality." *Saving Belief,* xi.
51. *The Essential Sermons,* 54.
52. Ibid., 62–64.
53. Ibid., 73–75.
54. See Jeffrey Eaton, "Divine Action and Human Liberation," in *Divine Action: Studies Inspired by the Philosophical Theology of Austin Farrer* (ed. Brian Hebblethwaite and Edward Henderson; Edinburgh: T & T Clark, 1990), 211–29.
55. *The Essential Sermons,* 207–11.
56. Davies, *Worship and Theology in England: The Ecumenical Century,* 212.
57. Austin Farrer, *The Crown of the Year: Weekly Paragraphs for the Holy Sacrament* (London: Dacre, 1952), 49.
58. *The Essential Sermons,* ix.
59. Ibid., 20.

BIBLIOGRAPHY OF WRITINGS ABOUT AUSTIN FARRER WITH OTHER RESEARCH AIDS

The following bibliography is divided into four sections. The first section, "Articles, Review Discussions, and Other Short Items," includes essays that focus exclusively or primarily on Farrer's thought, book reviews that offer substantive discussion, and one cassette tape of a conference presentation. Most of these items are located in learned periodicals, a few are in handbooks or encyclopedias, and some are in collections devoted either entirely or largely to Farrer. The second section lists books that include significant discussions of Farrer's thought or are significantly formed by engagements with it or by uses of it, even though they are not focused solely on it.

It would be wrong to suppose that these lists are complete. Other discussions surely exist — in journal articles, books, conference papers, and book reviews — that we have not discovered. Furthermore, there will be disagreement about what should be included. Do a few brief mentions of Farrer's name constitute a significant discussion? Citation in a note? When do such references amount to significant engagement with Farrer's thought? When do they signal the formation of an author's mind by Farrer's thought? Indeed, may there not be discussions that are significantly shaped by Farrer's thought but do not mention his name?

It is more reasonable to hope for completeness in the third and fourth sections. The third section lists theses and dissertations with a substantial focus on Farrer; and the fourth section, published monographs about Farrer.

We have not thought it necessary to provide a complete listing of Farrer's own works, as such lists are available elsewhere. See Philip Curtis, "Chronological List of Published Writings by Austin Farrer, 1933–76," in *A Hawk among Sparrows*. In *For God and Clarity,* Charles Conti provides a list of Farrer's writings that is updated through 1983; and in his 1995 monograph, *Metaphysical Personalism,* he provides a list that is further updated. We have found only two published items by Farrer that are not included in these lists: "An Ordination Sermon," *Theology* 94 (1991): 166–67; and *Austin Farrer on the Rosary* (Church Literature Association, 1989).

Another category of Farrer's writings is not included at all in the bibliographies: letters. Many of his letters to friends and scholars contain philosophical and theological discussions. Only a few letters have been published. Philip Curtis includes two of them in his biography of Farrer, *A Hawk among Sparrows* (pp. 242–44); and Charles Conti gives us four sets in *Metaphysical Personalism* (pp. 261–75). The Bodleian Library of Oxford University possesses many letters in its collection of Austin and Katharine Farrer's papers. If there are individuals, archives, or other libraries that have letters by Farrer, it would be a boon to scholars were they to donate them to the collection at the Bodleian.

Finally, Diogenes Allen indexed several of Farrer's works, and these indexes were published in *Divine Action: Essays Inspired by the Philosophical Theology of Austin Farrer* (pp. 230–81). The books indexed are *Faith and Speculation, Finite and Infinite, The Freedom of the Will, God Is Not Dead* (published in Great Britain as *A Science of God?*), *Interpretation and Belief, Love Almighty and Ills Unlimited, Reflective Faith,* and *Saving Belief.*

ARTICLES, REVIEW DISCUSSIONS, AND OTHER SHORT ITEMS

Allen, Diogenes. "Faith and the Recognition of God's Activity." Pages 197–210 in *Divine Action: Essays Inspired by the Philosophical Theology of Austin Farrer.* Edited by Brian Hebblethwaite and Edward Henderson. Edinburgh: T & T Clark, 1990.

———. "The Restoration of Sacramentality in a Post-Modern World." *Reformed Liturgy and Music* 19 (Spring 1985): 85–88.

Alston, William. "How to Think about Divine Action." Pages 51–70 in *Divine Action: Essays Inspired by the Philosophical Theology of Austin Farrer.* Edited by Brian Hebblethwaite and Edward Henderson. Edinburgh: T & T Clark, 1990.

Badham, Roger A. "Conti's Reclamation of Farrer's Cosmological Personalism: A Pragmatist's Response." *Personalist Forum: Special Issue on "Metaphysical Personalism"* 12 (1996): 18–34.

Baker, John Austin. Introduction to *The End of Man,* by Austin Farrer. Edited by Charles Conti. London: SPCK, 1973.

Bastin, Ted. "Review Discussion of Austin Farrer's *A Science of God?*" *Theoria to Theory* 1(1966): 59–64.

Bigger, Charles. "L'hermeneutique d'Austin Farrer: Un Modele Participatoire." Translated by Marcel Regnier. *Archives de Philosophie* 55 (1992): 49–76.

Blakesley, John. "Pictures in the Fire." *Literature and Theology* 1 (1987): 84–90.

Brown, David. "God and Symbolic Action." Pages 103–22 in *Divine Action: Essays Inspired by the Philosophical Theology of Austin Farrer.* Edited by Brian Hebblethwaite and Edward Henderson. Edinburgh: T & T Clark, 1990.

Brümmer, Vincent. "Farrer, Wiles and the Causal Joint." *Modern Theology* 8 (1992): 1–14.

Buckley, James J., and William McF. Wilson. "Rational Theology and the God of Knowledge: The Case of Barth and Farrer." *Heythrop Journal* 26 (1985): 274–93.

Burrell, David. "Divine Practical Knowing: How an Eternal God Acts in Time." Pages 93–102 in *Divine Action: Essays Inspired by the Philosophical Theology of Austin Farrer.* Edited by Brian Hebblethwaite and Edward Henderson. Edinburgh: T & T Clark, 1990.

Butler, Basil C. "Dr. Farrer's Bampton Lectures." *Downside Review* 67 (1949): 237–46.

Conti, Charles. "Austin Farrer and the Analogy of Other Minds." Pages 51–91 in *For God and Clarity: New Essays in Honor of Austin Farrer.* Edited by Jeffrey C. Eaton and Ann Loades. Allison Park, PA: Pickwick, 1983.

———. "The Author Responds." *Personalist Forum* 12 (1996): 81–121.

———. "Farrer's Christian Humanism." *Modern Theology* 7 (1991): 403–34.

———. "The Personalism of Austin Farrer." *Personalist Forum* 5 (1989): 83–118.

———. Preface to *Reflective Faith: Essays in Philosophical Theology,* by Austin Farrer. Edited by Charles C. Conti. London: SPCK, 1972.

Curtis, P. "The Rational Theology of Dr. Farrer." *Theology* 73 (1970): 249–56.

———. "The Biblical Work of Dr. Farrer." *Theology* 73 (1970): 292–301.

Dalferth, Ingolf. " 'Esse Est Operari': The Anti-Scholastic Theologies of Farrer and Luther." *Modern Theology* 1 (1985): 183–210.

———. "The Stuff of Revelation: Austin Farrer's Doctrine of Inspired Images." Pages 71–95 in *Hermeneutics, the Bible and Literary Criticism.* Edited by Ann Loades and Michael McLain. New York: St. Martin's Press, 1992.

Davies, Ian. "Inverse Analogy." *Downside Review* 113 (1995): 196–202.

Donovan, Peter. "Theology as Rhetoric." *Personalist Forum* 12 (1996): 11–34.

Downing, F. G. "Towards the Rehabilitation of Q." *New Testament Studies* 11 (1965): 169–81.

Duncan, Steven M. "Experience and Agency." Pages 149–61 in *Human and Divine Agency.* Edited by F. Michael McLain and W. Mark Richardson. Lanham, MD: University Press of America, 1999.

Dungan, D. L. "Mark: The Abridgement of Matthew and Luke." *Perspective* 11 (1970): 51–97.

Dupré, Louis. "Themes in Contemporary Philosophy of Religion." *New Scholasticism* 43 (1969): 577–601.

Eaton, Jeffrey. "Divine Action and Human Liberation." Pages 211–29 in *Divine Action: Essays Inspired by the Philosophical Theology of Austin Farrer.* Edited by Brian Hebblethwaite and Edward Henderson. Edinburgh: T & T Clark, 1990.

———. "The Problem of Miracles and the Paradox of Double Agency." *Modern Theology* 1 (1985): 211–22.

———. "Three Necessary Conditions for Thinking Theistically." Pages 151–61 in *For God and Clarity: New Essays in Honor of Austin Farrer.* Edited by Jeffrey C. Eaton and Ann Loades. Allison Park, PA: Pickwick, 1983.

Eaton, Jeffrey C., and Ann Loades. "Austin Marsden Farrer (1904–1968)." Pages xi–xiii in *For God and Clarity: New Essays in Honor of Austin Farrer.* Edited by Jeffrey C. Eaton and Ann Loades. Allison Park, PA: Pickwick, 1983.

Emmet, D., et al. "Review Discussion of Dr. Farrer's *A Science of God?*" *Theoria to Theory* 1 (1966): 55–59.

Forsman, Rodger. " 'Apprehension' in *Finite and Infinite.*" Pages 111–30 in *For God and Clarity: New Essays in Honor of Austin Farrer.* Edited by Jeffrey C. Eaton and Ann Loades. Allison Park, PA: Pickwick, 1983.

———. " 'Double Agency' and Identifying Reference to God." Pages 123–42 in *Divine Action: Essays Inspired by the Philosophical Theology of Austin Farrer.* Edited by Brian Hebblethwaite and Edward Henderson. Edinburgh: T & T Clark, 1990.

———. "Revelation and Understanding: A Defence of Tradition." Pages 46–68 in *Hermeneutics, the Bible and Literary Criticism.* Edited by Ann Loades and Michael McLain. New York: St. Martin's Press, 1992.

Galilee, David, and Brian Hebblethwaite. "Farrer's Concept of Double Agency: A Reply." *Theology* 85 (1982): 7–10.

Gill, Jerry. "Divine Action as Mediated." *Harvard Theological Review* 80 (1987): 369–78.

Glasse, John. "Doing Theology Metaphysically." *Harvard Theological Review* 59 (1966): 319–50.

Goulder, M. "Farrer on Q." *Theology* 83 (1980): 190–95.

Grayston, Kenneth. "Farrer Fares Far." *The Presbyter: A Journal of Reformed Churchmanship* 7 (1949): 10–14.

Gundry, Dudley W. "Philosophy of Religion: The Banner of a Sect." *Scottish Journal of Theology* 10 (1957): 113–21.

Hanson, Philip J. "Austin Farrer and Jacques Ellul." *Cross Currents* 35 (1985): 81–83.

Harries, Richard. Introduction to *The One Genius: Readings through the Year with Austin Farrer.* Edited by Richard Harries. London: SPCK, 1987.

———. " 'We Know On Our Knees . . .': Intellectual, Imaginative, and Spiritual Unity in the Theology of Austin Farrer." Pages 21–33 in *Divine Action: Essays Inspired by the Philosophical Theology of Austin Farrer.* Edited by Brian Hebblethwaite and Edward Henderson. Edinburgh: T & T Clark, 1990.

Hartt, Julian N. "Austin Farrer as Philosophical Theologian: A Retrospective and Appreciation." Pages 1–22 in *For God and Clarity: New Essays in Honor of Austin Farrer.* Edited by Jeffrey C. Eaton and Ann Loades. Allison Park, PA: Pickwick, 1983.

———. "Dialectic, Analysis, and Empirical Generalization in Theology." *Crozer Quarterly* 29 (1952): 1–17.

Hauge, Hans. "The Sin of Reading: Austin Farrer, Helen Gardner and Frank Kermode on the Poetry of St. Mark." Pages 113–28 in *Hermeneutics, the Bible and Literary Criticism.* Edited by Ann Loades and Michael McLain. New York: St. Martin's Press, 1992.

Hebblethwaite, Brian. "Austin Farrer's Concept of Divine Providence." *Theology* 73 (1970): 541–51.

———. "The Doctrine of the Incarnation in the Thought of Austin Farrer." *New Fire* 4, no. 33 (1977): 460–68. Reprinted, pages 112–25 in *The Incarnation: Collected Essays in Christology.* Cambridge: Cambridge University Press, 1987.

———. "The Experiential Verification of Religious Belief in the Theology of Austin Farrer." Pages 163–76 in *For God and Clarity: New Essays in Honor of Austin Farrer.* Edited by Jeffrey C. Eaton and Ann Loades. Allison Park, PA: Pickwick, 1983.

———. "Finite and Infinite Freedom in Farrer and von Balthasar." *CTNS Bulletin* 12, no. 1 (Winter 1992): 10–16. Enlarged and reprinted, pages 83–96 in *Human and Divine Agency.* Edited by F. Michael McLain and W. Mark Richardson. Lanham, MD: University Press of America, 1999.

———. "Freedom, Evil, and Farrer." *New Blackfriars* 66 (1985): 178–87.

———. "On Understanding What One Believes." *New Fire* [no vol. no.], no. 7 (1971): 11–15.

———. "Providence and Divine Action." *Religious Studies* 14 (1978): 223–36.

———. " 'True' and 'False' in Christology." Pages 227–38 in *The Philosophical Frontiers of Christian Theology: Essays Presented to D. M. MacKinnon.* Edited by Brian Hebblethwaite and Stewart Sutherland. Cambridge: Cambridge University Press, 1982.

Hebblethwaite, Brian, and Edward Henderson. Introduction to *Divine Action: Essays Inspired by the Philosophical Theology of Austin Farrer.* Edited by Brian Hebblethwaite and Edward Henderson. Edinburgh: T & T Clark, 1990.

Hebert, Arthur G. "Dr. Austin Farrer on St. Mark's Gospel." *The Reformed Theological Review* 12 (1953): 61–74.

Hefling, Charles C. "Austin M. Farrer." Pages 146–47 in *The Westminster Dictionary of Christian Spirituality.* Edited by Gordon S. Wakefield. Philadelphia: Westminster, 1983.

———. "Origen Redivivus: Farrer's Scriptural Divinity." Pages 35–50 in *For God and Clarity: New Essays in Honor of Austin Farrer.* Edited by Jeffrey C. Eaton and Ann Loades. Allison Park, PA: Pickwick, 1983.

Henderson, Edward Hugh. "An Appreciation of Austin Farrer." *Interface: A Journal of Opinion* 1 (1978): 46–56.

———. "Austin Farrer and D. Z. Phillips on Lived Faith, Prayer, and Divine Reality." *Modern Theology* 1 (1985): 223–45.

———. "The Divine Playwright." *Personalist Forum* 12 (1996): 35–80.

———. "Knowing Persons and Knowing God." *The Thomist* 46 (1982): 394–422.

———. "Knowing the World: The Process View of Austin Farrer." *Philosophy Today* 12 (1968): 204–24.

———. "Philosophie et Theologie chez Austin Farrer." Translated by Marcel Regnier. *Archives de Philosophie* 53 (1990): 49–72.

———. "The Supremely Free Agent." Pages 97–119 in *Human and Divine Agency.* Edited by F. Michael McLain and W. Mark Richardson. Lanham, MD: University Press of America, 1999.

———. "Valuing in Knowing God: An Interpretation of Austin Farrer's Religious Epistemology." *Modern Theology* 1 (1985): 165–82. Translated by Marcel Regnier as "L'Affirmation de l'existence de Dieu selon Austin Farrer." *Archives de Philosophie* 54 (1991): 65–90.

Hick, John. Foreword to *Reflective Faith: Essays in Philosophical Theology,* by Austin Farrer. Edited by Charles C. Conti. London: SPCK, 1972.

Hobbs, Edward C. "A Quarter Century without Q." *Perkins School of Theology Journal* 33 (1980): 10–19.

Howatch, Susan. Introduction to *Saving Belief: A Discussion of Essentials,* by Austin Farrer. Library of Anglican Spirituality. Harrisburg, PA: Morehouse, 1994.

Huston, Hollis. "The 'Q' Parties at Oxford." *Journal of Bible and Religion* 25 (1957): 123–28.

Kenny, Anthony. "The Problem of Evil and the Argument from Design." *Archivo di Filosofia* 56 (1988): 545–55.

King, Robert H. "The Agent's World: Farrer's Contribution to Cosmology." Pages 23–34 in *For God and Clarity: New Essays in Honor of Austin Farrer.* Edited by Jeffrey C. Eaton and Ann Loades. Allison Park, PA: Pickwick, 1983.

Lewis, C. S. Preface to *A Faith of Our Own,* by Austin Farrer. Cleveland: World, 1960.

Lewis, John Underwood. "Austin Farrer's Notion of 'Conscience as an Appetite for Moral Truth': Its Metaphysical Foundation and Importance to Contemporary Moral Philosophy." Pages 131–50 in *For God and Clarity: New Essays in Honor of Austin Farrer.* Edited by Jeffrey C. Eaton and Ann Loades. Allison Park, PA: Pickwick, 1983.

Loades, Ann. "Austin Farrer on Love Almighty." Pages 93–109 in *For God and Clarity: New Essays in Honor of Austin Farrer.* Edited by Jeffrey C. Eaton and Ann Loades. Allison Park, PA: Pickwick, 1983.

———. "Austin Marsden Farrer." Pages 120–23 in *The SPCK Handbook of Anglican Theologians.* Edited by Alister E. McGrath. London: SPCK, 1998.

Loughlin, Gerard. "Making It Plain: Austin Farrer and the Inspiration of Scripture." Pages 96–112 in *Hermeneutics, the Bible and Literary Criticism.* Edited by Ann Loades and Michael McLain. New York: St. Martin's Press, 1992.

Mascall, Eric L. Foreword to *Interpretation and Belief,* by Austin Farrer. Edited by Charles C. Conti. London: SPCK, 1976.

———. Review of Austin Farrer, *Reflective Faith. Religious Studies* 9 (1973): 241–44.

Masterman, Margaret. Review of Austin Farrer's *A Science of God? Theoria to Theory* 1 (1966): 64–71.

McLain, F. Michael. "Austin Farrer's Revision of the Cosmological Argument." *Downside Review* 88 (1970): 270–79.

———. Introduction to *Human and Divine Agency.* Edited by F. Michael McLain and W. Mark Richardson. Lanham, MD: University Press of America, 1999.

———. "Narrative Interpretation and the Problem of Double Agency." Pages 143–72 in *Divine Action: Essays Inspired by the Philosophical Theology of Austin Farrer.* Edited by Brian Hebblethwaite and Edward Henderson. Edinburgh: T & T Clark, 1990.

MacIntyre, Alasdair C. "Analogy in Metaphysics." *Downside Review* 69 (1950–51): 45–61.

Mitchell, Basil. "Austin Farrer." Pages 41–44 in *The Anglican Spirit.* Edited by P. Wignall. Cuddesdon: Ripon College, 1982.

———. "Austin Marsden Farrer." Pages 13–16 in Austin Farrer, *A Celebration of Faith.* Edited by Leslie Houlden. London: Hodder & Stoughton, 1970.

———. "Austin Farrer: The Philosopher." *New Fire* 7, no. 57 (1983): 452–56.

———. "Overview and Analysis." *Personalist Forum* 12 (1996): 1–10.

———. "The Place of Symbols in Christianity." Pages 184–97 in *How to Play Theological Ping-Pong.* Edited by William J. Abraham and Robert W. Prevost. London: Hodder & Stoughton, 1990.

———. "Two Kinds of Philosophy of Religion." Pages 177–90 in *For God and Clarity: New Essays in Honor of Austin Farrer.* Edited by Jeffrey C. Eaton and Ann Loades. Allison Park, PA: Pickwick, 1983.

Morris, J. N. "Religious Experience in the Philosophical Theology of Austin Farrer." *Journal of Theological Studies,* n.s., 45 (1994): 569–92.

Muddiman, John. "John's Use of Matthew: A British Exponent of the Theory." *Ephemerides Theologicae Lovaniensis* 59 (1983): 333–37.

Oliver, Simon. "The Theodicy of Austin Farrer." *The Heythrop Journal* 39 (1998): 280–97.

Pasewark, Kyle A. "Predestination as a Condition of Freedom: Reconsidering the Reformation." Pages 49–66 in *Human and Divine Agency.* Edited by F. Michael McLain and W. Mark Richardson. Lanham, MD: University Press of America, 1999.

Peterson, Jeffrey. "A Pioneer Narrative Critic and His Synoptic Hypothesis: Austin Farrer and Gospel Interpretation." Society of Biblical Literature Seminar Paper Series 39. Pages 651–72 in *Society of Biblical Literature Seminar Papers 2000.* Atlanta: Society of Biblical Literature, 2000.

Polkinghorne, John. "Conversations with John Polkinghorne: The Nature of Physical Reality." *Zygon* 35 (2000): 927–40.

———. "The Laws of Nature and the Laws of Physics." Pages 429–40 in *Quantum Cosmology and the Laws of Nature: Scientific Perspectives on Divine Activity.* 2nd ed. Edited by Robert John Russell, Nancey Murphy, and C. J. Isham. Vatican City State and Berkeley, CA: Vatican Observatory Publications and The Center for Theology and the Natural Sciences, 1996.

Proudfoot, Wayne. "Conceptions of God and the Self." *Journal of Religion* 55 (1975): 57–75.

Purtill, Richard. "The Success of C. S. Lewis' Apologetics." Paper presented to the First C. S. Lewis Institute. Sound cassette. Seattle, WA: Seattle Pacific University, 1978.

Ramsey, Michael. Foreword to *The One Genius: Readings through the Year with Austin Farrer.* Edited by Richard Harries. London: SPCK, 1987.

Richardson, W. Mark. "A Look at Austin Farrer's Theory of Agency." *CTNS Bulletin* 12 (1992): 1–9. Enlarged and reprinted, pages 121–48 in *Human and Divine Agency.* Edited by F. Michael McLain and W. Mark Richardson. Lanham, MD: University Press of America, 1999.

Routley, Erik. "When Preaching Is Poetry." *The British Weekly,* February 11, 1960.

Russell, Robert John. Introduction to *Quantum Cosmology and the Laws of Nature: Scientific Perspectives on Divine Activity.* 2nd ed. Edited by Robert John Russell, Nancey Murphy, and C. J. Isham. Vatican City State and Berkeley, CA: Vatican Observatory Publications and The Center for Theology and the Natural Sciences, 1996.

Settle, Tom. "The Dressage Ring and the Ballroom: Loci of Double Agency." Pages 17–40 in *Interpreting God's Action in the World.* Vol. 4 of *Facets of Faith and Science.* Edited by Jitse M. van der Meer. Ancaster, Ontario, and Lanham, MD: Pascal Centre for Advanced Studies in Faith and Science and University Press of America, 1996.

Slocum, Robert B. "Light in a Burning Glass: The Theological Witness of Austin Farrer." *Anglican Theological Review* 85 (2003): 365–73.

Smart, Ninian. "Revelation and Reasons." *Scottish Journal of Theology* 11 (1958): 352–61.

———. Review of Austin Farrer, *Faith and Speculation. Philosophical Quarterly* 20 (January 1970): 93.

Springsted, Eric O. "Theology and Spirituality; Or, Why Religion Is Not Critical Reflection on Religious Experience." Pages 49–62 in *Spirituality and Theology: Essays in Honor of Diogenes Allen.* Louisville, KY: Westminster John Knox, 1998.

Stahl, J. T. "Austin Farrer on C. S. Lewis as 'The Christian Apologist.'" *Christian Scholar's Review* 4 (1975): 231–37.

Stocker, Margarita. "God in Theory: Milton, Literature and Theodicy." *Literature and Theology* 1 (1987): 70–88.

TeSelle, Eugene. "Divine Action: The Doctrinal Tradition." Pages 71–91 in *Divine Action: Essays Inspired by the Philosophical Theology of Austin Farrer.* Edited by Brian Hebblethwaite and Edward Henderson. Edinburgh: T & T Clark, 1990.

Thomas, Owen C. "Recent Thought on Divine Agency." Pages 35–50 in *Divine Action: Essays Inspired by the Philosophical Theology of Austin Farrer.* Edited by Brian Hebblethwaite and Edward Henderson. Edinburgh: T & T Clark, 1990.

Tortorelli, Devin. "Some Contributions of Balthasar and Farrer on the Subject of Analogy of Being." *Downside Review* 107 (1989): 183–90.

Tracy, Thomas F. "Evil, Human Freedom, and Divine Grace." *CTNS Bulletin* 12 (1992): 17–27. Enlarged and reprinted, pages 165–90 in *Human and Divine Agency.* Edited by F. Michael McLain and W. Mark Richardson. Lanham, MD: University Press of America, 1999.

———. "Narrative Theology and the Acts of God." Pages 173–96 in *Divine Action: Essays Inspired by the Philosophical Theology of Austin Farrer.* Edited by Brian Hebblethwaite and Edward Henderson. Edinburgh: T & T Clark, 1990.

Vaughn, J. Barry. "Resurrection and Grace: The Sermons of Austin Farrer." *Preaching* 9 (March–April 1994): 61–63.

Vogel, Arthur A. "Essential Reading." *Anglican Theological Review* 81 (1999): 767–68.

Wiles, Maurice. "Farrer's Concept of Double Agency." *Theology* 84 (1981): 243–49.

Wilson, M. P. "Austin Farrer and the Paradox of Christology." *Scottish Journal of Theology* 35 (1982): 145–63.

———. "St. John, the Trinity, and the Language of the Spirit." *Scottish Journal of Theology* 41 (1988): 471–83.

Wilson, William McF. "A Different Method, a Different Case: The Theological Program of Julian Hartt and Austin Farrer." *The Thomist* 53 (1989): 599–633.

DISCUSSIONS IN BOOKS

Allen, Diogenes. *Christian Belief in a Postmodern World: The Full Wealth of Conviction.* Louisville, KY: Westminster John Knox, 1989.

———. *The Reasonableness of Faith.* Washington, DC: Corpus, 1968.

Baillie, John. *The Idea of Revelation in Recent Thought.* New York: Columbia University Press, 1964.

Barton, John. *People of the Book? The Authority of the Bible in Christianity.* Louisville, KY: Westminster John Knox, 1988.

Bloom, Harold. *The Revelation of St. John the Divine.* New York: Chelsea House, 1988.

Brümmer, Vincent. *Speaking of a Personal God: An Essay in Philosophical Theology.* Cambridge: Cambridge University Press, 1992.

Clayton, Philip. *God and Contemporary Science.* Edinburgh Studies in Constructive Theology. Edinburgh: Edinburgh University Press, 1997.

Como, James T. *C. S. Lewis at the Breakfast Table, and Other Reminiscences.* New York: Macmillan, 1979.

Ernst, Cornelius. *Multiple Echo.* London: Darton, Longman & Todd, 1979.

Franklin, R. L. *Freewill and Determinism: A Study of Rival Concepts of Man.* London: Routledge & Kegan Paul, 1968.

Gardner, Helen. *The Business of Criticism.* Oxford: Clarendon, 1959.

Goulder, Michael, ed. *Incarnation and Myth: The Debate Continued.* Grand Rapids, MI: Eerdmans, 1979.

Harned, David Baily. *Images for Self-Recognition: The Christian as Player, Sufferer, and Vandal.* New York: Seabury, 1977.

Hart, Ray L. *Unfinished Man and the Imagination: Toward an Ontology and a Rhetoric of Revelation.* New York: Seabury, 1979.

Hebblethwaite, Brian. *Ethics and Religion in a Pluralistic Age: Collected Essays.* Edinburgh: T & T Clark, 1997.

———. *Evil, Suffering and Religion.* London: Sheldon; New York: Hawthorn, 1976.

———. *The Incarnation: Collected Essays in Christology.* Cambridge: Cambridge University Press, 1987.

———. *The Ocean of Truth.* Cambridge: Cambridge University Press, 1988.

Helm, Paul. *The Providence of God: Contours of Christian Theology.* Downers Grove, IL: InterVarsity Press, 1994.

Hick, John. *Evil and the God of Love.* New York: Harper & Row, 1966.

Kermode, Frank. *The Genesis of Secrecy: On the Interpretation of Narrative.* Cambridge, MA: Harvard University Press, 1979.

King, Robert H. *The Meaning of God.* London: SCM, 1974.

Lewis, H. D. *Our Experience of God.* London: Allen & Unwin, 1959.

Long, Thomas, and Cornelius Plantinga. *A Chorus of Witnesses.* Grand Rapids, MI: Eerdmans, 1994.

Mascall, Eric. *Existence and Analogy.* London: Darton, Longman & Todd, 1949.

McClendon, James William. *Pacemakers of Christian Thought.* Nashville: Broadman, 1962.

McFague, Sallie. *Metaphorical Theology: Models of God in Religious Language.* Philadelphia: Fortress, 1982.

McIntosh, Mark. *Mysteries of Faith.* Cambridge, MA: Cowley, 2000.

Micklem, N. *The Abyss of Truth.* London: Bles, 1956.

Mitchell, Basil. *Faith and Criticism.* Oxford: Clarendon, 1994.

Oppenheimer, Helen. *The Hope of Happiness: A Sketch for a Christian Humanism.* London: SCM, 1983.

———. *The Hope of Heaven.* Cambridge, MA: Cowley, 1988.

———. *Incarnation and Immanence.* London: Hodder & Stoughton, 1973.

Polkinghorne, John. *Quarks, Chaos & Christianity: Questions to Science and Religion.* New York: Crossroad, 1994.

———. *Science and Christian Belief: Theological Reflections of a Bottom-Up Thinker.* London: SPCK, 1994.

———. *Science and Providence: God's Interaction with the World.* Boston: Shambhala, 1989.

Proudfoot, Wayne. *God and the Self: Three Types of Philosophy of Religion.* Lewisburg, PA: Bucknell University Press, 1976.

Roberts, Tom-Aerwyn. *History and Christian Apologetic.* London: SPCK, 1960.

Stratton, S. Brian. *Coherence, Consonance, and Conversation: The Quest of Theology, Philosophy, and Natural Science for a Unified World View.* Lanham, MD: University Press of America, 2000.

Thomas, Owen C. *God's Activity in the World: The Contemporary Problem.* Chico, CA: Scholars Press, 1983.

White, Vernon. *The Fall of a Sparrow: A Concept of Special Divine Action.* Devon: Paternoster, 1985.

THESES AND DISSERTATIONS

Conti, Charles C. "Descriptive Metaphysics: An Examination of Austin Farrer's Use of Cosmological Inference." DPhil thesis, University of Oxford, 1973.

Day, J. F. "Austin Farrer's Doctrine of Analogy: A Study in the Metaphysics of Theism." PhD diss., Yale University, 1959.

Duncan, Steven Merle. "Transcendence and Image: Austin Farrer on the Existence of God." PhD diss., University of Washington, 1987.

Eaton, Jeffrey C. "The Logic of Theism: An Analysis of the Thought of Austin Farrer." PhD diss., Princeton Theological Seminary, 1979.

Eumurian, Daniel John. "Analogy and Paradox in Austin Farrer." MA thesis, Wheaton College, 1978.

Forsman, Rodger. "Austin Farrer's Notion of Apprehension: An Analysis and Appraisal of His Claim to Knowledge of Substance." PhD diss., University of Toronto, 1974.

Glasse, J. H. "Creation and Creativity: An Essay in Philosophical Theology." PhD diss., Yale University, 1961.

Guthrie, Clifton Floyd. "Creation, Freedom, and Moral Choice in the Thought of Austin M. Farrer." MDiv thesis, Emory University, 1987.

Hart, R. L. "The Role of the Imagination in Man's Knowledge of God." PhD diss., Yale University, 1959.

Hefling, Charles C. "Scripture and Metaphysics: The Unity of Austin Farrer's Christian Theism." ThD diss., Harvard Divinity School, 1981.

Henderson, Edward Hugh. "Language and Reality: The Solution of Austin Farrer." MA thesis, Tulane University, 1964.

———. "Two Metaphysical Theories of the Self: C. A. Campbell and A. M. Farrer." PhD diss., Tulane University, 1967.

Ortiz Mutti, Dionisio S. "A Critical Examination of Austin M. Farrer's Concept of Religious Language." PhD diss., Southwestern Baptist Theological Seminary, 1977.

Richards, Jerald Homer. "The Nature, Function, and Validity of Religious Language in the Thought of Austin Farrer." PhD diss., Boston University, 1966.

Richardson, W. Mark. "Human Action and the Making of a Theist: A Study of Austin Farrer's Gifford Lectures." PhD diss., Graduate Theological Union, 1991.

Rothman, Kenneth I. "Austin Farrer's Language of Images." PhD diss., Princeton Theological Seminary, 1999.

Schedler, Norbert O. "Methodology in the Metaphysics of Theism: A Philosophical Analysis of the Method of Austin Farrer and Ian Ramsey." PhD diss., Princeton University, 1967.

Tracy, Thomas Frederick. "God, Action, and Embodiment: A Study in Philosophical Theology." PhD diss., Yale University, 1980.

Wilson, William McFetridge. "A Proof of the Faith: Austin Farrer's Case for Theism." PhD diss., University of Virginia, 1983.

Yee, M. M. "A Critical Examination of the Theology of Austin Farrer with Special Reference to *The Glass of Vision*." MA thesis, University of Sydney, 1976.

———. "The Validity of Theology as an Academic Discipline: A Study in the Light of the History and Philosophy of Science and with Special Reference to Relevant Aspects of the Thought of Austin Farrer." DPhil thesis, University of Oxford, 1987.

BOOKS ABOUT FARRER

Conti, Charles. *Metaphysical Personalism.* Oxford: Oxford University Press, 1995.

Curtis, Philip. *A Hawk among Sparrows: A Biography of Austin Farrer.* London: SPCK, 1985.

Eaton, Jeffrey C. *The Logic of Theism.* Lanham, MD: University Press of America, 1981.

Eaton, Jeffrey C., and Ann Loades, eds. *For God and Clarity: New Essays in Honor of Austin Farrer.* Allison Park, PA: Pickwick, 1983.

Hebblethwaite, Brian, and Edward Henderson, eds. *Divine Action: Essays Inspired by the Philosophical Theology of Austin Farrer.* Edinburgh: T & T Clark, 1990.

Hefling, Charles C. *Jacob's Ladder: Theology and Spirituality in the Thought of Austin Farrer.* Cambridge, MA: Cowley, 1979.

Loades, Ann, and Michael McLain, eds. *Hermeneutics, the Bible and Literary Criticism.* New York: St. Martin's Press, 1992.

CONTRIBUTORS

DIOGENES ALLEN is Stuart Professor Emeritus of Philosophy at Princeton Theological Seminary.

O. C. EDWARDS is Professor Emeritus of Preaching at Seabury-Western Theological Seminary, where he also served as President and Dean.

JULIAN N. HARTT is William R. Kenan Jr. Professor Emeritus of Religious Studies at the University of Virginia.

CHARLES HEFLING is Associate Professor of Theology at Boston College.

DAVID HEIN is Professor of Religion and Philosophy at Hood College.

EDWARD HUGH HENDERSON is Professor of Philosophy at Louisiana State University.

ANN LOADES is Professor Emeritus of Divinity at the University of Durham.

WILLIAM MCF. WILSON is Assistant Dean of Arts and Sciences and Lecturer in Religious Studies at the University of Virginia.

INDEX